THE ECONOMICS OF CULTURAL LOSS

The Economics of Cultural Loss

Harm and Resilience in North American Indigenous Communities

Mukesh Eswaran

OpenBook
Publishers

ISBN Paperback: 978-1-80511-648-6
ISBN Hardback: 978-1-80511-649-3
ISBN PDF: 978-1-80511-650-9
ISBN HTML: 978-1-80511-652-3
ISBN EPUB: 978-1-80511-651-6
DOI: https://doi.org/10.11647/OBP.0477

Cover image: Crosswalk painted orange with white feathers for Truth and Reconciliation to honor Indigenous children who died in Canada's residential schools. Photo by madsci at iStock

Cover design: Jeevanjot Kaur Nagpal

To the xʷməθkʷəy̓əm (Musqueam) Band of British Columbia
(on whose traditional, ancestral, and unceded territory the
University of British Columbia is located)
With gratitude

Table of Contents

Foreword

Ronald L. Trosper, Emeritus Professor of
American Indian Studies, University of Arizona

I had thought that standard economics, dominated by neoclassical economics, is ill suited for understanding Indigenous societies. I wrote a book presenting an alternative approach (Trosper 2022). Some may be surprised that it is possible to describe many features of Indigenous responses to settler colonialism using the language and techniques of standard economics. I reviewed a draft of this book, was surprised by its analysis, and recommended it be published. I pointed out a few technical errors and suggested additional reading, including my own work, and revealed myself to the author. He responded by asking me to write this introduction.

The book answers this question: What economic models might a sympathetic economist develop to explain to other economists why Indigenous Peoples have fared so poorly in the settler societies of North America? Because economics is an important part of the dominant culture, an economist's efforts to fit Indigenous reality into its analysis is an important exercise; it explains Indigenous Peoples to those with a different culture.

Although Eswaran needs to work hard to squeeze Indigenous history and experience into a neoclassical model, he succeeds in producing some striking results. He explains how imposing individualism and private property can reduce welfare in an Indigenous community. He explains the consequences of the trauma imposed on Indigenous communities from the expropriation of land and removal of children from Indigenous families. He provides reasons that some Indigenous societies are surviving the onslaught.

To explain the devastation caused by the settler societies, Eswaran first

https://doi.org/10.11647/OBP.0477.00

must describe Indigenous economies in terms understandable to conventional economists. The basic tools of conventional economics are (1) commodities of many types, (2) utility functions for individuals about the value of the commodities, (3) production functions for creating private goods and public goods, and (4) a method that assumes outcomes result from individuals independently acting based on maximizing their utility subject to production constraints.

The commodities are private and public goods. Complexities are handled by creating simple variables to represent large parts of economies. Private goods are divisible among members of a community. Public goods are shared equally by all members of the community. Private goods are all the products that most people are familiar with when they shop. Private goods can be separated from each other and can be controlled by a person who holds them. Examples in this book are food and pain-relieving substances. These represent all the other goods that people use. Food represents clothing and other personal items as well as service such as restaurants. Pain-relieving substance represents alcohol, medicines, and the services of physicians. The simplification of using just two specific private goods makes it easier to explain the analysis.

The book uses one public good represented by the letter G, called "culture." Culture thus represents the many community goods of identity, trust, solidarity, joint connections to land, among others. "We belong to the land" is a shared idea that is part of identity. Common pool goods are also part of the one public good. Common pool goods can be divided into parts, but access to them is difficult to control. Examples are fisheries, wild fruits like huckleberries, wild animals like deer, elk, and bison. Details about the composition of the common public good, culture, is available in Trosper (2022).

Individuals are represented by their utility functions, which are based on the idea of an economic agent used in economics, individuals. This work expands the idea of an individual as a person only interested in his or her own consumption; a component of an individual is development of an "us." If an individual belongs to an "us," then he or she is concerned about the utilities of others in the "us" group. Being part of an "us," an individual is willing to work for the production of a common good, culture, that is shared equally among all members of the community, the group of individuals who make up the economy. Although altruism of this sort is usually left out of formal analysis in introductory texts, the field of behavioural economics has established that altruism is included in many people's utility functions.

The individual provides labour and with that contribution can obtain consumption goods. It is common to model an individual's labour contributions into two categories, work and leisure, as done in this book. It is also common to examine the allocation of work among several different production activities. Leisure has to be included if only to give people time to sleep!

Most economic models contain production functions for the goods in the model. This book has food produced by inputs of labour and land, using a common form for the production function, known as the Cobb-Douglas function, which is easy to use and complies with diminishing returns. The work also uses the Cobb-Douglas formula for the utility functions. The public good is produced only by input of labour, and the quantity of the public good is the sum of labour input by individuals. Relief of pain is also only achieved by use of labour.

Once the goods, utility functions, and allocation of labour by individuals are defined, the economic question is then this: what are the amounts of labour allocated to production of each good and to leisure? The question is answered by a mathematical formulation using calculus: everyone maximizes their utility subject to the constraints of the production functions and the fact that all labour effort adds up to one unit. The production function for food is limited by the amount of land available. In mathematical formulation, the land amount is set to one unit.

Of course, the amount of labour available in a day is twenty-four hours, and the amount of land is equal to the acreage of the community. Setting both equal to one is done simply to facilitate the mathematical notation.

Another simplification is to assume that each person in the economy is the same. Each has the same utility function. The result is that the community's joint welfare function is the sum of the individual utility functions. Without assuming each individual has the same utility function, an analyst can't easily describe a community's welfare function. Although individual decisions determine the outcome, there is no individuality in the model because everyone is assumed to be the same, at least in regard to their allocation of labour time.

Persons in an Indigenous community are varied: men, women, kinship groups, young and old. These are all collapsed into one type, which can vary in their amount of work in each type of production. Other differences among people are ignored. What makes these individuals different from those in a non-Indigenous community is that they share community goods that are represented as a single public good. While each may assign the same amount of labour time to the public good, they may engage in different activities; such details are left aside.

Given these basic elements of economies, the book proceeds to use another typical strategy for economic analysis. Create different models, starting with simplest one with the fewest variables, add one variable at a time and compare the resulting Nash solutions. A Nash solution assumes each person maximizes their utility subject to constraint and they don't coordinate with each other. His first comparison is between a solution assuming land is held in common, compared to a situation where the land is divided into equal parcels while the community continues to produce the public good together. The second model applies to a private property situation.

By comparing the solutions of a model without private property to one with private property, Eswaran is able to argue that imposing a system of private property in land reduces the welfare of Indigenous Peoples by inducing them to consume too much food and not enough of the public good. Since the food represents all private goods and the public good represent Indigenous culture, Eswaran shows that reduction of the production of the public good reduces Indigenous welfare if the coefficient representing the value of the public good is large enough in the utility function. Those who advocated private property argued that such a policy would increase Indigenous welfare; Eswaran shows that it might not. The dominance of the private property equilibrium depends upon the value of the public good being low. At higher values, the communal equilibrium gives better welfare.

Eswaran then adds a third model, using a "belongingness" parameter to show the dependence on each individual's utility on that of other people. With this change, he can separately show the impact of the belongingness parameter on both of the previous equilibria. He stresses the comparison between the private equilibrium and the belongingness equilibrium. He picks values of the parameters in which the belongingness equilibrium at first is lower than that of the private equilibrium. When he increases the belongingness parameter, at higher levels the ratio of the belongingness equilibrium to that of the private equilibrium is greater than 1.

The result of comparing the solutions in the first three models shows fairly conclusively that private property is a bad idea for an Indigenous society. In the United States, the imposition of a limited form of private property occurred when Senator Dawes succeeded in passing the *General Allotment Act*, often known as the *Dawes Act*. In addition to imposing allotments on Indians, the Act also allowed land not allocated in allotments to be sold to homesteaders, thus opening Indian reservations to non-Indian settlement. Other laws passed after the *Dawes Act* also led to substantial loss of land, and the land not lost came under the control of the US Government. Private ownership creates a tragedy of the commons that Indigenous management avoids (Trosper 2022, Chapter 5).

Because imposition of private property led to lower welfare from using the land as well as less land, quite appropriately the author moves on to considering the impact of the loss of land, which was great. Land entered both the production of food and the production of culture. Had the analysis included the presence of common pool goods, the impact of private property could be shown to be even greater.

To these material losses, government policy also impacted families by removing children. Children were sent to boarding schools in both the US and in Canada. Both countries also allowed local governments to remove Indian children and place them in their child welfare programs. Children sent to boarding schools eventually returned. Children removed by the child welfare system were given to other parents and were much less likely to return to the community.

Both of these policies caused loss, and loss caused trauma. Eswaran reviews literature on historical trauma. After reviewing the substantial evidence that historical trauma is a real problem, Eswaran adds new variables to his models then compares the effects of adding those variables to the solutions in the previous three models.

In addition to allocating labour time between production of private goods, production of the community good, and leisure, he offers that individuals allocate some time to the alleviation of pain. Pain can be alleviated by consumption of pain-relieving substances. Sahlins (1996)

shows that the model of man used in economics is based on the story of
Adam being thrown out of Eden and forced to work for his pleasure as
a result. Since pain reduces pleasure, using pain as key to the individual
model of man is therefore quite reasonable in a work that complies with
the culture of economics. A way to provide pleasure is to alleviate pain.

Eswaran is able to examine the impact of devoting time to pain alleviation
on his results. He shows that diverting labour time to pain alleviation reduces
Indigenous welfare. This is itself not a surprising result. What is surprising is
that by creating a new variable, the ratio of time spent in the production of food
and the community good to time spent on leisure and pain alleviation, he can
analyse the parameters of the utility function to determine whether there is a
possibility that the dynamic effects of trauma depend upon the given parameters.
He shows that high levels of altruism and valuation of the community good
can be associated with lower levels of individual pain alleviation.

He also addresses another effect of historical trauma, suicide.
He suggests that suicide as a method of pain alleviation would be
less in communities with high levels of altruism and valuation of the
community's public good.

This analysis allows him to end the book with attention to the
observation that some Indigenous communities have reduced suicide
rates to very low levels. He suggests that these low levels are associated
with high valuation of the community's good and high levels of concern
for each other. He connects this to the idea of "survivance" as Indigenous
Peoples' response to the events that create historical trauma.

Because survival of Indigenous culture is so important, one can
understand why Indigenous Peoples insist on self-determination. If they
can control their own lives, they can address the serious issues raised
by allowing only individual consumption of goods to dominate life.
Community actions and community produced public goods are very
important.

References

Sahlins, Marshall (1996), "The Sadness of Sweetness: The Native Anthropology
of Western Cosmology," *Current Anthropology*, 37(3), pp. 395–428.

Trosper, Ronald L. (2022), *Indigenous Economics: Sustaining Peoples and Their
Lands*, University of Arizona Press, Tuscon.

Preface

Culture has a profound effect on the functioning of a society and the wellbeing of its members. What happens when culture gets eroded is not usually studied in the field of economics. This book examines some of the deleterious effects of the erosion of the cultures of Indigenous Peoples of North America over the past few centuries. It is written by a non-Indigenous economist and is intended for economists, students, and policy makers steeped in the mainstream tradition of the discipline, that is, neoclassical economics. Thus, its intended audience is *not* Indigenous Peoples of North America, though it is my hope that this book may show any reader how Indigenous insights can enrich mainstream economics and vice versa.

This book offers a formal economic analysis using the standard tools of mainstream economics, and many of the insights it offers are already well-known to Indigenous scholars. What is new here is a theoretical framework couched in the language of standard economics. The tools are neoclassical, but the assumptions are not. Rather, the book attempts to premise the analysis on assumptions that are more consonant with Indigenous cultures and world views than are standard neoclassical assumptions.

My knowledge of Indigenous cultures is certainly not obtained from lived experience but, rather, from what I have read. I have earnestly sought to understand differences between Indigenous points of view and those of neoclassical economics, and then tried to examine what follows from assumptions reflecting the lived experience of many Indigenous communities. The findings of this research suggest that there is great wisdom in Indigenous traditions that we miss when we view Indigenous societies through lenses more appropriate for western societies. I offer my understanding in the hope that subsequent researchers will remedy the shortcomings of this effort so that we can acquire a better understanding of Indigenous issues than we have to date.

©2025 Mukesh Eswaran, CC BY 4.0   https://doi.org/10.11647/OBP.0477.12

The reader might wonder why a non-Indigenous academic has written this book about serious matters pertaining to Indigenous Peoples. My motivation has been this. Except for a year-long stint at the beginning of my academic life, my career of more than forty years as an economist has been at the Vancouver campus of the University of British Columbia. This campus is located on expropriated ('unceded') Indigenous land. For about a decade I have been very conscious of the fact that I owe virtually my entire career to the Musqueam band, for even my PhD in economics was from UBC. Professionally, I was working in various fields of applied theory but I never worked on Indigenous issues. Then in mid-2021, I heard and read with horror about the unmarked graves of Indigenous children found in a residential school in Kamloops, British Columbia, Canada. It was so appalling that I was consumed by questions regarding how and why such a thing could happen. That is when I felt that, even though I am retired, I should investigate these matters, notwithstanding my limited knowledge and abilities. This book is the final outcome of that endeavour and contains what I have learned. It is offered as a small token of my gratitude to the Musqueam Band of British Columbia. And, more generally, it is my feeble attempt to honour the Indigenous Peoples of North America, who, at great cost to themselves, have afforded generations of immigrants like myself from all over the world to come to North America and improve their own lives.

For comments on work that has gone into Part I of this book, I would like to thank Curt Eaton, Kelly Foley, Nancy Gallini, John Helliwell, Jonathan Graves, David Green, David Scoones, and Michael Veall; and, for work that went into Parts I and II, anonymous referees of *Canadian Public Policy*. I also thank the seminar participants of the Indigenous Economics Study Group (IESG) and the Association for Economic Research of Indigenous Peoples (AERIP). I am extremely grateful to Ronald Trosper for his detailed, helpful, insightful, and encouraging comments on an earlier version of my entire manuscript. I greatly appreciate that he agreed to write a Foreword to my book.

I am particularly grateful to my wife, Viju, for her persistent encouragement and support over the years. I thank Nisha and Hari for being available to talk about Indigenous matters. I am indebted to the Vancouver School of Economics of the University of British Columbia for giving me access to resources for research even in my retirement.

Finally, I thank the editorial team at Open Book Publishers, especially the managing director Alessandra Tosi, Annie Hine (for excellent copy-editing), Jeremy Bowman for typesetting, and Jeevan Kaur Nagpal (for her cover design).

Vancouver School of Economics
University of British Columbia, Vancouver
June 2025

1. Introduction: Culture and Indigenous Wellbeing

1.1 The Issues and Motivating Questions

Among all the demographic groups in North America, Indigenous Peoples are known to unambiguously experience the worst average outcomes in terms of wellbeing, socioeconomic status, and health outcomes (Gracey and King, 2009; King, Smith, and Gracey, 2009).[1] Poverty and unemployment rates are much higher for Indigenous Peoples. The life expectancy of Indigenous individuals in the United States is about five years less than that of non-Indigenous peoples. The incidence of most of the highly prevalent diseases (heart disease, diabetes, respiratory disease, liver disease, alcohol-related disease, PTSD, and many others) is higher than those among the rest of the population.[2] In Canada, the life expectancy is considerably lower (up to nine years) for First Nations Peoples than non-Indigenous peoples; infant mortality rates are much higher in regions with high concentrations of Indigenous Peoples (Tjepkema, Bushnik, and Bougie, 2019; Public Health Agency of Canada, 2018; Feir and Akee, 2019). According to the Human Development Index, non-Indigenous Canadians ranked as twelfth on an international ranking scale in 2016, while Indigenous

---

1   By 'North America' in this book, I shall mean the United States and Canada only. Although there are numerous other countries (like Mexico and Panama, among others) that are geographically in the North American continent, they are generally considered to belong to Latin America.

2   https://www.ihs.gov/newsroom/factsheets/ See also Barnes et al. (2010), Blanchflower and Feir (2023), Feir and Akee (2019), Espey et al. (2014), and Walls and Whitbeck (2011) for more detailed analyses.

    https://doi.org/10.11647/OBP.0477.01

Canadians would have ranked as fifty-second (Cooke, 2019).[3]

A very serious problem facing North American Indigenous communities pertains to suicide. The suicide rate among Indigenous Peoples of Canada relative to non-Indigenous people for the period 2011–2016 was approximately three times higher for First Nations, twice as high for Métis, and nine times as high for Inuits (Kumar and Tjepkema, 2019). In the United States, the American Indian and Alaskan Native (AIAN) suicide rate in 2020 was 41% higher than for the non-Hispanic white population (Center for Disease Control and Prevention, 2022). The suicide rates among youth are even more concerning. For example, the suicide rate for First Nations youth in the age group of 15–24 years is about 6.3 times that for the corresponding non-Aboriginal group (Kumar and Tjepkema, 2019), and would rank among the highest in the world. In the U.S., the teen suicide rate among Native Americans is 3.5 times the national average.[4]

What are the reasons for the appalling condition of North American Indigenous Peoples, where they are in abject poverty and die at excessively high rates due to alcoholism, drug consumption, and suicide? How and why could particular historical events of the past few centuries have led to the current predicament? What factors contribute to the resilience of Indigenous communities that resist and flourish even under adverse conditions? Many scholars from several disciplines have pondered these questions and have offered valuable insights. How can economics contribute to an understanding of the grave contemporary conditions of North American Indigenous Peoples? Can we examine the wellbeing of Indigenous communities with rigorous modelling in a manner that is consistent with mainstream economics? What policy measures would economic analysis suggest in order to ameliorate the serious problems leading to Indigenous 'Deaths of Despair'?[5] These are some of the questions that I shall attempt to modestly contribute to answering in this book, drawing on the immense amount of work done by Indigenous and non-Indigenous scholars from disciplines other than economics.

---

3   A broad-brush overview of contemporary Indigenous economies within Canada is provided by Chernoff and Cheung (2024).

4   https://www.cnay.org/suicide-prevention/

5   'Deaths of Despair' is a phrase coined by Case and Deaton (2015, 2020) in the context of non-Hispanic whites without college education in the United States in recent decades.

Both Canada and the United States have dozens of ethnic groups that have immigrated in the past 200 years and faced various setbacks that could result in adverse health effects. Trovato (1998) finds that cultural support for immigrants to Canada tempers suicide rates; more specifically, greater ethnic cohesion among immigrants lowers suicide rates. This raises a natural question. Given the community orientation of Indigenous Peoples that has been traditionally so important (see e.g. Walters, Simoni, and Evans-Campbell, 2002), why is this protective factor against substance abuse and suicide so weak now for the original inhabitants of North America? This book complements studies in disciplines other than economics in proposing an answer.

Being the dominant paradigm in economics, neoclassical economics exercises a 'conceptual hegemony'—to borrow a term coined by Tomm (2013) for jurisprudence into economics where it is equally applicable. In effect, Indigenous claims have to be couched in the language of neoclassical economics to be taken seriously, and this disempowers Indigenous world views because the dominant paradigm has no place for Indigenous beliefs.[6] In this book, I attempt to include some aspects of traditional cultures that are important to many Indigenous communities while using the tools of neoclassical economics. The hope is that the loss in translation when undertaken by a non-Indigenous academic is not so great as to render the effort worthless.

1.2 The Role of Culture

Culture is a cement that binds a society together and ensures that it is functional. It largely stays in the background and it is more or less taken for granted until we try to do something that is deemed unconventional. As we might expect, there is an intimate connection between the smooth functioning of the culture of a society and the wellbeing of its members. The destruction of culture usually wreaks havoc among the people. A precise definition of culture is notoriously difficult to pin down, of course, and the accepted definition depends on the discipline—scholars in anthropology, sociology, economics, and cultural studies all have

---

6   As the Indigenous political philosopher Turner (2004, p. 66) put it, "The dominant culture has dialogued with Aboriginal peoples on the assumption that Aboriginal peoples' ways of understanding the world can be explained away".

different definitions of this core concept. Economists broadly use the idea that culture refers to the passing of a group's beliefs and values across generations.[7] If we accept this, the erosion or destruction of culture undermines the common understanding of members in a society of what may be taken as given and as the norms that prescribe usual behaviour. At the very least, this lowers wellbeing by disrupting routine daily transactions based upon shared understanding and throws society into confusion. At worst, it can unravel the very basis of the structures and cultural practices that form buffers against upheavals, bringing about death and devastation.

A society's institutions seek to prevent the unbridled exercise of self-interest and enforce behaviour in accordance with society's interests. The police, the judiciary, etc. are all institutions that ostensibly serve the interests of society when uncorrupted. They also evolve over time in response to circumstances in order to serve the interests of society or those with political power (North, 1981; Acemoglu and Robinson, 2012). Different cultures have different institutions. The institutions of a society are dependent on the culture, for the cultural norms dictate what is acceptable and feasible (enforceable) and what is not. Cultural norms of appropriate behaviour established over generations support and determine the efficacy of institutions (Guiso, Sapienza, and Zingales, 2016; Greif, 1994). On the other hand, a drastic change in the institutions will also change the culture, for norms that are no longer needed will erode and those that are required will gradually tend to get normalized. Institutions can have an impact on culture, and culture can also have an impact on institutions.[8] Neither culture nor institutions are written in stone; they change over the long haul, albeit generally quite slowly.

This link between culture and institutions is quite important for the study undertaken in this book. For example, a very important measure of institutional quality is the extent to which property rights are protected. In western societies, property rights in land are seen as private individual property, and the state's laws are devoted to

---

7   The economists Guiso, Sapienza, and Zingales (2006, p. 23) define culture as "those customary beliefs and values that ethnic, religious, and social groups transmit fairly unchanged from generation to generation."

8   Alesina and Giuliano (2015) give an exhaustive discussion of this two-way causality, along with the historical and empirical evidence for it.

protecting private property. In Indigenous communities, typically land (and all it contains) is collectively held, and Indigenous cultures have evolved institutions that effectively manage commonly owned property. This difference between the notions of property rights is a key difference between Indigenous communities and western societies and has been a source of considerable upheavals in Indigenous communities when private property has been sought to be foisted on them by European colonizers. The attempted change in the institution has a detrimental effect on the cultures of Indigenous Peoples that, in turn, have serious consequences for wellbeing. How this happens will be investigated in this book.

Cultural erosion in history has had pernicious effects on Indigenous Peoples.[9] The effects I refer to are due to the phenomenon called historical trauma. This concept was first brought up in the context of Indigenous Peoples by the scholars Brave Heart and DeBruyn (1998).[10] Historical trauma refers to the continuing trauma arising from unresolved grief due to extremely traumatic events of the past. Indigenous Peoples of North America have been relentlessly subjected to upheavals since the arrival of Europeans 500 years ago. Before they could recover from one, another arrived at its heels, leaving little time for healing (Wesley-Esquimaux and Smolewski, 2004; Wiechelt, Gryczynski, and Lessard, 2019). More recent discussions of this topic can be found in Gone (2023, 2025).

Historical trauma, it is claimed, gets passed down from generation to generation, so it is long-lasting. According to the evidence from psychology and the medical sciences, it has very severe emotional, psychological, and even physical consequences. Post-traumatic stress disorder (PTSD), which is a well-studied phenomenon, is part of the manifest symptoms of historical trauma. Historical trauma has much to do with the destruction of Indigenous cultures. It is important to examine the mechanisms by which historical trauma arises and generates its effects.

---

9   In economics, there is literature that attributes contemporary outcomes, especially those pertaining to development, to historic events. See Nunn (2009) for a review. Particularly relevant to the context of Indigenous Peoples is Feir, Gillezeau, and Jones (2024).

10   A very similar concept was also introduced by Duran and Duran (1995) with the term 'soul wound'.

1.3 The Ends and Means of Cultural Destruction

The destruction of the cultures of groups has frequently been identified as a form of genocide. This book is not about determining whether what happened to Indigenous Peoples in North America is or is not genocide; a large number of scholars outside the discipline of economics have debated the issue. Nevertheless, many of the issues that are relevant to that question are obviously also relevant to the issue of the effects of colonization on the wellbeing of Indigenous Peoples. The characteristic feature of genocide—as opposed to other grave atrocities like crimes against humanity—in Raphael Lemkin's (1944) pioneering work and definition of the term is that in genocide, the obliteration of a group by its oppressors is *intentional*, which is usually very difficult to establish.[11] In fields outside economics, Indigenous scholars do not appear to have a consensus view amongst themselves on whether, according to this stringent definition, genocide broadly took place with Indigenous Peoples of North America.[12] There seems to be no doubt, however, that the consequences of colonization for the Indigenous Peoples have been utterly devastating. It is the underlying mechanisms that have wrought these consequences that I first investigate in this book before initiating an investigation into the phenomenon of Indigenous resilience in the face of these dire consequences.

Lemkin's work on genocide has typically been associated with the Holocaust (Lemkin, 1944). However, in his study of what happened to Indigenous Peoples of the Americas since the Spanish invasions, he showed that genocide preceded the Holocaust. European colonization, in Lemkin's thinking, has been associated with genocides. The Spaniards, operating under the Papal 'Doctrine of Discovery' which assured them that lands occupied by non-Christians can be taken to be unoccupied,

---

11   The UN Genocide Convention that was finally adopted in 1948 states that genocide means any of the following acts committed with intent to destroy, in whole or in part, a national, ethnical, racial, or religious group, as such: (1) killing members of the group; (2) causing serious bodily or mental harm to members of the group; (3) deliberately inflicting on the group conditions of life calculated to bring about its physical destruction in whole or in part; (4) imposing measures intended to prevent births within the group; (5) forcibly transferring children of the group to another group.

12   Stannard (1992) and Sinclair, C.M. (2015) in the *Report of Truth and Reconciliation Commission* claim that it was.

assumed that their monarchy was universal, and so they were entitled to the land they invaded. They ruthlessly put down resistance, setting a precedent that was somewhat taken up by the English (Mcdonnell and Moses, 2005).

Lemkin and subsequent scholars have realized that, though physical violence is often an accompaniment of colonization, the violence need not be physical if the goal is to obliterate a group (Greenland and Gocek, 2020). One means that might suffice for this is the destruction of the group's culture.[13] Cultural suppression and erasure can greatly undermine the wellbeing of a group and even result, ultimately, in deaths. This is the avenue of investigation followed in this book. Through the lens of economics, some of the mechanisms by which this occurs are identified and their logical consequences laid bare.

The primary goal of settler colonialism is the acquisition of land; that is, the aim is fundamentally economic and territorial in nature. Cultural destruction is merely a means to this end, and there are many ways in which a group's culture can be undermined. A short and incomplete list is the suppression of religion, the banning of cultural practices, the breaking down of kinship relations and family networks, the suppression of language, the replacement of the educational systems, the destruction of cultural artifacts, relics, and sacred sites, the sidelining of cultural conceptual constructs, and general systemic oppression that insinuates discrimination into everyday transactions. *All* of these have been done to North American Indigenous Peoples, and some of these forms of colonial oppression are still in effect (see e.g. Sinclair, C.M., 2015).

The erasure of Indigenous religions and their replacement by Christianity is one of the routes of cultural assault in North America. This is not to suggest that Christian missionaries were overtly and consciously involved in the colonialization project of Europeans. Much of the proselytization may have been well-intended but the effects, nevertheless, were not benign. Tinker (1993) offers a compelling view of how missionaries were complicit in the colonial treatment of Indigenous

---

13   Though Lemkin sought to incorporate cultural destruction as a part of the UN Genocide Convention, he did not succeed because western countries did not wish to be implicated in cultural genocide. There is renewed interest in this concept in recent years. In the *Report of the Truth and Reconciliation Commission*, Sinclair, C.M. (2015) clearly stated that what happened to Indigenous Peoples in Canada was cultural genocide.

Peoples. His argument is that European missionaries were so persuaded of the superiority of their own culture that they couched Christianity's message of salvation in a manner that also sought to transmit European culture. Consequently, the religious message was confounded with missionaries' cultural orientations. This did damage to the cultural integrity of North American Indigenous Peoples. Furthermore, Tinker (1993, p. 6) claims it damaged the Indigenous self-image "by attacking or belittling every aspect of native culture". We shall see in this book how damage to self-image—that is, identity—has extremely pernicious effects through despair, to the point that it can and does lead to Indigenous deaths. The graphic phrase 'Deaths of Despair' coined by Case and Deaton (2015) is certainly applicable to North American Indigenous Peoples.[14]

Deaths of despair are not unique to Indigenous Peoples. For example, Giles, Hungerman, and Oostrom (2023) have made the case that deaths of despair in recent decades among middle-aged, non-Hispanic whites without college education, as identified by Case and Deaton (2015), may be attributed to the loss of importance of religion. If a decline in the role of religion—which is only one aspect of culture—can by itself account for deaths of despair in a demographic group, the devastation from a simultaneous decline in several crucial aspects of culture can be expected to be far more serious. While Indigenous Peoples may not be unique with regard to deaths of despair, what stands out is the comprehensiveness of the assault on Indigenous cultures in North America.

Kinship is an integral part of a society's culture, and it determines the bloodlines and lineage links that are important, and how family ties are set up. In western culture, at least since medieval times, the nuclear family has been the norm (Schultz et al., 2019). In Indigenous cultures, typically the extended family has been important (Red Horse, 1978; Killsback, 2019). As a result, it is not just the parents who are involved in raising children but also aunts, uncles, grandparents, community members, etc. There is an extensive support system in place for children and youth. European colonizers devoted many policies to deliberately breaking these kinship ties. The forced enrolment of

---

14   The statistics revealed by Friedman, Hansen, and Gone (2023) justify this claim.

Indigenous children in residential schools and the prevention of contact between these children and their parents is one example. The attempted Europeanization of Indigenous children automatically meant distancing them from their own kin, so the weakening of Indigenous kinship systems inevitably followed. This decline was complemented by a ban on Indigenous religious practices. These practices are typically collective in nature, emphasizing the importance of community. Christian religious practices typically involve nuclear families, in accordance with western kinship relations. This, and even restrictions on Indigenous attire and the length of one's hair, served to separate an Indigenous person from their community (Tinker, 1993).

The culture of a society provides a framework for its members on how to think about and navigate their world. And by being raised in a culture, they unconsciously incorporate this framework into their identity—which is how they respond to the query 'Who am I?' Identity has an individual component to it, and this pertains to one particular body and mind. But, as social psychologists emphasize, identity also has a collective component—involving the group that the individual is part of. This collective aspect of identity embodies the group members' values, their preferences, and their notions of what is honourable, and what is appropriate.[15] When culture is destroyed, the identity of the society's members is undermined and this has deleterious effects on their behaviour and wellbeing (Sinclair, C.M., 2015). Some of the colonial strategies outlined here bring about precisely that.

1.4 The Approach Adopted in this Book

Though there is excellent empirical work on Indigenous issues that is increasingly being done in the field of economics, there is a paucity of theoretical frameworks. By way of theory, the tendency has been to apply routine off-the-shelf economics that, in my view, is just not relevant to Indigenous communities. Any serious attempt at providing an economic

---

15 Trosper (2022) argues that Indigenous identity is formed through relationships and that each individual is as unique as their relationships. In that view, terms like 'community' and 'communal' may not strictly apply, but expediency in modelling forces me to invoke these concepts that, nevertheless, seem like good approximations to examine the issues dealt with in this book.

framework—however simplified—of Indigenous communities requires a deliberate examination of whether the assumptions of standard economics are applicable and, if they are found not to be, how they should be replaced. A major drawback in economics in the study of Indigenous issues is the almost complete absence of relevant theory. My book attempts to take some small steps towards remedying this, because suitable policy measures need to be grounded not only in good empirical work but also in relevant economic theory.

Neoclassical economics, the dominant paradigm in western economics, lends itself to the belief that it is an objective science uninfluenced by cultural considerations. This presumption, however, is not true. The essential premise of economic behaviour is that individuals make choices based on preferences and their budgets. The emphasis is on the individual aspect of identity as opposed to the collective aspect. This predilection is decidedly a cultural position characterizing the cultures that emerged from western Europe and then spread across the western world through colonization. However, this bias towards the individual view is not shared by the rest of the world, as shown by Schultz et al. (2019). And it most decidedly is not shared by the Indigenous Peoples of North America. The implicit role that culture plays in economic analysis is extremely important, because analysis that is valid for one society is not necessarily so for a society with a different culture. When the policies derived from the former are foisted on the latter, much damage can result. We shall see precisely how this happens in the context of North American Indigenous Peoples even when the policies might be genuinely well-intended. However, even in western societies, the objectives of culture are not necessarily identical to those of economics, for culture tends to offset too-individualistic an orientation. In fact, Throsby (2001) characterizes this difference by claiming that economics tends to be more individualistic whereas culture tends to be more collective.

The literature outside the discipline of economics emphasizes the importance that Indigenous communities place on culture. A core feature of my approach is to respect this preference and to incorporate it into the economic analysis. There are two aspects of culture that I shall focus on. The first is the importance of land (and all the resources it contains) and the second is the importance of community and communal activities. Land is so significant and sacred to Indigenous Peoples that even the Supreme Court of Canada acknowledges the special status of Indigenous land.[16] Since the land of an Indigenous community is deemed to be owned collectively, this common ownership is a crucial aspect of Indigenous economic and social organization. This common ownership also includes common pool resources like lakes, rivers, forests, etc., as emphasized by Trosper (2022). When this cultural practice is tampered with in attempts to privatize land by converting it to privately owned plots, it can have very adverse cultural consequences that ultimately translate into a serious decline in Indigenous wellbeing. I demonstrate this with an economic model that explicitly incorporates a role for culture—something that previous analyses in economics have not done.[17]

To discuss Indigenous issues pertaining to physical and mental health while ignoring culture is to leave out what may be one of the most critical factors. To address the role played by culture in health issues, the second part of this book deals with the community orientation of Indigenous Peoples. This includes collective activities, the extended family system, 'alloparenting' (parenting by relatives), and many other features that are not present to anywhere near the same extent in western societies. This aspect of culture leads to a special space for communal support that is intimately connected to the wellbeing of Indigenous Peoples. When this community aspect is undermined, it has serious health consequences. Drawing on the work of Indigenous scholars, I argue that precisely this has occurred as a result of what has been called 'historical trauma' (unresolved trauma that is passed down across generations).[18]

To proceed, this monograph incorporates into an economic model the one universal feature of historical trauma: deep and persistent psychological pain, and sometimes even physical pain. The question then becomes, 'How does one cope with pain?' Taking the cue from a large number of empirical studies in diverse fields that examine this, the model explicitly incorporates pain in an economic framework—

---

16   See Slattery (2000).
17   I draw heavily on Eswaran (2023a) here.
18   Brave Heart and DeBruyn (1998), Evans-Campbell (2008), Kirmayer et al. (2007), Sinclair, C.M. (1998), Wesley-Esquimaux and Smolewski (2004), Wiechelt , Gryczynski, and Lessard (2019), Bombay, Matheson, and Anisman (2014), Gone (2023, 2025).

something that economic models have never done, to my knowledge. One is then able to examine how resources get reallocated in the presence of pain. This approach sheds some light on the consequences of historical trauma, especially for Indigenous communities that highly value culture.

By setting up a formal economic model that extends the one introduced in the first part of the book, I will show in the second part how, *because the colonial legacy has rendered positive means of pain treatment unavailable,* historical trauma can lead to alcoholism, substance abuse, and, ultimately, suicides—deaths of despair, in short. This book provides an economic theory for the deaths of despair among Indigenous communities. Historical trauma perpetuates the colonial dismantling of Indigenous culture by undermining traditional support systems of family and community, which function as buffers against despair and substance abuse. This is consistent with the writings of numerous Indigenous scholars. The approach also demonstrates the exorbitant cost of historical trauma in terms of deaths of despair.

Focusing on the adverse effects of historical trauma may be a natural instinct for economists interested in understanding how these grave effects can be alleviated. However, there is a great deal of variation across Indigenous communities, in their manner of functioning and in the severity of the effects of colonization on them. Health and mortality statistics most certainly do not exhibit homogeneity across communities (Chandler and Dunlop, 2018), and this is also reflected in the disparities in the incidence of deaths of despair. There is much to be learned from communities that have proved to be 'resilient' under adverse conditions. A natural question, then, is: 'What makes a community resilient?'

The model in the second part of this book also speaks to the phenomenon of Indigenous resilience. The testable predictions of the model allow us to infer what is implied when the underlying parameters of a community are changed. To the extent that these parameters are different across communities, the predicted outcomes would be commensurately different. This allows the model to offer explanations for the observed variation in outcomes across Indigenous communities. In particular, it enables us to speak to the notion of resilience and to suggest what separates resilient Indigenous communities from those that are less so. Furthermore, the model emphasizes the collective role of communities in addressing deaths of despair and improving outcomes, in line with what Indigenous scholars have been suggesting (e.g. Ansloos, 2018).

1.5 Outline of the Book

Part I considers the role of culture in what is deemed to be of great importance to Indigenous communities: the Indigenous relationship with land. Chapter 2 introduces a model of a hypothetical Indigenous community premised on two assumptions that distinguish many Indigenous communities, as revealed by evidence in the literature. Culture is explicitly included in the model and it is modelled as a public good that everyone benefits from and everyone can contribute to. It is shown that, when a community places a great deal of importance on culture—as the literature suggests is the case with many Indigenous communities—a transition from commonly owned land to privately owned land actually decreases the wellbeing of community members, a finding that flies in the face of the common presumption in economics.

Chapter 3 incorporates into the economic model another important feature that distinguishes many Indigenous communities: the view that land (and all its contents) is not their owned property, even collectively, but that it is *they* who belong to the land.[19] It is argued that this deeply rooted sentiment alters the weight put on others in an individual's welfare. In effect, a person's self-image puts an increased weight on the 'Us' aspect of self at the expense of the 'I' aspect of it. This sense of belonging to the land is shown to change an individual's allocation of resources within a community. It counters free riding in communal contributions, which is overly emphasized in standard economic models. The incorporation of this additional feature is seen to complement and strengthen the role of culture in determining Indigenous wellbeing. The consequences of forcing privatization of property are even worse than those seen in Chapter 2.

Chapter 4 discusses the attempts that have been made to privatize Indigenous reserve land in the United States and Canada.[20] It first

---

19 See Akiwenzie-Damm (1996).
20 Indigenous land called 'reserve' in Canada is referred to as 'reservation' in the United States.

discusses the motivation and the effects of the best documented of such attempts—the *Dawes Act of 1887* in America, also known as the *General Allotment Act*. This was a piece of legislation that was a key component of the attempt to erase Indigenous cultures and to assimilate the Peoples into mainstream American life. The chapter discusses how this was attempted and why it failed dramatically. There have also been Canadian attempts at privatizing Indigenous property (though not through legislation) and promoting the enfranchising of Indigenous Peoples. The chapter analyses these attempts and explains the reasons for Indigenous resistance to the privatization of reserve land.

Part II of this book considers the even more dire consequences of the erosion of Indigenous cultures since colonization. Specifically, using the vehicle of economics, it addresses the health consequences of historical trauma. Chapter 5 discusses the origin of the concept of historical trauma, drawing on literature from fields outside of economics. It then provides a brief history of the major events that are deemed to have led to historical trauma—in particular, the appropriation of Indigenous land, the residential school system, and the child welfare system. Finally, it provides evidence for the links between Indigenous health outcomes and historical trauma from the empirical literature, again from outside the field of economics. This chapter lays the groundwork for a formal economic consideration of historical trauma.

Chapter 6 sets out an economic model that offers one approach to analysing the effects of historical trauma. Drawing on evidence for the link between historical trauma and psychological pain, it extends the model from Part I to incorporate the endogenous responses of individuals to historical trauma. In particular, the model is suited to examine the resource allocation effects of persistent pain, where the response takes the form of attempts at pain alleviation. The chapter derives the equilibrium in a hypothetical Indigenous community experiencing shared historical trauma.

Chapter 7 presents an investigation of the adverse effects of historical trauma on Indigenous wellbeing. De facto, psychological pain shifts the weight of identity from the 'Us' component to the 'I' component. One of the effects of historical trauma is the destruction of the traditional means of pain treatment. In their absence, by diverting resources to pain alleviation, an increase in historical trauma reduces the individual contributions of Indigenous community members to collective activities. This results in an inferior equilibrium where family and community outcomes are worse in the short run. In the long run, the reduced communal contributions erode the sense of belonging that characterizes many Indigenous communities. This further worsens outcomes. The model shows how and why the causal effects of historical trauma are durable: they do not diminish with time. It is seen that high levels of historical trauma can lead an Indigenous community to get stuck in a 'bad' equilibrium in which individual, family, and community outcomes are extremely compromised. The model reveals why colonization casts a long shadow and why Indigenous communities still have to struggle with the consequences of past events. Added to these outcomes are the effects of the ongoing colonization that undoubtedly exists but which the model is somewhat less equipped to formally capture.

In Chapter 8, the book turns its attention to what the economic model has to say about the health status of and deaths of despair among the North American Indigenous Peoples. It theoretically traces the effects of pain, and the reduced sense of belonging induced by historical trauma, on the reallocation of resources to pain alleviation. This links the extent of historical trauma to substance abuse (excessive drug and alcohol consumption) and to suicides and, generally, to deaths of despair. A key to understanding Indigenous suicides is the disruption to the sense of self, as emphasized by the landmark study of Chandler and Lalonde (1998). In this chapter, the economic model of this book highlights how trauma and the associated psychological pain wreak havoc on Indigenous identities and facilitate suicide in the absence of suitable means of treating pain. The model offers the hypothesis that variation in the extent of historical trauma across North American Indigenous communities may explain the large disparity in deaths of despair observed.

It might be inferred that an economic approach is limited to this analysis of the deleterious effects of the erosion of Indigenous cultures due to historical trauma. This is far from the truth. The model offered in this book also speaks to the phenomenon of resilience of Indigenous communities in the face of repeated and ongoing hardships. In fact, the careful investigation of the colonial mechanisms that have wrought devastation to Indigenous Peoples also reveals the factors that have contributed to Indigenous resilience. A term more appropriate than resilience in the case of historical trauma is 'survivance', a term coined by Vizenor (2008). The economic model that offers explanations for the adverse effects of historical trauma also suggests what it is that contributes to the flourishing of Indigenous communities. Chapter 9 gives a tentative theory of when an Indigenous community spirals into a 'bad' equilibrium and when it exhibits survivance. It is seen that the greater is a community's emphasis on culture and sense of belonging, the more likely it is to exhibit survivance in the face of historical trauma. Communities with high levels of historical trauma are seen to be less likely to exhibit survivance. The analysis, which brings out the importance of community activities instead of individualistic therapies as a remedy, is consistent with Indigenous practices that are intended to promote survivance (White and Mushquash, 2016; Ansloos, 2018; Chandler and Dunlop, 2018).

Chapter 10 offers some concluding thoughts on this study.

PART I

Effects of the Erosion of Indigenous Land Rights

This part of the book, which draws on Eswaran (2023a), comprises three chapters. It focuses on why land has a very special place in many Indigenous cultures. These chapters investigate some of the important economic consequences that follow from this deep attachment to land, what this implies for Indigenous community orientation, and what it entails for the organization of production in Indigenous economies. There is then a discussion of how Indigenous wellbeing is undermined when traditional property rights in land are tampered with and are made to conform to the western notion of private property. Finally, the last chapter in this part discusses inappropriate policy measures with regard to land that have been implemented or espoused in North America in the past and are frequently proposed in the present.

2. A Simple Economic Model of an Indigenous Community

2.1 Introduction

In this chapter, I introduce a theory that offers an answer to the question 'how would the division of commonly owned Indigenous reserve land into privately owned individual plots affect the wellbeing of the Indigenous Peoples in North America?' The answer, which hinges on the importance of Indigenous cultures, provides one explanation for the extreme reluctance of Indigenous communities to privatize reserve land.[1]

In proposing a framework for analysis, the attempt here is to imbed ideas that are central to some Indigenous cultures and identities. The model allows us to investigate the possibility that the erosion of culture and communal property rights can result in a decline in the level of Indigenous wellbeing. To do so, instead of invoking standard neoclassical theory in identifying the most proximate causes, I adopt an approach that takes a more deliberate view of what Indigenous elders, leaders, and scholars say about the important aspects of Indigenous cultures. In contrast to standard models in economics, the assumptions

---

1   Nisga'a and Tsawwassen are the only First Nations that voluntarily opted to have private property in the over-600 First Nations in Canada. (Even here, there are some restrictions that should be noted. In Nisga'a, the private property cannot exceed 0.2 hectares and can be transferred to non-Nisga'a citizens, too. Only 0.05% of Nisga'a land has been earmarked for private property, and it can only be used for residential purposes. In the case of Tsawwassen, the private property cannot be transferred to a person who is not a member of the Tsawwassen First Nation.) In the U.S., the Dawes' Act of 1887 forcibly introduced private property on Native American reservations and its regime lasted for around half a century, and this complicates reservation ownership patterns in that country.

     https://doi.org/10.11647/OBP.0477.02

of the theoretical model here are more in alignment with "the truth of lived experiences", to borrow a telling phrase of C. Murray Sinclair in his report as Chair of Canada's *Truth and Reconciliation Commission* (2015, p.12). This is particularly important because policies based on assumptions more pertinent to the Indigenous Peoples could be very different from those generated by standard western (neoclassical) economic theory. It is a recurring claim made by Indigenous Peoples that land is of central importance in Indigenous societies. Land is often the lynchpin around which Indigenous identities, cultures, and economies were and are built.[2] This is reflected in the claim 'I belong to the land', which is in sharp contrast to the western, neoliberal view of property that asserts 'this land belongs to me' (Akiwenzie-Damm, 1996; Noble, 2008).

In this chapter, I propose a very simplified economic model of an Indigenous community. The model envisages a hypothetical community comprising of Indigenous people with a common culture and language, sharing the same land. There is a great deal of variation across the communities of various Indigenous Peoples in North America, and one cannot construct a theory that fits all of them. That is why I refer to the model as one of a *hypothetical* Indigenous community. Different Indigenous communities will have varying degrees of resemblance to the one modelled here. I am constrained here by what is possible for economic modelling; some of the richness of real-world Indigenous communities will be lost due to the needs of analytic tractability. There is no intention here to 'essentialize' particular features of cultures as defining *all* Indigenous Peoples. The purpose in this chapter and the next is to model a hypothetical Indigenous community in a manner that would resonate with the world view of at least some Indigenous communities.

A reading of the literature makes it clear that Indigenous economies are not separate from Indigenous cultures; economic life is woven into the fabric of everyday cultural life (Trosper, 2022). One sharp difference from the western tradition is that, in contrast to the individualism and the nuclear families that are characteristic of Western Europeans (and European immigrants to North America, Australia, and New Zealand),

---

2   Hageman and Galoustian (2024, esp. Ch. V) offers a very helpful introduction to traditional Indigenous values, as does Trosper (2022).

Indigenous kinships systems comprise extended families (Red Horse et al., 1978; Killsback, 2019).[3] Thus, the allocation of food, childcare activities, etc. is best modelled as a sharing arrangement in a simplified treatment. This sharing aspect of many Indigenous cultures is one of the features built into the model of this chapter.

Another immensely important aspect of life for Indigenous Peoples is the significance of land in daily life. This is not just because hunting, gathering, and farming all require land as an indispensable input. It is rooted, rather, in the view that many Indigenous Peoples see themselves not as individuals in possession of themselves but as individuals who commonly owe their existence to the land. (This special role of land is discussed in detail in the next section of this chapter.) Thus, land forms an integral part of the lives of Indigenous Peoples; the cultural activities (storytelling, ceremonies, rituals, religions, etc.) were and are largely collective activities in which ancestral land figures importantly. In this book, land stands for the resources given by nature and thus includes other resources like forests, lakes, rivers, etc., all of which are commonly owned.[4]

Not all goods or activities are consumed or undertaken collectively; some are naturally individual. There is the strictly individual consumption of food and leisure, because the evolutionary process of natural selection has also shaped humans to be individuals. Humans have two components to their sense of self: an individual component, and a collective component, which I will refer to as the 'me' aspect and the 'Us' aspect, respectively. Individual leisure activity and consumption are dictated by the 'me' aspect of the sense of self; the collective cultural activities are more influenced by the 'Us' aspect of self. The 'Us' component of identity is weighted more heavily among Indigenous societies than in western societies. This view on Indigenous identity is consistent with that presented in Trosper (2022, pp. 192–196).

Before spelling out the model, I should clarify the land tenure

---

3   Trosper (2022) emphasizes that Indigenous relationships even include those with conscious non-humans.

4   Citing the proposed American Declaration on Rights of Indigenous Peoples, Daes (2001, p. 9) quotes, "[I]n many indigenous cultures, traditional collective systems for control and use of land and territory and resources, including bodies of water and coastal areas, are a necessary condition for their survival, social organization, development and their individual and collective well-being".

system I shall be assuming here for the analysis. The natural assumption to make for an Indigenous community is to presume that the land is commonly owned. It may be argued, however, that in reality Indigenous communities did and do have various forms of property rights, including private property.[5] This is indeed correct: a variety of property rights exist, depending on the circumstances and the nature of the resource. Bailey (1992) has examined the various land tenure systems that exist within Indigenous communities and identified conditions under which incentives are maximized by private property and by common property. When there are scale economies, advantages to group production, risky outputs etc., then common property is favoured. Otherwise, private property is assigned. But it has to be emphasized that when an Indigenous community gives its resources for private use such as housing, fishing, hunting, agriculture, etc., it is always on a *usufruct* basis (Hoelle, 2011).[6] That is, the private 'owners' can only receive the *flow benefits* of the resources, but this right can be revoked by the community because of disuse or abuse. The person or family with these rights cannot appropriate Indigenous land and sell it for profit. This important distinction has to be kept in mind because the explicitly usufruct nature of the resource among Indigenous Peoples does not inculcate a sense of exclusive ownership as in the western, economic concept of private property—and this is consistent with the belief 'I belong to the land; the land does not belong to me'.[7]

To avoid a tiresome taxonomy in the model below, I compare the

---

5   Many examples can be found in the volume edited by Anderson (1992) and in the paper by Hoelle (2011). Alcantara (2003) offers a history of the evolution of Indigenous property rights in Canada, with his view of its strengths and weaknesses.

6   Sometimes Indigenous communities have private property with institutional practices like the potlatch. Johnsen (1986) has argued that the ostentatious gift-giving activity observed among Southern Kwakiutl Indians was, in fact, a mechanism for protecting the property rights of their communities in the salmon fishery from encroachers. I offer an alternative explanation. The inefficiency of over-exploitation associated with a common property fishery is corrected by private property in a usufruct sense. The mutual sharing, in my view, in competitive potlatches may well have been a way of maintaining the equal sharing ethic common in many Indigenous cultures while fixing the common property inefficiency at the same time. In a similar vein, Trosper (2009, Ch. 4) has argued that potlatches equalize wealth and thereby solve the prisoner's dilemma problem that is endemic to common pool problems.

7   Interestingly, Penner (1997, p. 5) says that from the point of view of western law, "[T]he ownership of property is intimately connected to giving and sharing [...] having the right to property does not entail the right to sell what one owns."

outcomes for wellbeing in only two sharply different scenarios: common property and property that is private in the western sense. In my analysis, in the former scenario I shall simply model food production using land (hunting/fishing and/or farming) as communal.

2.2 Evidence for the Model's Assumptions

There is some evidence for the two important premises of my model: *the importance of land* (and its common ownership) in many Indigenous cultures, and the attendant *ethic of sharing*. However, the evidence is not quantitative because this is not available. Therefore, I shall quote frequently from the writings and sayings of Indigenous elders and scholars, given that even the Supreme Court of Canada now accepts oral testimony as evidence (as in e.g. *Delgamuukw v. British Columbia*) due to the importance of the oral tradition in Indigenous cultures.

2.2.1 The Importance of Land to Indigenous Peoples

As noted, numerous Indigenous communities in Canada and the U.S. exhibit an exceptionally deep attachment to land. Since the historical trauma following the loss of land and the erosion of culture still plagues Indigenous Peoples, it is important to learn about the sources of this bond. The following is a brief overview of the reasons as I understand them.

In the Introduction of this chapter and also in Chapter 1 it was suggested that, among Indigenous Peoples, the view is often that it is not individuals who own the land; rather it is *they who belong to the land*. This special meaning of land to Indigenous Peoples has even been recognized by the Supreme Court's decisions in Canada (Slattery, 2000). If land is claimed by an Indigenous community as 'theirs', the claim is a collective one, not an individual one (Akiwenzie-Damm, 1996; Noble, 2008).[8] The reason why land cannot typically be claimed by individuals and bought and sold resides in the belief that ancestral land is sacred. The economy is not compartmentalized in many Indigenous societies but is inextricably interwoven with religion and culture.

---

8   There were other usufruct uses of property, as noted before (Bailey, 1992; Hoelle, 2011).

Among Indigenous Peoples, it is the entire land of the nation that is considered sacred, and this includes all the common pool resources and conscious non-humans (Trosper, 2022). Indigenous religions often have Creation stories that interpret the nation's land as a gift from the Creator, and there is a deeply embedded belief that a community should live within the bounds of the gifted territory and act as its stewards (Akiwenzie-Damm, 1996). This may explain why there are numerous communities in North America, each localized in a particular geographical area that is deemed sacred to the community. The cultures and religions that subsequently arose were specific to the land, even though they share broad commonalities. This geographical specificity of culture and belongingness gives rise to a deep attachment among numerous Indigenous communities to the land of their forebears, and is the source of the belief 'We belong to the land'.

Furthermore, Indigenous cultures are infused with the idea of mutual belongingness to the nation's particular landscape, the animals, and the earth through an indivisible but conscious bond—for, in this view, what others may take as inanimate is seen by Indigenous Peoples as conscious (Booth, 2003; Trosper, 2022). The Indigenous scholar Mills (2010, pp. 115–116) says, "[F]or the Anishinaabek, everything is alive. In our language, Anishinaabemowin, almost everything is considered alive—even rocks, drums or tea kettles. [...] For most (but certainly not all) Canadians personhood is a category limited to *Homo sapiens sapiens*, yet Anishinaabe world views hold that many animate non-human beings are fully persons, with temperaments, volitions and preferences". And again, "Because everything is made by the Great Spirit, all life is imbued with the sacred: from the smallest insect to the biggest animal; from the tiniest grain of sand to the largest galaxy, all is alive and everything is intimately and spiritually connected" (p. 118). From this view, there seems to arise a deep sense of the sacred that informs the lives of Indigenous Peoples. It is for this reason that, when the particular land Indigenous Peoples believe has been given to them as its stewards is taken away, the loss is accompanied by a profound sense of grieving and a deep longing for its return. Indigenous identity is so deeply fused with the land that the person feels everything it is perceived to contain, visible and invisible, is their very self.

The *Truth and Reconciliation Committee's Report* reveals how deeply the

Indigenous connection with land and the environment runs: "As Elder Crowshoe explained further, reconciliation requires talking, but our conversations must be broader than Canada's conventional approaches. Reconciliation between Aboriginal and non-Aboriginal Canadians, from an Aboriginal perspective, also requires reconciliation with the natural world. If human beings resolve problems between themselves but continue to destroy the natural world, then reconciliation remains incomplete. This is a perspective that we as Commissioners have repeatedly heard: that reconciliation will never occur unless we are also reconciled with the earth" (Sinclair, C.M., 2015, p. 18). In other words, even reconciliation with the natural world is viewed as part of the truth and reconciliation process in the eyes of Indigenous Peoples— so important is land and the environment to Indigenous ways of life. Trosper (2002) maintains that Indigenous bonds extend also to non-human inhabitants of the land. The Métis Elder Ghostkeeper trenchantly captures the difference between the Métis use of land as "living *with* the land", and the western use of land as "living *off* the land" (Jobin, 2020, p. 106, emphasis in the original).

Indigenous literature in reference to land is replete with analogies to that human relationship which is universally deemed to be the most sacred and unbreakable bond: the relationship to one's mother. "Tribal territory is important because the Earth is our Mother (and this is not a metaphor, it is real). The Earth cannot be separated from the actual being of Indians," says Little Bear (2000), for example.[9] Attachment to the land in which one is raised may be common, but there are very few cultures other than the Indigenous in which people would identify the land with their *being* and vice versa. In other words, the Indigenous concept of property is *ontological* in nature (that is, it pertains to being) as opposed to the western concept whereby property is defined by geographical territory (Bryan, 2000). Egan and Place (2013, p. 136) point to how, for Indigenous Peoples, everything is bathed in spirit and objects have relationships to kin: "The point is not to romanticize or essentialize indigeneity or Indigenous worldviews, but rather to recognize that there are other ways of understanding land and property and geography, where the world is not divided neatly into exclusionary

---

9   The paper by Bakht and Collins (2017), which also quotes Little Bear, documents the sacredness of land among Indigenous Peoples the world over.

categories of inanimate and animate, human and non-human, and where the idea of land as a commodity that can be broken up into pieces and sold for profit is alien." In light of such worldviews, we begin to understand why the Anishinaabe Nation Elder Fred Kelly says of the effect of the dispossession of land on the Indigenous, "[T]o take the territorial lands away from a people whose very spirit is so intrinsically connected to Mother Earth was to actually dispossess them of their very soul and being; it was to destroy whole Indigenous nations" (Sinclair, C.M., 2015, p. 225).

The courts in Canada have been taking the particularly deep attachment of Indigenous Peoples to traditional lands seriously. A good example is the case of Platinex Inc v. Kitchenuhmaykoosib Inninuwug First Nation, which arose because Platinex was involved in mining that was contested by the First Nation. Although the outcome favoured the company, the judge's statement in the Ontario Court of Appeal is revealing: "It is critical to consider the nature of the potential loss from an Aboriginal perspective. From that perspective, the relationship Aboriginal peoples have with the land cannot be understated. The land is the very essence of their being. It is their very heart and soul. No amount of money can compensate for its loss. Aboriginal identity, spirituality, laws, traditions, culture and rights are connected to and arise from this relationship to the land. This is a perspective that is foreign to and often difficult to understand from a non-Aboriginal viewpoint."[10] When even Canadian courts—firmly embedded as they are in common and civil law—are beginning to arrive at this position, it is incumbent on economists to take seriously the especial importance of land to Indigenous Peoples.

The attachment to land is reinforced by the performance of collective rituals, storytelling, drama, and other social activities among Indigenous Peoples (Akiwenzie-Damm, 1996) and also in most religions (Mazumdar and Mazumdar, 2004). These activities would acquire an even greater significance when the land and nature itself form the basis of a group's daily cultural and religious life.[11] The collective activities

---

10   https://miningwatch.ca/blog/2006/9/15/analysis-platinex-inc-v-
      kitchenuhmaykoosib-inninuwug-first-nation-case

11   "It is not a matter of 'worshiping nature,' as anthropologists suggest: to worship
      nature, one must stand apart from it and call it 'nature' or 'the human habitat'

would forge even stronger interpersonal bonds. These activities, by their very nature, would tend to diminish the 'me' component of identity and enhance the 'Us' component.

Kant, Vertinsky, and Zheng (2016) make the important point that, since the value system of Indigenous Peoples is very different from that of westerners, quite different factors will inform Indigenous subjective wellbeing (utility). After extensive discussion with Indigenous elders on factors considered important, the authors collected data from 316 First Nations households in Canada and examined the correlation between general life satisfaction and satisfaction with various domains that are important to Indigenous Peoples—domains such as finance, health, housing, social, cultural, and land use, etc. Their empirical estimation found that the correlation of general life satisfaction among the sample of Indigenous Peoples was quantitatively much stronger with the social, cultural, and land use domains than with satisfaction in the financial domain. This provides some quantitative evidence for the importance of land and culture to Indigenous Peoples.

In sharp contrast to Indigenous views, in western economies land is largely but not entirely viewed mainly as an input in production—whether in agricultural, manufacturing, retail, or residential services.[12] Much of its value stems from the fact that it is viewed as an economic asset that can be bought and sold in land markets. One's attachment to a piece of land is built into one's assessment of its present value, which may somewhat exceed what others are willing to pay for it—a phenomenon that is not uncommon and is referred to as the endowment effect (Kahneman, Knetsch, and Thaler, 1990). The unwillingness of some Indigenous Peoples to entertain the idea of trading Indigenous land for money may be viewed as an extreme case of the endowment effect, but there is much more to it than this. The reluctance to trade would especially arise because there is no adequate substitute available for land that is deemed sacred. In all liberal democracies, individuals can obviously trade land as private property because this sense of sacredness is absent.

---

or 'the environment.' For the Indian, there is no separation. Man is an aspect of nature". Matthiessen, quoted in Booth (2003, p. 334).

12 Land is not always viewed entirely in monetary terms. So as not to 'otherize' the Indigenous Peoples, we may note that some people from the general population are usually willing to defend, and often die, to protect their countries against foreign aggression.

In sum, the above discussion shows why land, having ontological significance, is of utmost importance to many Indigenous communities. The importance far exceeds that which might be attributed by societies with economies that merely rely on land for hunting, gathering, and farming—that is, for production. Given the holistic nature of many Indigenous cultures, land, interpersonal relations, and spirituality are interwoven in generating a sense of identity and wellbeing among Indigenous Peoples.

2.2.2 Communal Ownership of Indigenous Land and Sharing

In modelling an Indigenous community in this chapter, it is not presumed that agriculture is the main use for land, though in North America Indigenous groups have practiced agriculture since prehistoric times. Here, land—in terms of production—also stands in for an essential input into hunting, trapping, and fishing. For these activities, since the animals and fish are migratory, it is clear that this model's aggregate called 'land' would be seen as a 'common pool' resource and, therefore, tend to be communally owned and shared across Indigenous communities. The near extinction of the bison by the 1880s, partly as a strategy of the U.S. Army to subdue Indigenous Peoples through starvation (Smits, 1994) and partly due to international trade (Taylor, 2011), increased the importance of agriculture to Indigenous Peoples, at least in the plains.

Hurt (1987, Ch. 5) documents what little is known about land tenure in Indigenous agriculture in America. His review clarifies that Indigenous land was communally owned. While individual plots were assigned, often on the basis of family lines, they were for use only. When not used, they were reverted to the community, which suggests that these usufruct rights cannot be interpreted as property rights in the western sense as has been done by Flanagan, Alcantara, and Le Dressay (2010). Land tenure was established in terms of the household or lineage—sometimes matrilineal and sometimes patrilineal. There could be no absolute claim of individual possession in the nature of western ('fee simple') property rights; that is, an individual could not sell land. In fact, even the community could not dispose of the land freely because the land belonged to the future generations, too. Because Indigenous communities in America practiced subsistence farming, the demand for land from each community was limited. And because a community had no rights to unused land, this resource did not lend itself to pre-emptive appropriation of the sort one saw after the arrival of European settlers, where even land that is not used can be owned under the fee simple property rights regime.

As seems to have been the case in all subsistence economies, many Indigenous communities routinely practiced sharing (see Hageman and Galoustian, 2024, Ch. V). Enloe (2003) discusses hunter-gatherer societies in general and argues, from ethnographic studies, that food sharing is seen to be a universal and important practice that, in fact, played a role in human evolution. The sharing of effort is seen in the cooperative hunting of large animals and also in the transportation of the carcasses; sharing of the carcass in consumption was expedient due to the absence of refrigeration. Sharing in general arises in periods of scarcity because it is a risk-sharing mechanism. It is not difficult to see why this would become a social norm. Such arrangements were stronger between kin, it is true, but sharing also occurs between non-kin on the understanding of reciprocity.

Morales and Thom (2020) write about sharing in Hul'qumi'num communities on Vancouver Island. For Hul'qumi'num people, the authors claim, sharing is a legal principle. Drawing on Blomley (2010), the authors point out that property is determined in terms of *relationships* across peoples rather than being neatly defined by geographical boundaries as in the western concept of property. So, there can be overlapping claims to a given piece of geographical territory—ownership is not a mutually exclusive, constant-sum phenomenon, in other words—and this implies joint ownership, sharing, and mutual respect. Even where resident groups exclusively owned hunting or fishing grounds, sharing with outside groups was possible, although this required permission and reciprocity. Morales and Thom (2020, p. 150) sum up the land rights as follows: "Common property tenures are enshrined in laws of Island Hul'qumi'num peoples, guided by the nuances of complex kin networks and strategic residence choices." This is consistent with the general view that the desired social relations of the society determine, and are determined by, property rights.[13] Drawing

---

13 As Singer (2000, p. 139) puts it, "Our choice of a particular property regime alters

on Hyden's (2012) concept of 'the economy of affection' as applied to African countries but applicable universally, Kelly (2017) examines the development of the Coast Salish of British Columbia, Canada. Crucial to this concept is the idea that society is built on informal relationships that solve otherwise difficult problems.[14] Building reciprocal relationships is one such example.

   Natcher (2009) characterizes Indigenous communities in northern Canada—which continue to engage in hunting, fishing, gathering, etc.—as social economies in which sharing and reciprocity are cardinal features. Relying on other research, he argues that "[T]he economies of Aboriginal peoples not only entail highly specialized modes of resource production, but also involve the transmission of social values" (p. 84). In other words, cultural norms dictate production and exchange, of which sharing is an important component and is also key to promoting the continuity of Indigenous communities. Collings, Wenzel, and Gordon (1998) describe the practice of sharing wild and 'country' food obtained by hunting among Holman Inuit even in the present day. Bodenhorn (2000) gives a detailed description of the elaborate, institutionalized sharing rules among the Alaskan and Canadian Inuit Peoples. Ziker (2007) discusses food sharing amongst Indigenous groups in Northern Siberia. While there is a bias towards sharing with kin (presumably for plausible evolutionary reasons), he finds that sharing also occurs with more distant relatives. Sharing is seen as a commitment to participating in a cultural and social arrangement.

   In a study using a sample of twenty-two modern, small-scale groups (eighteen from America and four from Siberia), Ahedo et al. (2019) did not find any significant bivariate correlations between sharing practices and any of their ecological, geographic, and economic variables. The authors suggest that sharing practices may be driven by complex cultural variables and cannot be attributed to local conditions. This inference is not inconsistent with the premise of this chapter that highlights the role of culture.

---

the social world. It will determine what expectations people have a legal right to expect. It will impose duties and vulnerabilities in a certain pattern."

14   Hyden (2012, p. 75) offers a definition of what is meant by the term 'economy of affection': "[I]t is constituted by personal investments in reciprocal relations with other individuals as a means of achieving goals that are seen as otherwise impossible to attain."

The evidence presented in this section supports this chapter's model's assumptions regarding the importance of land to numerous Indigenous communities and the prevalence of sharing practices. The premises of the model introduced in the next section appear to reasonably approximate, to the extent possible, the lived experience of many Indigenous Peoples. With this assurance in hand, I now introduce the model.

2.3 A Simple Model

I write down the utility function, $u(c, G, \ell)$, of a typical person in an Indigenous community as a function of their consumption of food (c), their group cultural activity (G), and their private leisure activity (ℓ). For analytic tractability, I shall work with the following simple Cobb-Douglas form, $u(c, G, \ell)$, of the utility function:

$$u(c, g, \ell) = c^{\alpha} G^{\beta} \ell^{\gamma}, \tag{2.1}$$

where the exogenous parameters in the exponents satisfy $0 < \alpha < 1, 0 < \beta < 1$, and $0 < \gamma < 1$—restrictions that ensure diminishing marginal utility. I assume that each person has 1 unit of time available. If t is the amount of time they devote to food production, g that devoted to the group cultural activity, and ℓ to private leisure activity, the time constraint may be written as $t + g + \ell = 1$. The variable G is the sum of the individual's contributions to the community's cultural activities. This aggregate communal good may be viewed as a 'relational good', to use a term invoked by Uhlaner (1989) and Trosper (2022). The essence of this concept in the present context is that G is a good that every individual enjoys and contributes to, and this enjoyment is enhanced by the contributions of others in the community. It is analogous to the sort of investments in reciprocal relationships referred to by Hyden (2012).

The function in (2.1) will be referred to as the 'egoistic' utility function of a typical community member in order to distinguish it from one to be introduced in the next chapter that incorporates preferences that extend overs others' wellbeing, too, or what are referred to as other-regarding preferences.

For convenience, I model hunting/gathering/farming as the economic activity of the community. For brevity, I shall refer to this activity as production. Assume there are n (≥ 2) people in the Indigenous community. I posit that the output, Q, of food is given by the production function

$$Q = A L^{1-\mu} T^{\mu}, \tag{2.2}$$

where L and T denote, respectively, the land area and total effort applied, and A the total factor productivity of the technology, and $0 < \mu < 1$. The total amount of land in the economy is hereafter normalized to 1 unit. The variable T is the sum of the time inputs towards food production of all the group members.

I model an Indigenous community operating under two different regimes of property rights. The one taken as the norm among many Indigenous Peoples is common property, as already explained. Land cannot be claimed exclusively in the sense that it can be privately sold or disposed of. The other scenario modelled is one in which the communities operate—or are forced to operate—under the notion of private property as understood in the western, neoclassical sense of exclusive, fee simple property rights. In this case, the land is assumed to be divided into n equal-sized private plots and the Indigenous Peoples here hypothetically abandon the cultural notion of 'I belong to the land', and reverse it by claiming 'I own this land'. Food production occurs on these individually-owned plots.

2.3.1 Model with Common Property

Here I take the land of an Indigenous community as commonly owned, and so food production is jointly undertaken. Denoting the production effort of individual i by t_i, $i = 1,2,...,n$, we may write the total effort as $T = \sum_{i=1}^{n} t_i$. With an ethic of equal sharing, the consumption, c_i, of person i will be given by $c_i = Q/n$. While the ownership of the asset land is usufruct, the sharing of the flow output from it (food) does not derive from this but, rather, from a social convention.[15]

Thus, the utility maximizing problem of person i can be written as

---

15 Whether the food is cultivated privately on usufruct land and then shared or is cultivated jointly, there will be a moral hazard in the application of effort—which is the important thing to capture. I have opted for the latter route.

$$\max_{t_i,\, g_i,\, \ell_i} \quad \left(A\left(t_i + T_{-i} \right)^{\mu} / n \right)^{\alpha} \left(g_i + G_{-i} \right)^{\beta} \left(\ell_i \right)^{\gamma}$$

$$\text{subject to} \quad t_i + g_i + \ell_i = 1, \qquad\qquad (2.3)$$

where T_{-i} and G_{-i} are the total time contributions to production and to the group cultural activity, respectively, by all members other than i. That is, $T_{-i} = \sum_{j \neq i}^{n} t_j$ and $G_{-i} = \sum_{j \neq i}^{n} g_j$. We shall eliminate the time constraint by setting $\ell_i = 1 - t_i - g_i$.

Note that the cultural good is a pure public good for the community.[16] There are two activities of the Indigenous community in this model that entail externalities: production for food consumption and participation in group cultural activities. Increase in individual effort in each case benefits the individual and also benefits the group. In food production, any free riding by an individual (by shirking) lowers output, but the person bears only $1/n$ of the fall in output due to the equal-sharing arrangement. In the cultural activity, which is a pure public good, any free riding lowers the cultural output but the free rider bears the full cost of the subsequent decline in output (and so do all the others). Thus, while free riding can also occur in the contribution to cultural good, it is more consequential to the free rider. Therefore, the application of effort towards the cultural good reduces free riding tendencies, all else constant. This underscores the difference between culture and food production in the model: the participation in culture, which is so important to many Indigenous communities, is nonexcludable; whereas food, once shared, is not.

I examine below the outcome when members of the community entertain Nash conjectures. In this scenario, each individual makes conjectures about the choices of others and takes them as given while non-cooperatively making their own choices. In the Nash equilibrium, which I focus on, the assumed conjectures are borne out for all members of the group; no one has any regrets about their choices.[17] It is easy to

---

16 In his influential paper on why religious sects may self-impose restrictions that seem to stigmatize themselves in the eyes of the rest of society, Iannaccone (1992) refers to an analogous religious good as a 'club good'. More generally, as pointed out, the cultural good is a 'relational good', a concept coined earlier by Uhlaner (1989) and emphasized by Trosper (2022) in the Indigenous context.

17 It may be objected that (the less-tractable) cooperative behaviour may be more appropriate than Nash behaviour in a community-oriented setting. But by showing the effects of culture under the assumption of Nash behaviour, I am rigging the case

show (see the Appendix to this chapter) that, in the symmetric Nash equilibrium, the time allocations $\{t^*, g^*, \ell^*\}$ of any member of the community are given by

$$t^* = \frac{\alpha\mu}{\alpha\mu + \beta + n\gamma} \; ; \; g^* = \frac{\beta}{\alpha\mu + \beta + n\gamma} \; ; \; \ell^* = \frac{n\gamma}{\alpha\mu + \beta + n\gamma} \; . \quad (2.4)$$

An increase in the community size, n, reduces the time devoted to common food production and to group cultural activities, which may be expected given our standard intuition of free riding in teams (Alchian and Demsetz, 1972). This captures the self-interested aspect of the production of the consumption good (food) and the cultural good: free riding off the common effort makes more time available for private leisure.

The equilibrium egoistic utility, U^*, of a member of this community can be readily shown by substitution of the expressions in (2.4) into (2.1) as

$$U^* = \frac{A^\alpha}{n^{(1-\mu)\alpha-\beta-\gamma}} \frac{(\alpha\mu)^{\alpha\mu} \beta^\beta \gamma^\gamma}{(\alpha\mu + \beta + n\gamma)^{\alpha\mu+\beta+\gamma}} \; . \quad (2.5)$$

2.3.2 Model with Private Property

Land as private property in the neoclassical conception is *not* the norm among Indigenous Peoples. Nevertheless, as discussed in Chapter 4 the governments in the U.S. and Canada on various occasions have sought to privatize land on reserves (or reservations in the U.S. context) by dividing up common land into individual parcels. To investigate the effect of this, assume that of the total land of 1 unit, each community member gets a private allocation of $1/n$ unit.[18] The difference now is that each member is the sole proprietor of their own food production, applies their own effort to it, and solely consumes the output without sharing. Since the fixed factor land goes from 1 to $1/n$ in this case, the

---

against myself; with cooperative behaviour, the role of culture would be even more pronounced.

18   As mentioned, land in this model is a stand-in for all the natural resources in the community, many of which have a common pool nature. One can conceive of agricultural land and forests being divided in shares of $1/n$, but what about the division of a fishery or of game that move across boundaries? The tacit assumption of the model in the privatization scenario is that individual quotas are put in place. For example, in the fishery, each individual can harvest only $1/n$ of the total allowable catch determined by the community. Likewise with game hunting.

output, q_i, of person i's assigned land becomes

$$q_i = A (1/n)^{1-\mu}(t_i)^\mu. \tag{2.6}$$

Thus the (egoistic) utility maximizing problem of a person i can be written in this case as

$$\max_{t_i, g_i, \ell_i} \left(A (t_i)^\mu / n^{1-\mu}\right)^\alpha (g_i + G_{-i})^\beta (\ell_i)^\gamma$$

subject to $t_i + g_i + \ell_i = 1.$ (2.7)

As before, we can eliminate ℓ_i by using the time constraint and setting $\ell_i = 1 - t_i - g_i$. By mimicking the steps in the Appendix that led to (2.4), we obtain the solution, denoted by $\{t^+, g^+, \ell^+\}$, as

$$t^+ = \frac{n\alpha\mu}{n\alpha\mu + \beta + n\gamma} \ ; \ g^+ = \frac{\beta}{n\alpha\mu + \beta + n\gamma} \ ; \ \ell^+ = \frac{n\gamma}{n\alpha\mu + \beta + n\gamma}. \tag{2.8}$$

Using (2.1), (2.6), and (2.8), we obtain the Nash equilibrium utility, U^+, of a typical member of the community as

$$U^+ = \frac{A^\alpha}{n^{(1-\mu)\alpha - \alpha\mu - \beta - \gamma}} \frac{(\alpha\mu)^{\alpha\mu} \beta^\beta \gamma^\gamma}{(n\alpha\mu + \beta + n\gamma)^{\alpha\mu + \beta + \gamma}}. \tag{2.9}$$

By comparing the equilibrium solutions in (2.4) and (2.8), we obtain the following proposition.

Proposition 2.1: When the communal land of an Indigenous community is privatized through individual allotments to its members, the time devoted to (a) food production increases, (b) group cultural activity decreases, and (c) private leisure decreases.

The reason behind the above result is that, with the privatization of land, the reward for individual effort in food production is not diluted by sharing with others, thereby increasing food production effort at the cost of cultural activities (which entail team production) and private leisure. Standard neoclassical arguments suggest that privatization of land should curb the free riding in team production (Alchian and Demsetz, 1972). Naturally, as a corollary, the consumption of food will increase and, if this were a measure of wellbeing for Indigenous communities (which it is not), wellbeing would register an increase, too.

That food production theoretically increases with privatization is obvious.[19] The crucial question here, however, is not what happens to food production with privatization, but rather what happens to the level of wellbeing—that is, the utility in the equilibrium. It might appear that the privatization of land should certainly lead to higher welfare because an externality involving team production has been remedied. But this is not necessarily so, as we see when we compare (2.5) with (2.9). Since this comparison entails expressions that are highly nonlinear in the parameters, I make the point with a simple simulation that has a compelling intuitive explanation.

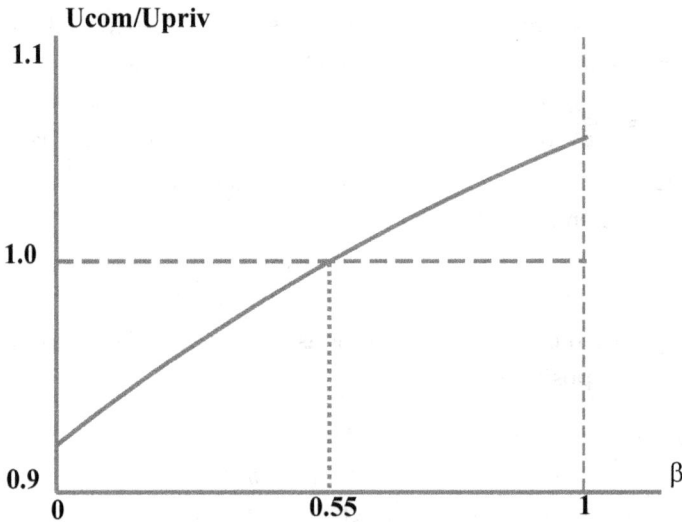

Fig. 2.1. Ratio of (egoistic) equilibrium utility under communal land ownership to that under private ownership as a function of the importance of cultural activities. (Parameter values: $A = 1, \alpha = 0.3, \gamma = 0.3, \mu = 0.6, n = 5$)

When β changes, the functional form of the utility function in (2.1) changes, and so comparisons of the utilities for different values of this parameter are meaningless. However, comparison of the utilities for the *same* value of β is meaningful. So, we can examine the *ratio* of the equilibrium utilities in communal and private property equilibria as a function of β. If this ratio

---

19   Nevertheless, it is not without interest, for it may explain why Sahlins (1972, Ch. 1) in his study of hunters and gatherers was surprised by the limited amount of time they devoted to subsistence activities and thus characterized them as "The Original Affluent Society".

is greater than 1, the communal equilibrium is better than the private one. This is illustrated in Figure 2.1. This figure plots this equilibrium utility ratio—denoted by $Ucom/Upriv$ in the Figure—as a function of β, which captures the importance put on culture in the preferences. The ratio is the upward sloping schedule shown.

When β is 'low'—that is, below about ≈ 0.55 in the Figure—the privatized outcome dominates in the ranking of the outcomes. However, for higher values of β, the communal equilibrium dominates in ranking. In other words, the privatized equilibrium is better when the cultural activity is relatively unimportant, as emphasized by standard models in economics that bring out the virtues of incentives. But when β is relatively large (greater than ≈ 0.55 in the Figure), the private land allotment of the common land of an Indigenous community *lowers* the utility of a typical member in the Nash equilibrium. The communal equilibrium is better when cultural activity is deemed to be important in the preferences—which fits the Indigenous context.

The reason for this finding is interesting. Private allotment increases food production effort at the expense of cultural effort and private leisure. But since this outcome is the result of endogenous choices, one may think that the private land outcome should be better than the common land one—as, indeed, it is when β is low. However, cultural activity entails team production, too, and the reallocation of individual effort to private food production ignores the externality inflicted on other community members in the generation of the group cultural good. Going from two activities that entail team production to only one does not guarantee an increase in the equilibrium utility. This, in fact, is an example of the influential theory of the second best of Lipsey and Lancaster (1956). Their general insight was that when there is one irremovable distortion in an economic system, there is no guarantee that getting rid of other distortions would improve welfare. In fact, welfare may be improved by introducing more distortions, depending on the context. Moral hazard in team production is one such distortion of the standard assumptions under which the equilibrium outcome is Pareto-optimal. In the present context, since there is an externality in the team production of cultural activities, the introduction of a second activity with team production (food production) actually increases welfare.

When land is privatized, effort gets redirected to private production, exacerbating the problem of free riding in cultural production. In Nash behaviour, under the assumed premise of purely egoistic preferences, each person does not take into account this negative externality on other community members. When the cultural good is important, the equilibrium outcome can be worse when land becomes privatized. Since the switch in the ordinal ranking of welfare occurs only at high values of β, we see why this outcome is particularly relevant to Indigenous communities (for many of which culture is very important).

2.4 Summary

This chapter introduced a simple economic model of an Indigenous economy based on two assumptions that deviate from those in standard models of neoclassical economics. The first is the insistence in many Indigenous communities on land ownership being collective, not individual. The second is that culture is deemed very important in Indigenous communities. The model reveals that privatizing land in such a community can lower individual wellbeing, contrary to the standard neoclassical claim that it should improve wellbeing by reducing the scope for free riding on others' effort. And the decline in wellbeing with privatization occurs precisely when culture is important—which is the case for Indigenous communities. We see that the logic that privatization of reserve land would improve wellbeing may hold true for non-Indigenous peoples, especially those of western origins, but is seriously misleading in the Indigenous context.

So far, the important conviction 'we belong to the land' of many Indigenous Peoples has not entirely figured in the economic analysis. The implications of this conviction go well beyond an insistence on collective ownership of the land; it also consolidates the sense of community. This aspect of Indigenous identity and its consequences are addressed in the next chapter.

2.5 Appendix

2.5.1 Derivation of the Nash Equilibrium

Taking the (monotonic) logarithmic transformation of the objective function in (2.3) of the text, we may rewrite the optimization, apart from an additive constant, as

$$\max_{t_i, g_i} \quad \alpha\mu\ln(t_i + T_{-i}) + \beta\ln(g_i + G_{-i}) + \gamma\ln(1 - t_i - g_i)$$

simplifies the algebra without altering the solution. In Nash behaviour, each person takes as given the choices of all the others. The first order conditions with respect to t_i and g_i, therefore, are simply given by the respective partial derivatives of the above objective function:

$$t_i: \quad \frac{\alpha\mu}{t_i + T_{-i}} = \frac{\gamma}{1 - t_i - g_i},$$

$$g_i: \quad \frac{\beta}{g_i + G_{-i}} = \frac{\gamma}{1 - t_i - g_i}.$$

The second order conditions for a maximum are satisfied, given the curvature of the objective function. We would expect that the equilibrium is symmetric because all members of the community have the same preferences and so their choices would be identical. Invoking symmetry and dropping subscripts, we see from the two first order conditions that

$$g = \frac{\beta}{\alpha\mu} t.$$

Using this in either of the first order conditions and solving, we obtain the Nash equilibrium allocations shown in the expressions in (2.4) of the text.

3. Incorporating Cultural Belongingness

3.1 Introduction

This chapter attempts to incorporate into the model of the previous chapter the persistently articulated Indigenous belief that it is they who belong to the land, not the other way around. In the field of social psychology, the need to belong is recognized as one of the most fundamental human needs (Baumeister and Leary, 1995). 'Belonging' means interacting positively with a significant number of others in a group on a regular basis. There are many ways in which humans fulfil this need. Indigenous cultures seem to fulfil this with the holistic manner in which the cultures are conceived. Trosper (2022) describes Indigenous societies as being based on relationships, and suggests that a person's identity comprises the unique relationships that they have. This relational aspect and the resulting relational 'goods' like trust and altruism are at the very core of the notion of belonging. This is important here, and becomes even more important in Part II of this book.

In an insightful essay entitled 'Owning as Belonging/Owning as Property', Noble (2008) brings home the core distinction between the western and Indigenous approaches to ownership. In standard economics, 'owning' means having the right to the exclusive use of an object, an object which can be alienated and disposed of at will. In contrast, when owning is conceived as belonging, as in many Indigenous traditions, the emphasis is on the nature of the transactions and on obligations accompanying the property that is deemed communal.

To my understanding, the Indigenous concept of 'belonging to the land' automatically brings into one's preferences the others who belong

 https://doi.org/10.11647/OBP.0477.03

to the same land, because mutual belonging requires mutual recognition and respect. Right away, we see that this conception requires a departure from the egoistic perspective that is articulated by the claim 'this land belongs to me'. Indigenous cultural beliefs of belonging immediately attenuate the 'me' aspect of self and magnify the 'Us' aspect. Working collectively on the land and engaging in cultural activities could be seen as sacred actions in themselves, thereby increasing their utility worth because they enhance the sense of belonging.[1] In other words, the sense of belonging will automatically induce altruism towards other members of the community.[2] This is in line with Trosper's (2022) emphasis on relationships in Indigenous societies. The first effect of the special nature of land to Indigenous Peoples is the importance of *common ownership* of the land, and some of the consequences of this were analysed in the previous chapter. The second important effect of the Indigenous view of land is the *sense of community* that it brings about. This chapter aims to analyse some consequences of this second aspect.

How does the key sense of belonging translate into transactions between the members of a community? I model this by incorporating other-regarding preferences. These preferences exhibit altruism towards community members relative to the general population. With these preferences, we discover that the findings of the previous chapter on the importance of culture are strengthened. Furthermore, this characterization of Indigenous cultures will be seen to have significant explanatory power in the rest of the book.

---

1   The idea that people may work even for modern organizations in a manner that bolsters their sense of belongingness is foreign to standard economic modelling but, nevertheless, there is empirical evidence to suggest its importance (Green, Gino, and Staats, 2017).

2   Biologists have had a difficult time explaining the observed *fact* of altruism from the point of view of Darwinian evolution. The basic problem was that, within a community, egoists always do better in perpetuating their genes than do altruists (who are willing to sacrifice resources to others). So, natural selection would always favour egoists over altruists. However, in recent decades scientists have made much progress by recognizing the phenomenon of multilevel selection, where evolutionary selection is posited to occur not only at the individual level but often also at the level of groups. As Wilson and Wilson (2007, p. 345) state in the conclusion of their review paper: "Selfishness beats altruism within groups. Altruistic groups beat selfish groups. Everything else is commentary." Therefore, there is a sound empirical and theoretical basis for incorporating altruism in economic models, especially for Indigenous communities. See also Hayes, Atkins, and Wilson (2021) for a discussion of multilevel selection.

3.2 Analytically Conceptualizing 'Belonging to the Land'

Since empirical and experimental work in economics has not investigated the link between belonging and altruism, I shall briefly offer a plausible theoretical justification supported by findings from the field of psychology. In his *The Theory of Moral Sentiments*, Adam Smith argued that we empathize with others essentially by imagining ourselves in their shoes and sensing how we would feel in their place. Furthermore, our empathy is more pleasant if the other person's sentiments are in agreement with ours: "[...] whatever may be the cause of sympathy, or however it may be excited, nothing pleases us more than to observe in other men a fellow-feeling with all the emotions of our own breast; nor are we ever so much shocked as by the appearance of the contrary" (Smith, A., 1759/2000, Ch. II). It would follow that the intensity of our empathy is greater towards people who share our views. Indeed, this probably explains the widely observed proclivity for favouritism towards people who, we believe, belong to the same in-group (and so share our views). In the field of psychology, there is a history of research done over four decades showing that there is a positive correlation between empathy and altruism (see Batson, Lishner, and Stocks, 2015 for a review). Furthermore, if community members consider themselves as belonging to the same land and view the land as their mother, as Indigenous Peoples frequently claim, then community members would view themselves as siblings because they are children with a common parent. That there are built-in prosocial attitudes and behaviours towards siblings is a fact that is too universal to warrant justification here.

The strength of family ties is an important characteristic of all societies. Schultz et al. (2019), who were alluded to earlier in Section 1.4 of Chapter 1, demonstrated a correlation between kinship ties and individuality, among other things. Societies with strong kinship ties— arising from marriages between cousins, for example—exhibit a greater cultural proclivity for obedience, respect towards elders, deference to authority, etc. The authors posit that this arises because, when kinship ties are strong, people reside in extended families, not nuclear ones. It is therefore significant that, in sharp contrast to western societies,

Indigenous communities are organized according to lineages and clans, where a substantial proportion of the people belonging to the community are related by blood or marriage even in contemporary urban settings (Red Horse et al., 1978; Killsback, 2019). These kinship arrangements and also the social ties emphasized by Trosper (2022) would themselves engender feelings of concern for others in the community, and also presumably serve as informal enforcement mechanisms that ensure norm conformity. As a result, Indigenous interpersonal ties were stronger than those between the European colonizers. There are also evolutionary reasons for being more favourably disposed towards members of the same group through preferences (Eaton, Eswaran, and Oxoby, 2011). In a review, Castenello (2002) identifies the extended family as the primary institution for mediating individual, social, and political interactions. Barrington-Leigh and Sloman (2016) find that, in the Canadian prairies, Indigenous Peoples (especially on reserves) place much more weight on family and friends than does the general population. This lends some quantitative empirical support for the other-regarding preferences that I posit below.

In light of this discussion, it is not a great leap to infer that in Indigenous societies the very nature of the cultures lends importance to other-regarding preferences and altruism. A person is not concerned exclusively with their own consumption of various goods, as captured by the egoistic utility function in (2.1) of the previous chapter, but also places some importance on that of others in the community. Subscripting the individual-specific consumptions of person i, as before, we may write the utility of this person with other-regarding preferences, $v i(\to c , G, \to p)$, as given by

$$v_i\left(\vec{c}, G, \vec{\ell}\right) = u_i\left(c_i, G, \ell_i\right) + \sigma\sum_{j\neq i}^{n}u_j\left(c_j, G, \ell_j\right), \qquad (3.1)$$

where $\vec{c}$ and $\vec{\ell}$ denote the vectors of consumption levels of the production output and private leisure of the entire community, respectively. The functions $u_i\left(c_i, G, \ell_i\right)$ are assumed to retain the earlier form given in (2.1). The parameter σ, with $0 \leq \sigma \leq 1$, captures the extent of a community member's concern for all the others who also belong to the same land. I refer to σ as the 'belongingness' parameter that induces altruism towards other community members. For simplicity, σ is assumed to be the same for all individuals in the community, with its magnitude being determined by the specific culture. The first term on the right-hand side of (3.1) captures person i's egoistic concern for themselves, and the remaining terms capture the person's concern for others in the community. When $\sigma = 0$, we are back in the scenario with purely egoistic preferences, considered earlier in Chapter 2. At the other extreme where $\sigma = 1$, each member places the wellbeing of every other member on par with their own (that is, they treat their neighbours as themselves). In this extreme case, each member's objective would clearly coincide with that of a Benthamite social planner, whose objective is to simply maximize the sum of the utilities of all members of the community.

The above rendition of 'belonging to the land' also allows us to model the important idea that the system of property rights is related to the social relations between community members by defining the boundaries between 'me' and 'Us', as discussed in Section 2.2 of Chapter 2. Preferences are captured by $\sigma = 0$ under private property, and by $\sigma > 0$ under communal property. Thus, the parameter σ simultaneously captures the notions of belongingness to the land and belongingness to the community.

3.3 The Belongingness Equilibrium

We are now ready to determine the allocation of resources in our Indigenous community with these preferences in what I call the 'belongingness equilibrium'. The land is assumed to be held in common. What is different from the communal equilibrium considered in the previous chapter is that each community member also has preferences for the wellbeing of others in the community, preferences that are induced by a sense of belonging to the same land, and preferences that stem from interactions being relational.

Person i has control only over their own decisions, and so under Nash conjectures will maximize (3.1) by their choice of t_i, g_i, and ℓ_i subject to the time constraint $t_i + g_i + \ell_i = 1$.[3] As in Chapter 2, this constraint can be used to eliminate ℓ_i and perform an unconstrained optimization with respect to t_i and g_i. The details of the derivation of the Nash equilibrium are shown in the Appendix to this chapter. Essentially,

---

3   As noted in the previous chapter, Nash behaviour understates the effect of 'belongingness' on equilibrium wellbeing.

taking the derivatives of (3.1) with respect to t_i and g_i, simplifying the corresponding expressions after invoking symmetry and dropping the subscripts, solving the two first order conditions, and using the time constraint, we obtain the solution for the 'belonging equilibrium'—denoted by the triplet $\left\{ \tilde{t}^*, \tilde{g}^*, \tilde{\ell}^* \right\}$—as

$$\tilde{t}^* = \frac{\alpha\mu\rho}{\alpha\mu\rho + \beta\rho + n\gamma} \; ; \; \tilde{g}^* = \frac{\beta\rho}{\alpha\mu\rho + \beta\rho + n\gamma} \; ; \; \tilde{\ell}^* = \frac{n\gamma}{\alpha\mu\rho + \beta\rho + n\gamma}, \quad (3.2)$$

where $\rho \equiv 1 + (n-1)\sigma$. This parameter ρ (with $1 \leq \rho \leq n$) captures the effect of social ties on resource allocation. When everyone in the community is purely egoistic, that is $\sigma = 0$, we obtain $\rho = 1$; at the other extreme, when everyone treats their neighbour as themselves, that is $\sigma = 1$, we have $\rho = n$. The effect of changes in the strength of social ties on the belongingness equilibrium, which we investigate below, works through the parameter ρ. Furthermore, when the group size n increases, the standard moral hazard within teams increases. However, when there are social ties present, that is $\sigma > 0$, this moral hazard is tempered because mutual goodwill is spread out across more people. This is why ρ is increasing in n. The effects of a relational society are captured by the parameter ρ.

The egoistic component of the individual utility, $\widetilde{U}^*$, for a typical band member generated in the Nash equilibrium is given by

$$\widetilde{U}^* = \frac{A^\alpha}{n^{(1-\mu)\alpha-\beta-\gamma}} \frac{(\alpha\mu\rho)^{\alpha\mu} (\beta\rho)^\beta \gamma^\gamma}{(\alpha\mu\rho + \beta\rho + n\gamma)^{\alpha\mu+\beta+\gamma}}. \quad (3.3)$$

From the above, the following result immediately follows.

Proposition 3.1: An increase in the parameter σ that captures belongingness monotonically increases the equilibrium egoistic utility of each community member.[4]

Note from (3.1) that when σ increases, the utility from extended preferences would mechanically increase even if the equilibrium resource allocation remains unchanged. To be meaningful, it is the effect on the *egoistic* component of the belongingness equilibrium that Proposition 3.1 refers to. This result shows that concern for others leads

---

4   This can be readily seen by rewriting the expression in (3.3)

as $\widetilde{U}^* = \dfrac{A^\alpha}{n^{(1-\mu)\alpha-\beta-\gamma}} \dfrac{(\alpha\mu)^{\bar{\alpha}\mu} (\beta)^\beta \gamma^\gamma}{(\alpha\mu + \beta + n\gamma/\rho)^{\alpha\mu+\beta+\gamma}}$. An increase in σ leads to an increase in

$\rho \equiv 1 + (n-1)\sigma$, and this reduces the denominator.

every individual to alter their behaviour in a way that results in greater utility for every individual, even when considering only the egoistic portion of their extended preferences and ignoring the utility they derive from others' wellbeing.

Table 3.1. Equilibria being considered, by types of property rights and preferences.

Type of Property Rights	Type of Preferences	Label for the Equilibrium	Equilibrium Egoistic Utility Notation
Private	Egoistic ($\sigma = 0$)	'Private'	$U^{\dagger}$
Common	Egoistic ($\sigma = 0$)	'Communal'	U^{*}
Common	Other-Regarding ($\sigma > 0$)	'Belongingness'	$\tilde{U}^{*}$

This occurs because concern for others reduces free riding in the activities of food production and cultural production, at the expense of private leisure. Thus, the belief 'I belong to the land'—rather than the other way around—is a conception of ownership that induces greater concern for fellow community members and brings about greater cooperation amongst the members.[5] This effect is compounded by the relationship aspect of Indigenous cultures, which is also captured by the belongingness parameter σ. The result in Proposition 3.1 further strengthens what we saw in Chapter 2: even without the sense of belongingness to community, an Indigenous community with private property can have lower welfare than one that has common property— if culture is sufficiently important and/or if members are concerned for one another.

We are dealing with three sorts of equilibria, dubbed 'private',

---

5   It may be noted that belongingness and cooperation are separate concepts; the latter derives from the former here.

'communal', and 'belongingness'. To keep these different scenarios clear in the mind, Table 3.1 may be useful as a mnemonic aid.

We are now ready to see why these equilibria can differ, and the reason is even more important than we might have surmised in Chapter 2. Suppose, for argument, that without a sense of belongingness (that is, $\sigma = 0$), the private property equilibrium welfare-dominates the communal equilibrium because the cultural good is not sufficiently important in the preferences (that is, β is low). Even in this case, introducing a sense of belonging to the land can induce concern for other community members so as to render the *egoistic* component of the belongingness equilibrium utility higher than in the private equilibrium. Figure 3.1 illustrates this point.

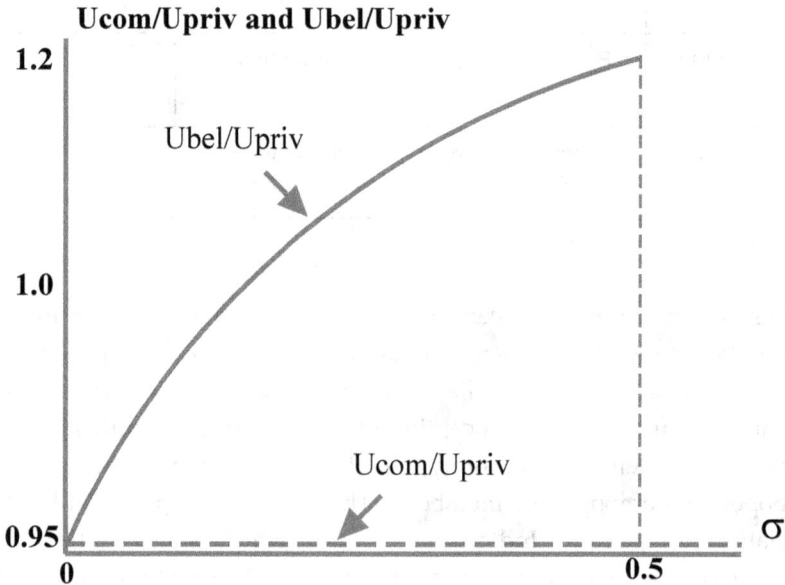

Ucom/Upriv and Ubel/Upriv

Fig. 3.1. Comparison of the egoistic component of equilibrium utilities in privatized, communal and belongingness scenarios as a function of the belongingness parameter σ. (Parameter values: $A = 1$, $\alpha = 0.3$, $\beta = 0.3$, $\gamma = 0.3$, $\mu = 0.6$, and $n = 5$)

It is simplest to compare the ratios of the egoistic utilities in the communal and belongingness equilibria with that in the private property equilibrium as a function of the belongingness parameter, σ. The first ratio is denoted in the Figure by *Ucom/Upriv* (mathematically,

U^*/U^+ of Chapter 2) and the second by *Ubel/Upriv* (mathematically, $\widetilde{U}^*/$ U^+). Recall that the former ratio simply compares the common property utility to the private property equilibrium, as was done in Chapter 2. Since σ played no role in the analysis there, the ratio *Ucom/Upriv* is independent of σ. For the parameter values indicated in the caption of Figure 3.1, this ratio is shown as the horizontal dashed line located at 0.95 along the vertical axis. Since this ratio is less than 1, it means that, for the chosen parameter values, the private property equilibrium dominates the common property one.

Now consider the ratio *Ubel/Upriv*. Since the egoistic utility in the belongingness equilibrium depends nontrivially on the parameter σ, this ratio is not constant. In fact, *Ubel/Upriv* is shown as the upward sloping schedule in Figure 3.1. When $\sigma = 0$, of course the utility in the belongingness equilibrium coincides with that in the communal equilibrium, and so the private equilibrium dominates the belongingness equilibrium, too. But as σ increases, *Ubel* increases and beyond some point the ratio *Ubel/Upriv* exceeds 1. Thus, we see that, even when the private equilibrium dominates the belongingness equilibrium when σ is low, when σ is sufficiently high, the latter dominates the one with private property. This result reinforces the fact that ignoring culture in the analysis of Indigenous societies gives us a misleading picture. Thus, when σ is high, if land is privatized and the collective sense of belonging is demolished, welfare would decline. This is the cost of ignoring culture when it is important to Indigenous communities.

As σ increases, the equilibrium becomes more cooperative even though the members are assumed to entertain (non-cooperative) Nash conjectures. This occurs because, when σ is positive, the wellbeing of others is given some consideration in each member's objective and, therefore, in their allocation of effort. (In fact, as noted in Chapter 2, when $\sigma = 1$ the equilibrium outcome reproduces the Benthamite social optimum.) Thus, the belongingness parameter σ also becomes a proxy for the extent of the cooperativeness embedded in Indigenous culture.

Since food output accrues entirely to oneself under private property but is shared under common property, it would follow that food output is higher under private property, as we saw in Proposition 2.1 of Chapter 2. Is it conceivable that greater cooperation through the cultural perspective of belongingness derived from commonly owned land increases food production and to perhaps the same level as under private property, as σ approaches 1? Greater cooperation due to communal orientation does increase food production but it never eliminates the shortfall relative to the private property output covered in Chapter 2. The reason is that the private property equilibrium is not the correct benchmark of efficiency that a Benthamite social planner (simulated by $\sigma = 1$) would adopt because, in that equilibrium, there is *overproduction* of food relative to what is in the best collective interest of the community.

To see this, consider the total output in the belongingness equilibrium. Using the individual equilibrium effort in (3.2) and substituting into expression (2.2) of Chapter 2, the total output in this equilibrium is given by $\widetilde{Q}^* = A\left(n\,\tilde{t}^*\right)^{\mu}$, which simplifies to

$$\widetilde{Q}^* = A\left(\frac{n\alpha\mu}{\alpha\mu + \beta + n\gamma/\rho}\right)^{\mu}. \tag{3.4}$$

In the private property equilibrium, the total output is the sum of outputs on n individual plots, each of size $1/n$. Thus, the total output of the community in the private property equilibrium, denoted by $Q^{\dagger}$, is given by $Q^{\dagger} = nA\left(\frac{1}{n}\right)^{1-\mu}\left(t^{\dagger}\right)^{\mu}$, where $t^{\dagger}$ is an individual's private effort. Substituting for $t^{\dagger}$ from (2.8) in Chapter 2, the total output under private ownership reduces to

$$Q^{\dagger} = A\,n^{\mu}\left(\frac{n\alpha\mu}{n\alpha\mu + \beta + n\gamma}\right)^{\mu}. \tag{3.5}$$

Using (3.4) and (3.5), the following result is derived in the Appendix to this chapter.

Proposition 3.2:
(*a*) *An increase in the belongingness parameter, σ, increases the food output in the belongingness equilibrium.*
(*b*) *In the private property equilibrium, the food production of the Indigenous community exceeds that in the Benthamite welfare optimum.*

This proposition is illustrated in Figure 3.2.

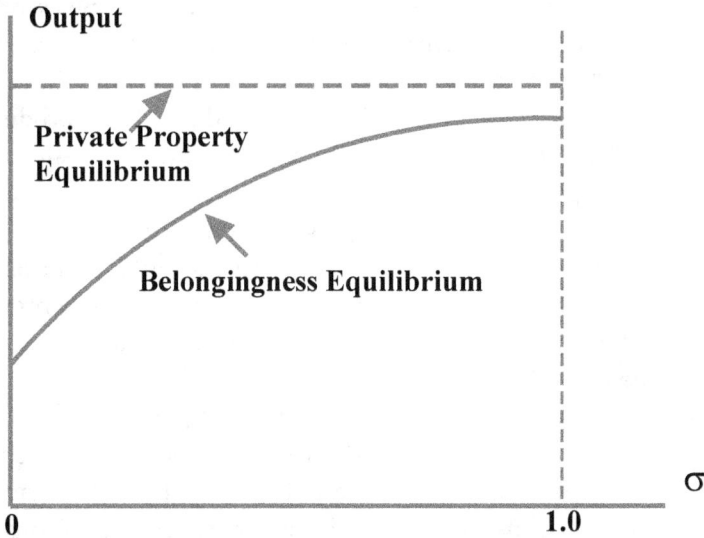

Fig. 3.2. Comparison of the food output in the private property equilibrium with that in the belongingness equilibrium.

The private property equilibrium output is independent of the belongingness parameter, σ, and is shown as the horizontal dashed curve in Figure 3.2. The output in the belongingness equilibrium is shown by the upward-sloping schedule. When the belongingness parameter σ increases, every member working the commonly owned land applies more effort (at the expense of leisure) because they place more weight on the wellbeing of others in the community. Output increases as a result. Note, however, that the entire upward-sloping schedule lies below the dashed line. The belongingness equilibrium output remains below the private property equilibrium output even when σ rises to its maximum value 1. When $\sigma = 1$, each member considers their neighbour's wellbeing on par with their own and is essentially maximizing the Benthamite welfare function. In this welfare optimum, the agricultural output is less than that in the private property equilibrium because, in the latter case, an excessive amount of cultural good is traded-off against the private good (food). That is, the externality in the production of the cultural good is not accounted for in the private property Nash equilibrium, whereas in the Benthamite welfare optimum it certainly is.

The increase in output of Indigenous land due to its reallocation as private property, therefore, says nothing about welfare. Since private food production is excessive, the welfare under private property is lower than what could be generated if some of the time devoted to food production were reduced and time devoted to cultural production increased. The above proposition emphasizes that we cannot take the private property food output as the efficient benchmark for the Indigenous food output in the belongingness equilibrium. In this model, food is the only material good produced and is a stand-in for income. In light of this, we see that the usual practice of using income as a proxy for welfare (a standard practice for non-Indigenous peoples) is misguided when applied to Indigenous Peoples.

There are very few studies that provide comparative measures of wellbeing for Indigenous and non-Indigenous peoples. One such rare study is that of Barrington-Leigh and Sloman (2016), who examined the difference in self-perceived wellbeing between Indigenous and non-Indigenous people in the Canadian prairies.[6] They found that, while income correlates positively with life satisfaction in the general population the world over, the correlation is insignificant for off-reserve Indigenous people and significantly negative for on-reserve Indigenous people. This cautions that we cannot assume incomes can proxy for subjective wellbeing among Indigenous people. This is precisely what can be expected if culture is deemed very important to wellbeing, but it is ignored when income is used as a measure of wellbeing. The preoccupation with income among empirical economists is understandable, given that it is the most widely available statistic, but for Indigenous Peoples it is a poor measure of wellbeing.

When a move from communal ownership to individual ownership takes place, in reality the culturally-induced cooperative behaviour that occurs in the former case is lost and this causes the decline in welfare. The ontological notion of property ('I belong to this land') is dropped in favour of the egoistic one ('this land belongs to me'). Likewise, the relationship orientation ('I am defined by my relationships') is dropped. That is, the community goes from a scenario with $\sigma > 0$ to one with $\sigma = 0$, and the tacit cooperation induced by concern for others is

---

6   In the burgeoning literature on subjective wellbeing, the measure used is a person's own assessment of their life satisfaction (or happiness), put on a suitable numerical scale. It gives us a comprehensive single measure of a person's utility.

forfeited. Note that this theoretical comparison is made here with the total amount of land held constant; a given amount of land simply gets subdivided. This results in a welfare loss because *the territorial boundary imposes a 'boundary' even on social relations*, as described by Nedelsky (1993) and Singer (2000).

Proposition 3.2 (a) can be interpreted in light of the work of Nobel Laureate Elinor Ostrom, who examined in detail what sorts of institutions facilitate the management of the commons. Her work is very relevant here because we consider land as commonly owned in the model's hypothetical Indigenous community. In Ostrom (1990), she laid out the principles that should dictate the management of the commons. More recent work has synthesized her insights with those of evolution in order to identify what sorts of groups behave in a cooperative manner to successfully manage common resources (see Hayes, Atkins, and Wilson, 2021, for a readable account). One characteristic of such groups is that the community should have a sense of shared identity and purpose, so that the group's norms are clearly understood by all. This is precisely satisfied by the Indigenous communities that deeply identify with the land and all its human and non-human beings. As noted earlier, if all community members see themselves as belonging to, and as stewards of, the land that is perceived as their common mother, this will automatically engender feelings of empathy and altruism among members towards one other, and thereby elicit more cooperation.[7] This view is also bolstered by the view of Trosper (2022, Ch. 5), who argues that the relational feature of Indigenous communities is conducive to trust, solidarity, and social capital. One consequence of these aspects of Indigenous communities is captured in part (a) of Proposition 3.2.

I must emphasize that there is a distinction to be made here between the importance of land in reality to Indigenous societies and land as it has been modelled in this book; the importance of the former greatly exceeds what can be captured in a simple economic model. In many Indigenous societies, land is the lynchpin of culture, which partially manifests as the practices of sharing and enhancing the sense of community. Technically, land in my model is only a production input in food and, therefore, is quite limited in its role. Much more importantly,

---

7   Hayes, Atkins, and Wilson (2021) provide a brief review of the evidence on the efficacy of shared values in managing the commons in non-Indigenous settings.

when land is privatized, there is a corresponding division between 'self' and 'others'. The introduction of a physical boundary also introduces a psychological boundary, and the latter reduces the equilibrium welfare of Indigenous Peoples with the privatization of reserves, even as it incentivizes the greater production of food.

As far as I understand, for many Indigenous Peoples it is not possible to separate communal land and culture. Economists may cavalierly draw a clean conceptual separation between the institutions of property and the norms of culture, but this is not actually possible in reality for Indigenous Peoples or, for that matter, any community elsewhere in the world. To assume that these factors can be separated is thus an unwarranted assumption for which there is no evidence, as far as I am aware. An egoistic orientation that sets up boundaries with respect to property ('mine' and 'not mine') also sets up boundaries in culture by drawing sharp distinctions between 'me' and 'not me', between 'self' and 'other'. Property relations and culture are interdependent everywhere. Assuming that they can be cleanly separated may provide some analytic convenience, but it does violence to the reality being analysed.

The pivotal role of land in many Indigenous cultures does not depend on Indigenous communities being largely agricultural. The welfare effects of the division of land into private property will hold even when Indigenous Peoples are workers in modern enterprises, writers, lawyers, academics, and the like. It is the 'I belong to the land' conviction rather than the specific economic use of the land that is the key. Culture has primacy over economics in this scenario.

Although it is welfare and not income that is the focus here, we may ask as an empirical matter: How does income compare across various tenure regimes on Indigenous land? Aragòn and Kessler (2020) investigated in First Nations reserves in Canada the effect of creating individual land holdings that could be transferred, though these fell short of the fee simple rights that would be construed as private property in the usual sense in the rest of Canada. In particular, they examine two sorts of property rights: certificates of possession, which confer legality to possessions, and land leases. They found that, while these land tenures improved investment in housing, they did not improve the incomes of those Indigenous members who were living on the reserves.[8] Pendakur and Pendakur (2018) extended the analysis to a broader range of treaties, and in Pendakur and Pendakur (2021), they confirmed these results and also demonstrated that self-government decreases income inequality.[9]

In the analytic exercises of this chapter and the previous chapter, the focus has been on private versus communal ownership of land, when the total amount of land is assumed to be constant. Historically, the total amount of Indigenous land certainly was not constant but rather experienced a catastrophic decline.[10] This, naturally, would have led to a drastic decline in Indigenous wellbeing—due to the loss of land and also, if the remaining land was subdivided, due to the loss of cooperation (Carlson, 1981a). Furthermore, the current level of Indigenous wellbeing is seriously affected by endogenous outcomes such as worse health, more prevalent substance abuse, trauma, and lower investment in human capital, among other things, as a result of the appropriation of Indigenous land, low employment and income levels, and the erosion of cultures.

3.4 Summary

This chapter has sought to incorporate into an economic model the implications for community ties of two important Indigenous cultural features: 'belonging to the land' and relationship orientation. Compared to Chapter 2, this represents an additional deviation from standard economic models relevant to non-Indigenous peoples, and the findings here further consolidate those of the previous chapter. It has been shown

---

8   Using data from areas in Canada with modern treaties between First Nations people and the federal government regarding land in the neighbourhood of reserves—where the jurisdictions of the First Nations, the government, and between various Indigenous communities were previously unclear—Aragòn (2015) found that the treaties increased incomes in these areas, with positive spillovers.

9   One might wonder why these communities opted for some forms of private property if, as I claim, they can lower welfare. I believe that it is because these changes were accompanied by *self-government*, a very empowering transition—and this is very different from private property being thrust on them by the state government (as in the Dawes Act that we shall discuss in the next chapter). For a different but insightful reason, based on the role played by Canadian government bureaucrats in masking privatization as restorative justice, see Schmidt (2018).

10 See Anderson and McChesney (1994) and Carlos, Feir, and Redish (2022) for analyses of the gradual appropriation of Indigenous land by the United States.

that scenarios that would appear to increase Indigenous wellbeing when culture is ignored and Indigenous land is privatized can, in fact, lower wellbeing. The sense of belongingness that revolves around the perceived sacredness of Indigenous land and the communal feeling it engenders delivers more efficient outcomes according to Indigenous preferences—more efficient relative to the results when income is used as a proxy for wellbeing (a proxy that is maximized with privatization). This sense of belongingness and community orientation will be shown to play an even more important role in the phenomena discussed in subsequent chapters.

3.5 Appendix

3.5.1 Derivation of the Belongingness Nash Equilibrium

Person i maximizes (3.1) of the text which, using (2.1) of Chapter 2, can be written as

$$\max_{t_i, g_i} \quad \left(\frac{A}{n}\right)^{\alpha\mu} (t_i + T_{-i})^{\alpha\mu} (g_i + G_{-i})^{\beta} (1 - t_i - g_i)^{\gamma}$$
$$+ \left(\frac{A}{n}\right)^{\alpha\mu} \sigma \sum_{j \neq i} (t_j + T_{-j})^{\alpha\mu} (g_j + G_{-j})^{\beta} (1 - t_j - g_j)^{\gamma},$$

where leisure has been substituted out using the time constraint. Each member takes the choices of the others as given. After they choose their actions, we would expect that the ensuing Nash equilibrium would be symmetric because all members have identical preferences. Taking the partial derivatives of the above objective with respect to t_i and g_i and then invoking symmetry by setting $t_i = t, g_i = g$, for $i = 1,2,3....,n$, we obtain the first order conditions:

$$t: \quad \frac{\alpha\mu[1 + (n-1)\sigma]}{nt} = \frac{\gamma}{1 - t - g},$$
$$g: \quad \frac{\beta[1 + (n-1)\sigma]}{ng} = \frac{\gamma}{1 - t - g}.$$

Since the right-hand sides of the two first order conditions are equal, the left sides must be too. Equating the left-hand sides, we obtain

$$g = \frac{\beta}{\alpha\mu} t.$$

Substituting for g in terms of t in either first order condition, we can solve for t, then for g, and finally obtain ℓ from the time constraint. This yields the solution shown in equation (3.2) in the text, assuming that the second order sufficient conditions are satisfied.

3.5.2 Proof of Proposition 3.2

(a) Since the logarithm is a monotonic function, we can more easily ascertain the behaviour of $\widetilde{Q}^*$ with respect to σ by taking the logarithm:

$$\log(\widetilde{Q}^*) = \log(A) + \mu\log(n\alpha\mu) - \mu\log\left(\alpha\mu + \beta + \frac{n\gamma}{\rho}\right),$$

where, recall, $\rho = 1 + (n-1)\sigma$. The parameter σ appears only in the last term on the right-hand side. Taking the derivative of this equation with respect to σ, we easily see that

$$\frac{1}{\widetilde{Q}^*}\frac{d\widetilde{Q}^*}{d\sigma} > 0,$$

which proves part (a) of the proposition.

(b) Setting $\sigma = 1$, which as we have seen would reproduce the Benthamite social planner's solution, we have $\rho = n$. Using (3.2), we obtain the output of the community in the belonging equilibrium for $\sigma = 1$, denoted by $\widetilde{Q}^*_{Ben}$, as

$$\widetilde{Q}^*_{Ben} = A\left(\frac{n\alpha\mu}{\alpha\mu + \beta + \gamma}\right)^\mu. \tag{*}$$

Comparing (*) above with (3.5) of the main text, we see that $\widetilde{Q}^*_{Ben} < Q^+$ if and only if

$$\left(\frac{n\alpha\mu}{\alpha\mu + \beta + \gamma}\right)^\mu < n^\mu\left(\frac{n\alpha\mu}{n\alpha\mu + \beta + n\gamma}\right)^\mu,$$

that is, if an only if

$$\frac{1}{\alpha\mu + \beta + \gamma} < \frac{1}{\alpha\mu + \beta/n + \gamma},$$

that is, if and only if $n \geq 2$, which is true. This proves part (b) of the proposition.

4. The Failure of the Dawes' Act in America and Canadian Attempts to Privatize Indigenous Reserves

4.1 Introduction

This chapter deals with attempts to privatize Indigenous lands in North America. *The Royal Proclamation of 1763* was the first law to specify how Indigenous land would be bought and sold in Britain's North American colonies. It declared that only the Crown could transact land deals with First Nations. This was, in part, to protect Indigenous land from settlers, but it was also strategic: Britain, being militarily vulnerable at the time, did not want to stir up wars with First Nations, and by becoming the only buyer of Indigenous land, the Crown could acquire land more cheaply from First Nations (Kades, 2000; Lavoie, 2016). The importance of culture to Indigenous communities did not appear to be a consideration.

In both the United States and Canada, the legal tradition maintained that Indigenous people themselves were not allowed to sell their land except to the government, even as their traditional territories were overrun with settlers. The reserve lands that were eventually conferred on Indigenous communities were intended to be held communally. In Canada it is only recently, with the negotiation of modern treaties, that a couple of First Nations hold some of their land in fee simple, allowing them to sell that land to people who are not members of their community.

As we saw in the previous chapter, privatization of the land of Indigenous Peoples based on the western concept of property rights contributes to an erosion of the culture that is cherished by Indigenous communities. It is difficult for a person to claim 'This is my land' in an

  https://doi.org/10.11647/OBP.0477.04

exclusive sense and also adhere to the belief 'I belong to this land' at the same time. The adoption of an egoistic perspective must come at the expense of the cultural perspective, with an attendant change in welfare on this count. As discussed in the previous chapter, institutions and culture cannot be neatly separated. In fact, the institutions of a society are reflections of its cultural values and also shape its cultural values. Since there is a two-way causality between institutions and culture, we cannot expect to change the institutions without affecting culture (Alesina and Giuliano, 2015; Rose, 2018; Throsby, 2001; Taiaiake Alfred, 2023).

It is important in this context, therefore, to consider historical attempts in the United States and in Canada to dismantle Indigenous culture with regard to land by replacing entrenched institutions shaped over millennia. Since land occupies a very special place in Indigenous cultures, this chapter will discuss attempts to dislodge the deep belief among many Indigenous communities in communal ownership of land and replace it with belief in individual private property. It will first outline the *General Allotment Act* (or the *Dawes Act*) of 1887 in the United States, and then describe the repeated attempts in Canada to bring about the same effects as this Act.

4.2 The *General Allotment Act*, 1887

In the United States of the 1870s, there was increasing sentiment among politicians and Christian religious groups that the solution to the 'Indian problem' lay in assimilating Indigenous Peoples into mainstream American culture. To accomplish assimilation, it was seen as necessary that Indigenous cultures be erased and the people 'civilized' by the adoption of agriculture and conversion to Christianity.[1] Assimilation was to be a prelude to becoming enfranchised as American citizens (which ultimately came through the *Indian Citizenship Act* in 1924). For assimilation to be accomplished, however, it was believed that the practice of communal ownership of land had to be destroyed. This was the vision that would inform one of the most influential pieces of

---

1   Agriculture was by no means an introduction of European settlers to the New World. Indigenous groups had been practicing agriculture in various parts of North America for millennia (see Dunbar-Ortiz, 2014).

legislation pertaining to Indigenous Peoples: *The General Allotment Act* or *Dawes Act of 1887*, which sought to break up and replace communal ownership and social bonds with selfishness. A few years earlier, Senator Henry Dawes, upon seeing some smoothly running Indigenous reserves, had this to say:

> They have got as far as they can go, because they own their land in common [...] *There is no selfishness, which is at the bottom of civilization.* Till this people will consent to give up their lands, and divide them among their citizens so that each can own the land he cultivates, they will not make much more progress. (*Lake Mohonk Conference Proceedings*, 1885, p. 43, emphasis added)[2]

As Stremlau (2005) has pointed out, communal ownership of land was the target of the Act because it engendered kinship relations that were given precedence over individual interests. (In terms of the model in the previous chapter, the attempt was to reduce the belongingness parameter σ from $\sigma > 0$ to $\sigma = 0$.)

Apart from the perceived sense of racial superiority of European Americans, who saw it as an obligation to civilize Indigenous Peoples and to Christianize them, the Act also resulted from pressure applied by European settlers and land speculators who wanted to lay hold of any land found to be in 'surplus' (Otis, 1973). As Carlson (1981b, Ch. 4) describes, "The reformers hoped the Dawes Act would accomplish at least six things: break up the tribe as a social unit, encourage individual initiative, further the progress of Indian farmers, reduce the cost of Indian administration, secure at least part of the reservation as Indian land, and open unused lands to white settlers" (p. 79). With the exception of a few reservations (deemed 'civilized'), the *Dawes Act* gave 160 acres of reservation land to every Indigenous family head, 40 acres to every adult over eighteen years of age, and 40 acres to every Indigenous person younger than eighteen. The land that was given to Indigenous persons was fee simple, private property that could be bought and sold

---

2   Fourteen years after the *Dawes Act* became law, in his first annual speech President Theodore Roosevelt said: "The General Allotment Act is a mighty pulverizing engine to break up the tribal mass. It acts directly upon the family and the individual. Under its provisions some sixty thousand Indians have already become citizens of the United States. We should now break up the tribal funds, doing for them what allotment does for the tribal lands; that is, they should be divided into individual holdings." https://www.presidency.ucsb.edu/documents/first-annual-message-16

after twenty-five years, during which period it was held in trust by the federal government and at the end of which the Indigenous person was to become a citizen of the U.S.[3] Indigenous Americans did not have the choice of accepting or refusing. The surplus land left over (around 90 million acres) after this allotment was sold to white settlers.

Matters may have been compounded by the *Homestead Act* (1862–1934), which gave away 160 acres of free land to those non-Indigenous people who wanted to farm. The homesteaders, through their aggressiveness and hunger for land, facilitated the process of appropriating Indigenous land by populating public lands whose ownership was contended by Indigenous Americans (Allen, 1991). Perhaps this also forced the government to protect Indigenous property by assigning fee simple property rights (Wilm, 2020). In the decades that followed, land ownership among Indigenous Americans haemorrhaged. The *Dawes Act* was repealed in 1934 by the *Indian Reorganization Act*, and during the period in between, Indigenous land holdings fell from 138 million acres to 48 million acres (Akee, 2020).[4] In the near half-century of operation, the *Dawes Act* may not have achieved its goal of assimilating Indigenous Americans, but it did dramatically reduce Indigenous land holdings and destabilize Tribal cultures.

In light of the results of the model in the previous two chapters, we see that even if it is assumed that the U.S. government's intention of private allotment of reservation lands through the *Dawes Act of 1887* was to improve the wellbeing of the Indigenous Peoples, it need not have worked—as, indeed, it did not (Carlson, 1981a; Roback, 1992). The reformers in the *Dawes Act* sought to weaken the culture of the communities because, as noted, sharing was perceived as an ethic that thwarts economic development; enlightened self-interest was seen as the driver of development (Carlson, 1981b, Ch. 4).[5] Based on a standard

3   Indigenous owners could lease out the land and, as it turned out later, even sell it before the twenty-five years expired.
4   McChesney (1990) has a different explanation for the *Dawes Act* and its repeal. He argues that the *Dawes Act* was in the interest of bureaucrats because its implementation in 1887 increased bureaucratic budgets, which also increased politicians' scope for patronage appointments. However, as more land was privatized, the need for the bureaucracy also declined, and so the bureaucracy and the politicians found it expedient to put a stop to any further privatization and the Act was repealed in 1934.
5   An Indian agent is quoted by Otis (1973, p. 18) as saying in 1882, "I do not think

model of agricultural production, Carlson (1981a) offered a theoretical reason for why the *Dawes Act* actually discouraged Native Americans from becoming farmers, causing food production to decrease. He argued that the land plots that were allotted had so many restrictions on them (e.g. initially they could not be used as collateral or be leased) that the Indigenous owners were incentivized to abandon farming and sell their land when they could. Using extant data, case studies, and reports, Carlson (1981a) suggests that the productivity of Indigenous farmers was improving before allotment (even though it was below that of white farmers) but it declined after allotment. My model in the previous chapters predicts an increase in food production upon privatization of reservation land because it does not account for any institutional restrictions but, despite this, it shows that Indigenous welfare could decline when the cultural good is deemed important.

Akee (2020) has examined the effect of the *Nelson Act of 1899* (a modified application of the *Dawes Act* to the state of Minnesota) that provided private plots to Native Americans to encourage farming. He found that farming actually declined among Indigenous individuals who were allotted private land. In fact, land- and home-ownership among them declined, which Akee attributes to lack of experience in dealing with property taxes, land sales, and accessing credit. As a result, peoples belonging to the poorest groups in the country lost a most important asset. They became renters and increased their participation in the labour market, which were not the intended goals of the *Nelson Act*. This graphically reveals some of the consequences of promoting assimilation through the erasure of Indigenous cultures.

The theoretical results of the previous two chapters suggest why the allotment of reservation land as private property among Indigenous Americans may have done more damage than good in a welfare sense. Theory implies that it loosened cultural bonds and reduced the degree of tacit cooperation in the communities. The reality was even more stark: Indigenous American communities were hurt even in a material sense. Carlson (1981a, p. 137; 1981b) pointed out that, contrary to the view that

---

that the results of labor ought to be evenly distributed irrespective of the merits of individuals, for that would discourage effort; but under the present communistic state of affairs such would appear to be the result of the labor of many." This is standard neoclassical thinking that emphasizes the aspect of free riding in teams.

Indigenous Americans had no property rights system in place before 1887, the truth was that the *Dawes Act* merely replaced an earlier system. Roback (1992) insightfully observes that the *Dawes Act* essentially dismantled Indigenous systems of dealing with externalities without replacing them:

> Allotment failed because it privatized land among individuals without understanding the existing family and tribal structure or the property rights structure that accompanied it. The Indians had developed these structures to solve their own problems and to internalize the externalities they faced. When the Department of the Interior made a conscious policy to break down Indian tribal and family life, these problem-solving structures were broken down as well... The irony is that the culture dissolved in its ability to keep order and produce wealth among its members, but this was not accompanied by a transfer of loyalty to white institutions and culture. (p. 23)

Recent findings of Baragwanath and Bayi (2020) may be interpreted as one example showcasing Indigenous efficacy in the control of externalities. These authors found that deforestation in the Brazilian Amazon was causally reduced when the Indigenous Peoples' territories were restored to full (collective) property rights. This shows that Indigenous institutions of management are well-equipped to deal with the externalities that plague the destruction of the Amazon forests, and that they work well when the Indigenous Peoples are given full rights.[6] Relationships within Indigenous societies are well-placed to solve problems involving externalities (Trosper, 2022).

Anderson and Lueck (1992) compared the agricultural performances of Indigenous land under three different land tenure systems in the United States. These three systems are the standard ones: fee simple land (private property), individual trust land, and tribal trust land. The latter two have various constraints imposed that, among other things, prevent Indigenous individuals from accessing credit in the manner that fee simple property does. The authors found that, compared to that in fee simple land, the agricultural productivity of an acre of land is 85–90% lower for tribal trust land and 30–40% lower for individual trust

---

6   See Ostrom and Hess (2008) for examples of efficient management of the commons in non-Indigenous scenarios.

4. The Failure of the Dawes' Act 75

land.[7] Although the authors' intention may have been to illustrate the superiority of fee simple land ownership, this finding has to be viewed in light of part (b) of Proposition 3.2 of the previous chapter. There it was shown that private property results in overproduction and is actually inefficient when culture is important. As my analysis indicated, there is nothing normative about the decline in output when culture matters; the fee simple outcome is simply not the right benchmark for comparison.

In the private allocation of Indian land in the *Dawes Act*, the land was held in trust by the government with the proviso that it could be converted to fee simple land if the owners showed they had been culturally assimilating. But this proviso ended in 1934. Dippel and Frye (2021) compared Native American landowners in 1940 by whether or not their land had been converted to fee simple by 1934. They found that households whose land had been converted to fee simple earned higher incomes and sent their children to school longer. But this, they found, was due to their cultural assimilation and *not* due to the fee simple nature of their land. In other words, the higher earnings cannot be attributed to the western-style property rights adopted by the subset of Indigenous people before 1934.

4.3 Canadian Attempts at Privatizing First Nations Reserves

The attitude of the Canadian government (pre- and post-Confederation) towards Indigenous Peoples was partly one of offering protection against exploitation by European immigrants. This is why Indigenous Peoples were given special status in the *Royal Proclamation of 1763* (Tobias, 1983). (This did not, of course, prevent colonial dispossession of Indigenous land, as chronicled by Harris (2004) for British Columbia.) But the long-term goal in Canada was to ultimately assimilate Indigenous Peoples into the rest of Canadian society.[8] Assimilation is a way of eliminating

---

7   Citing that culture and tribal integrity considerations may be important, the authors did not conclude that trust land systems should be replaced by fee simple systems. It must be noted that the authors do not seem to have had the data to control for the quality of land for all three categories.

8   Even as late as the 1920s, the Indian Superintendent Duncan Campbell Scott said,

future claims being made by Indigenous Peoples on the lands which belong to the Indigenous, as compellingly argued by Wolfe (2006). This assimilation, in Canada as in the United States, was to occur in three domains: economically by the adoption of agriculture, culturally by the shedding of Indigenous cultural beliefs (including belief in communal ownership of property), and religiously by conversion to Christianity.

By about 1830, the Canadian government's priorities started to shift towards faster assimilation leading to enfranchisement. The 1857 *Gradual Civilization Act* linked the education of a male Indigenous person over twenty-one to becoming enfranchised and no longer being deemed an Indian. An enfranchised Indigenous person would be given 50 acres of land from the reserve as their own—an early attempt at privatization of reserve land. This attempt at encouraging citizenship with the inducement of private property instead of communal property failed dramatically. In 1876, under the *Indian Act*, in which the government assumed sweeping powers over Indigenous issues, an Indigenous person obtaining a degree or joining the clergy would become a citizen, receiving a part of the reserve land for themselves and forfeiting their status as 'Indian'—the mandatory forfeiture of status being repealed only in 1961 (Canadian Encyclopedia, 2020). Indigenous Peoples in Canada finally got the right to vote in 1960, without having to lose their Indian status.

In 1969, the Minister of Indian Affairs and Northern Development, Jean Chrétien, in the government of Pierre Trudeau, issued the so-called *White Paper* (1969). This document proposed to do away with the *Indian Act* and the treaties in one stroke, thereby unburdening the Indigenous of reserve lands, rendering those lands private property, and also eliminating the government's fiscal responsibility towards Indigenous Peoples. The proposal—which was a wholesale attempt at privatizing reserve land and enfranchising all Indigenous Peoples as ordinary Canadians with no particular status—was vehemently rejected, and was subsequently withdrawn by the government.[9]

"I want to get rid of the Indian problem. Our object is to continue until there is not a single Indian in Canada that has not been absorbed." Quoted in Manuel and Derrickson (2015, p. 9).

9   A very strong response to the *White Paper* was given by the Indian Chiefs of Alberta (1970) in a paper that came to be known as 'The Red Paper'.

In Canada, too, as in the United States, we see that Indigenous Peoples' communal ownership of land was deemed an impediment to becoming 'civilized' and enfranchised. Also, impelled by the desire for land, European settlers claimed that Indigenous Peoples did not engage in agriculture (for only land on which labour was bestowed was counted as owned; the activities of hunting, fishing, trapping, etc. did not count).[10] Carter (1991; 2019, Ch. 6) documents the fact that, in 1880s Saskatchewan, Indigenous communities were quite successful in agriculture. However, the Indian Commissioner at the time, Hayter Reed, forced Indigenous farmers to individually practice subsistence peasant farming on 40 acres of land, which was presumed to be enough to feed a family. To thwart sharing and cooperation, Reed actively placed impediments to prevent the joint buying of machinery (and thereby sharing the large fixed cost of more productive technology) to exploit scale economies and to participate in local markets.[11] Carter (1991) observes that the Canadian government undermined Indigenous agriculture at a crucial juncture of its development. This was possibly to demonstrate that Indigenous Peoples could not succeed in agriculture and, therefore, could be relieved of 'surplus land' to make it available to settlers instead.[12] So we see that, even though Canada had no legislation like the *Dawes Act*, there were repeated attempts at privatizing reserve lands in Canada.

---

10   In the Americas, Indigenous populations fell drastically when they succumbed to diseases introduced by European settlers. As a result, agricultural land was left vacant for long periods and forests reclaimed the landscape (see e.g. Denevan, 1992; Liebmann et al., 2016). As Denevan (1992, p. 369) puts it: "A good argument can be made that the human presence was less visible in 1750 than it was in 1492". We may arguably infer that this would have made it easier for settlers to appropriate Indigenous land by claiming that the land was pristine and invoking the doctrine of Locke (1689/1967) that is discussed in the next chapter.

11   "He boasted that under his administration 'the policy of destroying the tribal or communist system is assailed in every possible way, and every effort made to implant a spirit of individual responsibility instead.'" Carter (1991, p. 355).

12   South of the border, Cheyenne communities were similarly handicapped by an absence of U.S. government help in their agricultural endeavour (Bateman, 1996).

4.4 Contemporary Canadian Debates on Privatizing Reserve Lands

In the current climate in Canada, there is an initiative to move towards privatizing reserve land, which this book has some relevance to.[13] The *Indian Act of 1876* took intrusive and oppressive control of the lives of First Nations Peoples. Even very routine transactions within reserves (such as land transfers between band members) required approval by the Minister of Crown-Indigenous Relations and Northern Affairs. Leasing reserve land to non-reserve members was an even more time-consuming process, which undermined possible business transactions and stunted economic development (Alcantara, 2007). Naturally, many First Nations wanted to control the management of their reserve land.

Starting with the initiative of 14 First Nations in the early nineties, in 1999 the *First Nations Land Management Act* (FNLMA) was passed by parliament. With this Act, First Nations could voluntarily opt out of sections of the *Indian Act* and opt in to administering their own land by developing land codes, instead of having transactions mediated by the dictates of the *Indian Act*. The FNLMA benefitted dozens of First Nations that chose to opt into it. However, there were also some drawbacks to the Act[14] and it was repealed and superseded in December 2022 by the Framework Agreement on *First Nation Land Management Act*.[15] These Management Acts were about governance and, to the extent that many First Nations acquired more control over reserve land, this was for the better. Fligg and Robinson (2020) reported welfare measures at the community level, called the community wellbeing index (CWB), for First Nations under the *Indian Act*, the FNLMA, and self-government (obtained by negotiation with the Canadian and provincial governments). The average index for each group was lowest for those under the *Indian Act* and highest for those with self-government. We may tentatively draw the inference that FNMLA improved First Nations wellbeing compared to the *Indian Act*.

---

13 Feir (2024) provides an informative review of the literature on Canadian policy on Indigenous issues in the past five decades.

14 For example, developing a land code was too expensive for some First Nations.

15 See the paper by Coates and Baumann (2023) for a discussion of recent developments in First Nations land management and for their drawbacks.

These Acts, however, were *not* about privatization per se. In 2006, the First Nations Tax Commission initiated a move to introduce opt-in private, individual, fee simple plots on reserve land through a scheme called the *First Nations Private Ownership Act* (FNPOA), which has not succeeded yet in being passed by Parliament. This proposal was strongly endorsed by Flanagan, Alcantara, and Le Dressay (2010) in their book *Beyond the Indian Act*, inspired by the thinking of De Soto (2003). The logic of De Soto, drawing on his experience from Peru, is that land that is not private property cannot be mortgaged and so cannot raise capital. Therefore, he argued, communal land is 'dead capital', unusable for economic development. The variation on the *Dawes Act* in the FNPOA proposal is that, if privatized reserve land were to be used as collateral, in the event of default on the loan the land would revert to the First Nation, not the provincial Crown, and so the land would stay within the reserve.[16]

Moving to individually owned plots in reserves will diminish cultural solidarity, for property then gets defined by geographical boundaries rather than by relationships. We have seen that relationships are the hallmark of Indigenous communities (Trosper, 2022). In terms of the model presented in the previous two chapters, this move towards individual ownership would emphasize the 'me' component of self at the expense of the 'Us' component. Thus, in contemplating the sale of a plot to a non-Indigenous person or entity, the shift in perspective will lower the perceived cost to an Indigenous owner of the reserve's attenuation and, therefore, raise the person's willingness to sell. And the larger the share of non-Indigenous owners in the reserve, the lower the cultural pressure on Indigenous owners to *not sell*.[17] In this manner, the entire Indigenous reserve will tend to unravel once private property is adopted by a community. In other words, even though the adoption of private property is voluntary, it is not innocuous. It undermines the collectivity by emphasizing selfishness—not by fiat, as did the *Dawes Act*, but by tacitly introducing a wedge between the individual and the

---

16   There have been several insightful critiques of the proposal earlier (see Dempsey, Gould, and Sundberg, 2011; Pasternak, 2015; Fabris, 2017; Carter and Kermoal, 2020).

17   Castro-Rea and Altamirano-Jimenez (2008) point out that 0.3% of non-Indigenous Americans live on reserves, making it difficult for Indigenous Peoples to self-govern.

collective. Neoliberalism, with its emphasis on individual freedom, is not optimal when there are externalities.

Under legislation such as the proposed FNPOA, the decision to adopt private property is a collective choice of the community, not an individual one. It becomes very important to ensure participation by *all* community members in expressing their vote, for once the choice of adoption of private property is made, the dissolution of the reserve may become inevitable.

If economic assimilation with the rest of Canada is deemed to *require* fee simple private property as a necessary condition, given the special cultural status of Indigenous land this will very likely result in cultural assimilation, too. Spurring economic development by integration with a globalized world through institutional changes like private property may spell the end of Indigenous aspirations to self-determination. The fact that only a couple of First Nations (the Nisga'a and the Tsawwassen) out of some 630 First Nations in Canada have opted for fee simple land ownership—and even that in a limited way—suggests that the FNPOA proposal is missing something that is important to First Nations. An understanding of the irreversibility of an action that would set the reserve on a slippery slope to inevitable disappearance probably explains the refusal of the overwhelming majority of communities to pursue fee simple land ownership.

All this is not to suggest that economic development requires private property. Proponents of the privatization of reserves often equate Indigenous communal ownership with communism—a serious error because such a view ignores the crucial role of Indigenous culture. When the lynchpin of Indigenous societies—the glue that is land-based cultures—is discounted, one is left only with the well-recognized and standard moral hazard problems of communism. What follows then is the well-worn but erroneous critique of presumed inefficiency based on the claim that sharing induces free riding and laziness. In reality, there is no presumption that private property is a necessary condition for economic development.

In any case, the limited evidence to date on the effects of western property rights on the welfare of Indigenous Peoples is not encouraging (Aragòn and Kessler, 2020). The erroneously presumed efficiency of private property rights in the Indigenous context bears repeating.

This claim may have validity in other societies and economies where the destruction of culture is not at stake. In my analysis of Indigenous communities, which takes Indigenous preferences seriously, the maximization of income or wealth is not the highest priority. Privatizing property rights would necessarily lead to a de facto abandonment of the deep cultural belief 'I belong to the land'.

We cannot ignore the history of the fur trade in bringing devastation to the lives of the Indigenous Peoples through market forces when resource use was not properly regulated. It induced Indigenous communities to abandon traditional ways of life to specialize in hunting to supply the European demand for fur that ultimately led to the undoing of the Indigenous suppliers according to Innis (1962), and to the dismantling of informal property rights regimes that conserved beaver stocks (Carlos and Lewis, 1999). Had property rights been well-defined or were the harvests well-regulated, trade need not have led to the devastation of beaver stocks.[18] But, with rising prices spurred by competition for fur in Europe and for a variety of Indigenous cultural constraints, the Indigenous Peoples came to treat the beaver as an open access resource—leading to its over-exploitation (Carlos and Lewis, 1999). In an illuminating analysis, Taylor (2011) brings home the importance of international trade in decimating the American bison stock, though he does not examine the effect of the extinction of the bison on Indigenous communities per se. Feir, Gillezeau, and Jones (2024) have demonstrated the lasting effect of this resource loss on the wellbeing of Indigenous Peoples. In light of persistent attempts at privatization of Indigenous land and subsequent exposures to markets, policies that are ahistorical in their approach to the problems confronting Indigenous Peoples are understandably and rightly met with much circumspection by the communities.

4.5 Summary

This chapter first discussed the disastrous attempt in the United States to privatize reserve land by the *Dawes Act of 1887*. Then, it summarized attempts in Canada to achieve the same ends—all largely unsuccessful.

---

18 There has been an extended debate on whether Indigenous Peoples have historically been conservationist. See Hames (2007) for a brief review of this contentious issue.

The Acts and proposals in Canada to move Indigenous communities outside the oversight of the *Indian Act of 1876* were then considered. To date, the proposal to make reserve land private property has not been adopted by an overwhelming majority of First Nations. This chapter provided reasons for this outcome. The argument is that the communities recognize that adoption of private property will inevitably erode the community's culture and will ultimately result in assimilation. The bottom line is that proposals with regard to Indigenous land must be premised on a deep understanding of the land- and relationship-based cultures of the Indigenous Peoples.

PART II

The Health Effects of the Erosion of Indigenous Community

This part of the book incorporates into the model of Part I the realities of historical trauma and the option of devoting resources to pain alleviation. It first explains the phenomenon of historical trauma and then examines the equilibrium outcome in an Indigenous community in the presence of this trauma. The model shows how the sense of community gets eroded in the short run and the long run. The analysis then investigates how this loss of the sense of community through historical trauma contributes to Indigenous deaths of despair, and why these effects are not only continuing but getting worse over time. The analysis also informs us about what in the economic model contributes to the important trait of resilience and why Indigenous approaches to healing are precisely the ones that the economics of the model would suggest because it consults Indigenous preferences and cultures in its analysis rather than using standard, off-the-shelf, western ones.

5. Indigenous Historical Trauma in the North American Context

The concept of historical trauma is invoked by Indigenous and non-Indigenous scholars to argue that the effects of European colonization continue to undermine the wellbeing of Indigenous Peoples of North America. Therefore, it is important to delve into what exactly historical trauma is, in the eyes of scholars and clinical psychologists.[1] Most of this literature falls outside the field of economics, but it is incumbent on economists to come to grips with this literature. If historical trauma impinges on behaviour, it is imperative that economic models should account for it, however tentatively, wherever it emerges. After clarifying the concept of historical trauma, this chapter will briefly outline the background events that led to Indigenous historical trauma.[2] The literature on this is quite vast, and entails many disciplines. The discussion here will be restricted mostly, but not entirely, to important events within the past 150 years or so because there is still some quantitative evidence from this period substantiating the concept.

5.1 Historical Trauma

Historical trauma is a concept that was first conceived in relation to survivors of the Jewish Holocaust. The grief and psychological symptoms of parents who faced losses but survived the Holocaust were seen to be present in subsequent generations (Barocas and Barocas, 1973;

---

1   Weaver (2019) provides a very readable account of the trauma of North American Indigenous Peoples.
2   See Sotero (2006) for a brief summary of the concept. Another readable account of Indigenous American historical trauma can be found in Wiechelt, Gryczynski, and Lessard (2019).

    https://doi.org/10.11647/OBP.0477.05

Felsen and Erlich, 1990). These symptoms—which resembled guilt for surviving and grief from the immediate survivors' incomplete mourning process—were not seen to be present in Jews whose family members lived elsewhere during the Holocaust and had not experienced losses. Brave Heart and DeBruyn (1998) found a similar phenomenon among the Lakota People, who experienced the Massacre at Wounded Knee in 1890 but were prevented from grieving by a ban on the traditional ways. The authors applied the concept of historical trauma to the Lakota People and now it is seen to be relevant more generally to Indigenous Peoples in North America.[3]

Trauma is the result of some threat or terror which causes anxiety and a sense of helplessness. Its effects last long after the event. Post-Traumatic Stress Disorder (PTSD) is one such effect that has high prevalence among Indigenous Peoples.[4] In PTSD, which is deemed to be a highly debilitating disease, there is a tendency to be hyperalert, angry and aggressive, reckless and impulsive, to have difficulty concentrating, to be prone to overreactions, and other symptoms. It is well-documented that PTSD, which is one of the characteristics of historical trauma, is correlated with chronic pain (psychological and physical), anxiety, depression, and suicidal tendencies, among other symptoms (Brennstuhl et al., 2015).

There are many characteristic features of historical trauma. It is *intergenerational*, being passed from parents to children not only through maladaptive behaviour of the parents but also genetically.[5] Therefore, the effects are not merely individual—they affect the whole family. Second, historical trauma affects the *collective*; many people in an Indigenous community share the trauma. There is now a fair amount of evidence that suggests the long-term effects of events that have led to historical trauma (Aguiar and Halseth, 2015; Matheson et al., 2022). Thus, through psychological scarring, traumatic historical events cast a long shadow, and their effects live on for many generations.

There is a whole range of very traumatic events that have been

---

3   As noted earlier, Duran and Duran (1995) also minted the same concept, which they called 'soul wound'.
4   See Beals et al. (2013), Basset et al. (2014).
5   This happens through what are called epigenetic changes, in which gene expressions change in response to stressors (Matheson et al., 2022; Conching and Thayer, 2019).

visited upon Indigenous Peoples in North America since the arrival of Europeans and which have resulted in historical trauma. These are chronicled by Wesley-Esquimaux and Smolewski (2004). First, since 1492 Europeans brought to the Americas infectious diseases like smallpox, measles, and influenza, among others, which the Indigenous Peoples of North America were not immune to. As a result, Indigenous populations were devastated. DNA evidence suggests that Indigenous American populations fell by 50% and that this decline was not localized (O'Fallon and Fehren-Schmitz, 2011). According to Thornton (1987), the Indigenous American population decreased from more than 5 million in 1492 to 0.25 million by the decade of 1890.

The loss of spiritual leaders, shamans, elders, and warriors made social and cultural continuity very difficult. Wesley-Esquimaux and Smolewski (2004) point out that, while Europe also experienced such devastations due to diseases and epidemics, the frequency there was less. As a result, European populations could recover and the disruptions in their cultures were only temporary: cultures could recover their former vibrancy. This was not the case with the Indigenous Peoples of North America, where a relentless series of epidemics visited roughly every 7–14 years. In addition, there were a whole series of other traumatic events, briefly described below, that compounded the effects of population decline.

5.2 The Appropriation of Indigenous Land

As mentioned earlier, the primary resource that is sought in settler colonialism is land, the acquisition of which requires the elimination of previous claimants, though not necessarily through genocide (Wolfe, 2006). Indigenous land was gradually appropriated over the centuries and the original inhabitants are now restricted to a very small fraction of the original terrain.[6] This was done through treaties signed (and often reneged on), squatting by white settlers, mass killings, forced relocations of Indigenous Peoples, privatization of Indigenous reservations as in the *Dawes Act* in the U.S. that we considered in Part I, and various attempts

---

6   Farrell et al. (2021) have shown that Indigenous people in North America lost more than 98% of their land, and now occupy land that is vulnerable to environmental shocks.

at enfranchisement. The process at a very broad level was similar in the United States and Canada. A particularly grievous forced relocation occurred in the U.S. in 1838 when, by an act of Congress, the Cherokee Nation were removed from east of the Mississippi and relocated to the west of it. In the long trek along the way—the 'Trail of Tears', as it is called—it is estimated that 8,000 Cherokees died (Thornton, 1984).

In Canada, the *Royal Proclamation of 1763* treated Indigenous Peoples as separate nations and stated an intention to protect Indigenous interests in land, but over time this eroded in practice, especially after 1812. Increased pressure on land due to larger numbers of white settlers led the government to seek access to Indigenous land through treaties with First Nations Peoples. The process was not uniform across Canada. In northwestern Ontario and the Prairies, Numbered Treaties were negotiated with First Nations, leaving them with small reserves. These First Nations were not in a strong bargaining position due to the decline of the fur trade, the decline of the bison population, and the encroachment of white settlers on traditional hunting and fishing territories. In British Columbia, much of the land was simply overrun without treaties being signed. The province of British Columbia became an immigrant society by displacing the Indigenous populations (Harris, 2004). The Métis too were forced out of their lands. Métis, as well as some First Nations reserve communities and some Inuit communities, faced forced relocations.

As Wood (2002) and Harris (2004) have argued, European colonizers found it handy to invoke the theory of property formulated by the English philosopher John Locke (1689/1967). Locke argued that, even though the Creator had granted human beings dominion over the earth in the Judeo-Christian tradition, we are expected to do what is required to survive. He then made the argument—which subsequently became the neoliberal foundation of property—that when people confer labour on a piece of commonly owned land, they can appropriate it as private property, provided enough is left over for others. As noted earlier, English settlers in the New World presumed that Indigenous ways of living off land by hunting and gathering did not entail labour on the land, and so Indigenous Peoples had no ownership rights to it. Therefore, the land was for free for appropriation.[7]

---

7   As Locke (1689/1967) put it, "In the beginning, all the world was America." Quoted
     in Harris (2004, p. 171).

As noted, Locke's theory that appropriation of land from the commons by conferring labour on it is contingent on there being enough land left over for others (subsequently called the 'Lockean Proviso'). This is because taking more land than one can cultivate will result in wastage. Arneil (1996) has pointed out that Locke was explicitly interested in the English colonization of America, especially given that his patron, the Earl of Shaftesbury, was active in Carolina. The Lockean Proviso provided more justification of the appropriation of Indigenous land, for any land in excess of Indigenous subsistence needs can be claimed by settlers to prevent wastage.[8] Furthermore, Arneil points out that, by introducing money into his theory, Locke also provided a rationale for colonials to appropriate land in excess of that warranted by their own needs. This is because the produce can be shipped abroad, thereby avoiding wastage. Of course, it was the English—not the Indigenous Peoples of America—who had the money (gold and silver) to do this. Locke's entire theory, therefore, worked to the detriment of the Indigenous Peoples. But his theory was certainly not the only enabler in the appropriation of Indigenous land. Carlos, Feir, and Redish (2022) have painted a compelling picture showing how the boundaries of the United States grew by transferring Indigenous land to itself in the nineteenth century. The means used were legitimate and illegitimate—treaties, reneging on treaties, immigration, squatting, violence, and the like.

Relatively more recent and extended events that have seriously undermined Indigenous health are the Indian residential school system and the child welfare system. I briefly describe these and their effects below. Canada has started coming to grips with these problems to some extent with its Truth and Reconciliation Commission (Sinclair, C.M., 2015) and the rulings of the Canadian Human Rights Tribunal regarding child welfare. This led to *Bill C-92*, an Act respecting the rights of First Nation, Inuit, and Métis children, youth, and families (2019), but there has been no analogue in the United States.[9] Therefore, the evidence I draw on below is tilted more towards Canada.

---

8   For an alternative interpretation of the Lockean Proviso, see Eswaran and Neary (2014). The authors provide an evolutionary rationale for Locke's labour theory of property and interpret the Lockean Proviso as a requirement imposed by the enforceability of property rights; rights in property that cannot be enforced are not of much value.

9   The U.S. has just begun taking a step in that direction (see the Newland Report, 2022).

5.3 The Residential School System

The American and Canadian governments started building boarding schools for Indigenous children in 1860 and 1883, respectively. It was decided by then that the most efficacious way to assimilate Indigenous Peoples was through education of the children. This led to the Indian residential school system (IRS), wherein Indigenous children were taken from their families and forcibly sent to residential schools. In Canada in 1930, about 60% of the schools were run by Catholics, 25% by the Anglican church, and the rest by the United and Presbyterian churches.[10] In the U.S., between 1860 and 1978, the boarding schools were run by the federal government, Christian churches (with federal funding), and various Christian missionary groups.[11]

In these schools, the children were taught English or French as well as the Christian religion. They were forbidden to speak their language, dress in traditional attire, perform traditional rituals, or practice traditional religions. They were prevented from seeing their families except in the summers, if then. In effect, this was an attempt to completely erase the Indigenous identity of the children and to instil white European identity in its place. The students were malnourished and kept in overcrowded conditions, and their illnesses were not speedily attended to. In addition, many children were physically and sexually abused. A large number of Indigenous students died in the residential schools. These historical events are comprehensively documented (see Adams (1995) for the U.S. and Milloy (2017) for Canada).

Since the children in the IRS grew up with little exposure to Indigenous cultures, without maternal and paternal care and that of the traditional extended family, and were exposed to apathy and abuse, many developed traumas and serious health problems associated with a fragmented identity, resulting in subsequent problems with coping (Sinclair, C.M., 2015). The trauma-driven behaviour of many attendees when they became adults, coupled with their lack of learned parenting skills, often passed on a degree of dysfunction to their children. This would have been compounded as multiple generations of the same families attended the IRS. The continued adverse effects of the IRS

---

10 https://www.thecanadianencyclopedia.ca/en/article/residential-schools
11 https://www.theindigenousfoundation.org/articles/us-residential-schools

spanning generations have been substantiated by evidence (see e.g. Wilk et al., 2017).

An important effect of the IRS on Indigenous children has been the disruption in the formation of the self-concept. We have already seen in earlier chapters that Indigenous identity is much more relational and society-oriented than western identities (Trosper, 2022). An important determinant of identity is the language one speaks. The shared experiences of a community over history are contained in the language. The banning of Indigenous languages in the IRS, along with the fact that children were separated from their parents, made learning and retaining the mother tongue much more difficult. This was not deemed an unfortunate but unintended consequence—it was by design. The loss of language was a strategy orchestrated as part of the colonial project of assimilation.[12] This language loss, along with isolation from others in the community, is now recognized to have very adverse health consequences (King, Smith, and Gracey, 2009; Khawaja, 2021). In the following chapters, we shall discuss what economics has to say about the grave consequences of the disruption of Indigenous identity formation.

A very important aspect of the IRS was the insistence that the enrolled children could not practice Indigenous religions or participate in the ceremonies. Generally, it is well-known that the proselytization of Christianity went hand-in-hand with colonization (Tinker, 1993; Niezen, 2000). These projects were complementary in their goals and execution: 'civilizing' Indigenous children also meant forcing them to shed their 'pagan' beliefs and practices. In 1884, the U.S. Congress banned the potlatch and the Sun dance. This ban was revoked only in 1934. In Canada, the potlatch was banned in 1885 and the Sun Dance was banned in 1895. The *Indian Act* was amended in 1951 to remove the ban. The banning of the practices of Indigenous shamans and medicine men was another grievous assault on Indigenous culture (Niezen, 2000). Since these ceremonies have deep meaning to Indigenous communities, the bans did considerable cultural damage. These ceremonies and practices involved the community at large and were not individual in nature, so they comported well with the community orientation

---

12 The Bishop of Avila is said to have remarked to Queen Isabella of Spain in 1492, "Your majesty, language is the perfect instrument of empire." Quoted in Crawford (1995, p. 25).

of Indigenous cultures. Attempting to force Indigenous Peoples into adopting a western-style individualistic orientation also damaged the Indigenous self-concept.

In a paper offering quantitative evidence on some of the effects of the IRS, Feir (2016a) has shown that attending an Indian residential school in Canada increased the rates of graduation of Indigenous students and their employment in the labour market; Gregg (2018) has found similar effects in the U.S. However, while it increased economic integration, the system also reduced connections within the Indigenous communities, with the attendees of these schools being less likely to participate in traditional ceremonies or speak an Indigenous language. Feir (2016a) also found suggestive evidence that, for students who went to residential schools which were abusive, even the economic benefits did not materialize. Feir (2016b) shows that residential school attendance by mothers had a negative intergenerational effect. Jones (2016) shows that children who had attended residential schools later exhibited increased smoking, drinking, social distance, and suicidal ideation. These are some of the empirically documented downsides of assimilation.

Since historical trauma is linked to many devastating effects on Indigenous Peoples, it is important to address some potential objections to the pervasiveness of the putative link based on the actual rate of attendance in the IRS. In the United States, the figure that is usually cited is that 83% of Indigenous American children were enrolled in the IRS in 1926 (Adams, 1995, p. 27). Therefore, it is reasonable to assume that the IRS affected most Indigenous Americans. However, matters were different in Canada. First, attendance in the IRS was required only of children with Indian status (those registered under the *Indian Act*) and, later, also Inuit children. But the record suggests that even by the 1930s, only around 30% of First Nations school-age children were enrolled in IRS.[13] This raises a question for Canada: if only a third of Indian-status children attended the IRS, how can it be claimed that historical trauma has pervasive and enduring effects down to current times? The answer lies in the fact that, even if the 30% figure remains relevant for subsequent decades after the 1930s, there were many generations that passed through the IRS. The children of those who attended are not

---

13   University of Manitoba, https://web.archive.org/web/20160420012021/http://umanitoba.ca/centres/nctr/overview.html
Fournier and Crey (1997, p. 61), however, put this percentage at 75% by 1930.

necessarily the only children who might have attended in subsequent generations. Consequently, the proportion of Indigenous people from families that were affected by the IRS would have been increasing over time. There were, in all, around 150,000 Indigenous students who went through the IRS in Canada (Sinclair, C.M., 2015, p. 3). Métis and Inuit communities in Canada were also affected by the IRS, though the attendance rates and process were different (RCAP, 1994; Logan, 2006; Qikiqtani Truth Commission, 2014).

The historical record, therefore, suggests that Indigenous Peoples in the U.S. and Canada all experienced substantial traumas, even if over different lengths of time and in non-identical ways. This was an exorbitant cost of the Indian residential school system, whose *raison d'être* was the assimilation of Indigenous children.

5.4 The Child Welfare System

Indian residential schools were only one means that separated Indigenous children from parents. By the 1930s in the U.S. and the 1950s in Canada, the governments began curtailing use of the IRS. The last such school closed in the 1960s in the U.S and in the 1990s in Canada. But from the 1950s onwards, the child welfare system (CWS) in both countries began removing Indigenous children from their parents and putting them up for adoption by non-Indigenous families or placing them in foster care (George, 1997; Fournier and Crey, 1997; Blackstock, 2007; Evans-Campbell, 2006). In the United States, inter-racial adoptions became restricted since 1978 with the passage of the *Indian Child Welfare Act* (ICWA), which gave Indigenous communities control over Indigenous American children.[14]

In Canada, from the 1960s until the 1990s—in what has been called the 'Sixties Scoop'—Indigenous children were placed in foster care in the 'best interests of the children' at such an alarming rate that Indigenous children were greatly over-represented (relative to their population) in the CWS. The ostensible reason for the removal of Indigenous children from their homes was to prevent maltreatment, which covered a range of

---

14   The law still allows adoptions of Indigenous American children by non-Indigenous American families, but only when no suitable Indigenous American family is available.

categories such as neglect, physical abuse, emotional abuse, and sexual abuse, among others. The majority of the children removed fell into the 'neglect' category, which covered criteria like poverty, poor housing, overcrowding, etc.

A significant proportion of Indigenous children taken from their families in Canada were placed in non-Indigenous foster homes up until the 1990s. In some cases, the foster parents adopted the children. Fournier and Crey (1997, Ch. 3) point out that the CWS was more isolating than the IRS because the CWS also separated Indigenous children from one another. Feir (2016a) finds suggestive evidence that the IRS may have preserved Indigenous cultural connectedness *within* the schools because Indigenous children were not separated from other Indigenous children (even though they were separated from their families).

The literature on transcultural adoptions finds that the outcomes are usually good (e.g. Silverman, 1993), while some are mixed (Godon-Decoteau and Ramsey, 2018). However, Indigenous children in transcultural adoptions do not seem to fare well; in fact, up to 50% of these adoptions break down (Bagley, 1991). R. Sinclair (2007) offers some plausible reasons for this. Indigenous adoptees facing discrimination outside their adoptive homes may not be able to fall back on the adopting family for help because the family may not perceive the discrimination. This leads to difficulties in the identity formation of Indigenous adoptees during adolescence, which brings on a host of psychological problems (Kim, 1978). A substantial proportion of Indigenous children were not adopted and were placed in foster care. But foster care, which is less permanent than adoption, also leads to serious psychological issues for these children. Kaspar (2014a) found, for example, that Métis children who came out of foster care were more likely to have depression and suicidal thoughts than children who had never been in foster care.

Child welfare placement of Indigenous children has been criticized for neglecting the option to place the children within Indigenous communities themselves. There is a strong extended family system in Indigenous cultures where grandparents, uncles and aunts, and, in fact, the entire community confer attention and affection on children (Red Horse, 1997; Hudson and McKenzie, 1981; Johnson, 1983; Killsback, 2019). The CWS was informed by a well-established theory in child psychology called 'Attachment Theory' which claims that, in order to develop 'normally', a child must form a stable attachment to a caretaker—usually the birth mother, or a substitute if the mother is unavailable—and that the window for this bond to form is fairly short. Attachment theory is based on a particular cultural view in which dyadic relationships between mother and child are typically the most observed. It has been persuasively argued that this view is based on empirical work done exclusively in Eurocentric cultures and does not apply to Indigenous cultures, where the norm is the extended family and there are usually many caretakers. As Keller and Chaudhary (2017) argue in their survey, many cultures practice alloparenting (that is, parenting by aunts, grandparents, older siblings, and even non-related individuals) and the children benefit from attachment to the many alloparents.

Carriere (2005) emphasizes the importance of 'connectedness' to birth families and ancestral culture as being crucial to the health of Indigenous adoptees via the sense of identity that this engenders. R. Sinclair (2016) argues that the separation of same-race siblings, families, and communities from each other greatly undermines the sense of belonging and safety. Furthermore—even if an Indigenous child forms a bond with a non-Indigenous family—at the crucial stage of adolescence when a child has to form an individual identity as a separate self, the bond can break as the children see that they are distinctly different from their adopted parents (Richard, 2007). When this happens, the adoptees tend to run away and neither return to their adopted homes nor to their birth homes; many end up homeless in urban areas (Belanger et al., 2013). Tait, Henry, and Walker (2013) identify and describe a host of challenges that confront children when they emerge from the CWS—homelessness, mental health issues, unwanted pregnancies, and encounters with the criminal justice system, to name a few—and the authors view the CWS itself as a social determinant of health. As Sinclair, R. (2016) argues, what may be perceived to be in the best interests of the children in the short run may not be so in the long run, and what should matter in child placements is the latter.

Colonial powers found it expedient to attempt to erase Indigenous cultures by separating children from parents. The Truth and Reconciliation Commission declared this to be "cultural genocide" (Sinclair, C.M., 2015, p. 1). In early and insightful work on this subject,

Hudson and McKenzie (1981) and Johnson (1983, esp. Ch. 3), suggested that this policy of child removal by the CWS was a continuation of the colonial strategy of assimilation, and subsequent scholarship has forcefully reiterated this claim (Sinclair, R., 2007).[15]

The over-representation of Indigenous children in the CWS is easily seen if we compare two numbers: (1) the percentage of children in foster care who are Indigenous, and (2) the percentage of all children in the population who are Indigenous. In the United States in 2015, for American Indian and Native Alaskan (AIAN) children, the ratio of (1) to (2) was 2.7 (NCJFCJ, 2017). In contrast, the corresponding figure for Indigenous children in Canada in 2021, according to Statistics Canada Census of Children, was 6.8. The over-representation of Indigenous children in the CWS is much greater in Canada than in the U.S., as noted earlier. This dramatic difference is due to the fact that the U.S. passed the *Indian Child Welfare Act* (ICWA) in 1978, giving American Indian tribes jurisdiction over Indigenous children. The analogue of ICWA in Canada is *Bill C-92* which came forty-one years later in 2019 and took effect only in 2020. This may explain differences between the two countries in some of the adverse effects (e.g. suicide rates) of the IRS and CWS, which are discussed later in Section 8.4 of Chapter 8 of this book.

Evidence shows that the disproportionate representation of Indigenous children in the CWS is driven by the risk factors present in households in which the parents have issues with substance abuse and mental health (Trocmé et al., 2004). Bombay, Matheson, and Anisman (2014) have shown that these conditions are linked to the parents or grandparents having attended the IRS. Recently, Bombay et al. (2020) demonstrated that there is a statistical link between children being involved with the CWS and having parents or grandparents who attended the IRS. McQuaid et al. (2022) found that, compared to Indigenous youths who had neither parents nor grandparents who attended the IRS, youths who had either a parent and/or grandparent who attended had higher odds of not living with either biological parent. They also experienced higher levels of psychological distress.

---

15   Rocha Beardall and Edwards (2021) have argued that, after appropriating Indigenous land via *terra nullius* ('nobody's land'), the governments were appropriating Indigenous children via *filius nullius* ('nobody's child') through IRS and the CWS.

5.5 Empirical Evidence on Historical Trauma

I now cite some correlational evidence for the concept of historical trauma (Brave Heart and Debruyn, 1998; Duran and Duran, 1995), having made the case for this in the previous two sections. An early attempt at quantifying historical trauma came from Whitbeck et al. (2004). The authors identified various losses associated with historical trauma (loss of community, family, land, language, etc.) and various symptoms associated with historical trauma (sadness, anger, isolation, distrust, etc.). They found an association between the frequency of times that Indigenous interview subjects thought of such losses and the negative feelings they experienced.

A rigorous test of historical trauma requires data from across generations, which can be provided by the relatively recent phenomenon of Indigenous residential schools (1880s to 1990s) in Canada. Since the IRS was a very disruptive institution imposed on Indigenous families that ended only a few decades ago, Bombay, Matheson, and Anisman (2014)—who also review the literature— have used the IRS data to examine intergenerational trauma. Drawing on families in which none, one, or two of the parents went through the IRS, the authors tested for depressive symptoms and suicidal ideation among children who did not attend the IRS. The results are consistent with those implied by historical trauma; children of parents who went through the IRS showed more of these symptoms. Furthermore, the authors showed the existence of an interaction between historical trauma and contemporary stressors like discrimination, stigmatization, assaults, etc. whereby historical trauma magnifies their negative effects.

Using 2006–2007 Aboriginal Peoples Survey data in a multivariate regression analysis, Kaspar (2014b) found that lifetime attendees of the IRS had lower self-perceived health than non-attendees. When socioeconomic factors (education, income, employment, and housing) were accounted for, the difference between the two groups declined but remained significant. IRS attendance had adverse effects on the socioeconomic variables. While the effect of IRS attendance worked through these socioeconomic variables, it also had an independent effect. The negative effect of IRS attendance on health remained even when communal adversity variables (suicides, alcohol and drug abuse, sexual violence, family violence, and unemployment) were accounted for in the statistical analysis.

In summary, the negative effects of the ill-treatment of children in Indigenous residential schools are seen to be *intergenerational* and pervasive, and to magnify the effects of other traumatic experiences.

In a systematic review of the literature on the health impacts of historical trauma as a scientific concept, Gone et al. (2019) found that the evidence from various studies in the United States and Canada is difficult to synthesize and the results are somewhat mixed. Citing the scholar Child (2014), they argue that historical trauma may be better construed as a metaphor for the sequential events that adversely affect Indigenous wellbeing rather than as a strictly scientific concept. Waldram (2014) refers to historical trauma as an "idiom of distress". I use the term 'historical trauma' as shorthand for various events leading to persistent trauma across generations, but the analysis would hold even if this concept was substituted with PTSD—which occurs at elevated levels among Indigenous Peoples, as demonstrated by ample and uncontested empirical evidence (Basset et al., 2014).[16] The intergenerational effects of historical trauma (that are not the focus of PTSD as a concept) are shown to arise endogenously in the model developed in the following chapters.

5.6 Conclusions

The brief summary above of the evidence strongly suggests that attendees of the Indian residential schools subsequently suffered serious mental and psychological problems, and that the child welfare system which quickly followed after the decline of the IRS has essentially perpetuated the same outcome of separating Indigenous children from their parents. The effects of the IRS became the causes for the withdrawal of Indigenous children by the CWS. The intergenerational transmission

---

16   It has been suggested, following Herman (1992), that people who have been subjected to traumatic events repeatedly and continuously show more symptoms than are covered by PTSD, which are hence grouped under the term 'complex PTSD'. But the American Psychiatric Association's latest *Diagnostic and Statistical Manual 5* does not include complex PTSD as a separate category, since the Association's definition of PTSD covers most of the symptoms of complex PTSD.

of the ill effects, in turn, threatens to inflict psychological problems on future generations of fragmented Indigenous families. Many Indigenous individuals, families, and communities have been fractured by PTSD and more general manifestations of historical trauma from oppression and the attempted elimination of Indigenous cultures to bring about assimilation. This is aggravated by ongoing contemporary conditions of racism and discrimination. In turn, the effects of colonialism experienced in the present are exacerbated by historical trauma.

Using historical trauma as a metaphor to collectively refer to the various adverse events the Indigenous Peoples confronted in colonial history, its consequences will be investigated through the lens of economics in the following chapters. How can we capture historical trauma in an economic model? What are the mechanisms through which the erosion of culture and historical trauma continue to undermine contemporary Indigenous wellbeing? Can we explain Indigenous deaths of despair in terms of historical trauma? What explains the resilience of many Indigenous communities? These are the questions we will now address.

6. An Economic Model to Capture Effects of Historical Trauma

"That colonialism is a fundamental determinant of health is inescapable."
—Editorial Comment in "The Past is Not the Past for Canada's
Indigenous Peoples," *The Lancet*, June 26, 2021.

6.1 Introduction

In approaching the subject matter of Part II of this book, I continue to invoke modelling assumptions based on the *lived experience* of Indigenous Peoples, whose manner of knowledge acquisition differs from the highly conceptual method of gaining knowledge that characterizes western scholarship.[1] I begin with the premise that communal orientation is of utmost importance to Indigenous societies; it is a central feature of life and culture and is inextricably tied to Indigenous land (and its contents). And, importantly, the ownership of land is communal, not individual. In addition to land ownership, the main cultural activities that are undertaken in Indigenous communities are also communal. This community orientation is a core feature of the economic model laid out in this book, in which it may be viewed as a formal rendition of the relational Indigenous society emphasized by Trosper (2022).

Culture provides a buffer against external shocks and consequent existential anxiety (Salzman, 2001; Walters et al., 2011). The belongingness characterizing communal cultural activities constituted the strength of Indigenous societies, but that strength became vulnerability when European settlers sought to erase Indigenous cultures. To demonstrate

---

1   As Elder Vee Whitehorse of Standing Buffalo Dakota Nation remarked, "[W]isdom cannot be given, it has to be experienced on your own." Quoted in Field (2022, p. 127).

     https://doi.org/10.11647/OBP.0477.06

how this and the spiralling effects of the trauma it induced may have come about, I will now adapt the model laid out in earlier chapters, which were based on Eswaran (2023a). Communal activities were represented in Part I as the production of a 'cultural good'.

For modelling purposes, I take as given the adverse psychological impact of the history of North American Indigenous Peoples, as established by scholars in other disciplines. My modest contribution here is to provide an economic framework to understand the mechanisms by which historical trauma facilitates the *continuation* of the dismantling of cohesion within Indigenous communities, and to examine how this impinges on Indigenous deaths of despair. I adapt the model of the previous chapters which incorporated an Indigenous person's concern for others through other-regarding preferences, for reasons already spelled out earlier. Such preferences enable one to conceive of the self as comprising the standard egoistic ('me') component and the somewhat non-standard, other-regarding ('Us') component. As noted earlier, these two aspects of an individual's self are well-established in social psychology (see e.g. Tajfel and Turner, 1979; Tajfel, 1982). A stronger sense of belonging to a community enhances the weight given to the 'Us' component of preferences (Trosper, 2022).

In an empirical investigation of suicide, Case, Deaton, and Cutler (2017) find little support for economic models of suicide but find *pain* to be consistently correlated with suicide, in accordance with findings in psychology (see Verrocchio et al. (2016) for a review). Therefore, a model dealing with deaths of despair (to be considered later in Chapter 8) has to seriously contend with the role of pain. Ill-health, taken here to follow exogenously from trauma, is attenuated in the short run by an endogenous response in which attention is drawn to pain and resources are diverted for managing it. As Douglas George-Kanentiio, Mohawk-Iroquois, said when speaking of his own pain and that of other Indigenous children in being forcibly removed from homes to residential schools, "This singular act of removing children by design, by federal policy, from their homes to institutions that were nothing short of penal colonies, *laid them wide open to substance abuse*" (Smith, H., 2005, p. 80, emphasis added).[2]

---

2   See Chansonneuve (2007) for more on Indigenous pain.

Jeremy Bentham (1789) claimed that pleasure and pain are our sovereign masters and that when the difference between them is maximized, utility is at its optimum.[3] Although all of economics is founded on the premise that we wish to maximize our wellbeing (pleasure net of pain), the analysis is usually couched in terms of allocating scare resources to maximize pleasure rather than minimizing pain. Pleasure and pain are two sides of the same coin, so mathematically there may be no difference. However, when cast in terms of maximizing pleasure, some expenditures of a person may be seen as wasteful or frivolous self-indulgence. When seen in terms of pain minimization, we are forced to confront the dire conditions under which the person is forced into certain choices—it compels us to comprehend what may well be desperate circumstances that the person is in. In emphasizing the role of pain, therefore, I follow my approach in Eswaran (2023b).[4]

Psychological trauma is a special form of pain in that it is *durable*, akin to what economists call a stock. That being the case, it informs an individual's decisions in the present and also over time, sometimes to a point beyond volition, until it is addressed and neutralized or, at least, managed. Specifically, unresolved trauma lowers a person's wellbeing at each instant in time and, simultaneously, calls for resources to diminish the pain felt.

This effect of trauma lowers wellbeing and diverts attentional resources away from other productive uses (for oneself, for family, and for community). This is the mechanism through which historical trauma in my model unravels Indigenous Peoples' organizations and devastates Indigenous wellbeing—individually and collectively. Consistent with what is observed in the lives of Indigenous Peoples in North America, the passage of time is seen not to ameliorate the effects of historical trauma.[5]

---

3   In an insightful essay, Sahlins (1996) has traced the effects on the social science disciplines of the Biblical story of Adam and Eve being ejected from the Garden of Eden for eating the forbidden fruit. The outcome of that act of disobedience to God, as the story goes, is that humans are condemned to live precariously in a world of scarcity by the sweat of their brow. All of life, one way or another, then became about avoiding pain and seeking pleasure.

4   More recently, Gone (2025) has emphasized the importance of suffering.

5   This approach, we shall see, also reconciles, as a byproduct, Durkheim's (1897/1951) well-known general theory of suicide with that of Chandler and Lalonde (1998) and Chandler et al. (2003) for Indigenous Peoples, which we shall discuss in the coming chapters.

In the next section, the model from Chapter 3 is adapted and set up to address the issue of historical trauma and its effects on the cohesion of an Indigenous community or any other community sharing a communal culture. The equilibrium will then be worked out and discussed, and the details and implications of this will be examined in the subsequent two chapters.

6.2 A Model Incorporating Psychological Pain

The intention here is not to derive sophisticated theoretical results from standard (neoclassical) premises that do not comport well with the context of Indigenous cultures. The purpose, rather, is to articulate in the simplest manner the implications for Indigenous health when we adopt premises that conform to the lived experience of Indigenous Peoples. This is addressed in a tractable but greatly simplified version of Indigenous culture by adapting the model introduced in the earlier chapters.

There is a great deal of variation among Indigenous communities. In Canada itself, for example, Indigenous languages come from eleven different language families. But there are commonalities. As Kirmayer, Macdonald, and Brass (2001, p. 6) point out, despite the great linguistic and genetic differences, Indigenous communities "share a common social, economic, and political predicament that is the legacy of colonialism". For tractability, the focus here is on the commonalities, and the consideration of variation is postponed to Chapters 8 and 9. Some results that are theoretically straightforward to derive but are important in their implications are presented here. These results go some distance towards explaining the present health condition and deaths of despair of Indigenous Peoples.

The utility function, $u(c, G, \ell, p)$, of a typical person in a hypothetical Indigenous community is now written as a function of their consumption of food (c), their group cultural activity (G), their private leisure activity (ℓ), and the amount of substance (p) devoted to alleviating their pain and anxiety caused by the historical trauma prevalent in the Indigenous community. The crucial additions to the model of Chapter 3 here are historical trauma and the consumption of substances for pain and anxiety alleviation. The former is modelled as exogenous and the latter in terms of the time spent acquiring substances used for dealing with it. An important correlate of trauma, especially PTSD, is chronic pain, both physical and psychological.[6] And pain is found to be strongly associated with suicides (Case, Deaton, and Cutler, 2017), even more strongly than with depression (Shneidman, 1993; Verrocchio et al., 2016). Since a vast collection of literature in neuroscience documents that pain increases with negative emotions (see Wieser and Pauli (2016) for a review), we would expect that emotions like those accompanying the experience of discrimination would exacerbate pain.

A comment is warranted on the assumption that psychological trauma, as determined by past historical events, is taken here as exogenous (given). The purpose of this is to maintain the tractability of the economic model. There are good empirical grounds for arguing that colonialism is still an ongoing process, though Canada and the United States ceased to be colonies a long time ago (Bombay, Matheson, and Anisman, 2009; 2014). So, one might wonder how historical trauma can be taken as an exogenous event. This is a compromise necessitated by having a static model, but we shall see in the next two chapters that the model generates insights on how the effects of colonialism are perpetuated. Therefore, even a static model will allow us to speak to the continuing effects of colonialism.

Group cultural activity, a core aspect of Indigenous community life, is very important for the issues under investigation. In the model, G is an aggregate that stands for collective activities such as religious rituals, healing ceremonies, storytelling, etc. These activities transmit Indigenous culture by allowing children and youth to imbibe the values, norms, traditions, and beliefs of the community, inculcating a strong sense of identity in children (Wexlar, 2009). This, in turn, creates a strong sense of self-esteem and resilience (Phinney, 1991; Heid et al., 2022). By their very nature, such cultural activities create bonds between community members which offer social support known to have many benefits and, specifically, are protective against anxiety, depression, PTSD, and other mental illnesses (Salzman, 2001; Southwick et al., 2005; Ozbay et al., 2007;

---

6   Brennstuhl et al. (2015) review evidence showing that PTSD and chronic pain occur together, possibly with mutual causation, but both occur invariably in response to trauma. They suggest that PTSD and chronic pain may be two alternative responses to trauma.

Bellamy and Hardy, 2015). The enculturation resulting from these activities has a moderating effect on alcohol abuse and so promotes resilience (Whitbeck et al., 2004). These activities also promote connectedness with the (extended) family, which is seen to serve as a protective factor against suicide attempts by AIAN youth (Borowsky et al., 1999). Religion has been causally shown in a non-Indigenous context to act as a buffer against depression (Fruehwirth, Iyer, and Zhang, 2019).

The collective contribution to the cultural good may also be interpreted as the community's social capital, an aspect of Indigenous communities emphasized by Mignone and O'Neil (2005) and Trosper (2025). Yet another important aspect of the cultural good is that cultural activities are deemed to cement Indigenous identities (Maracle, 2021). The Indigenous scholar Lyons (2010, p. 40) says, "Indian identity is something they do, not what they are" (also quoted by Maracle, 2021). The incorporation of cultural good into the model, then, enables us to investigate the potential effects of historical trauma on Indigenous identity and wellbeing.

For tractability, I shall use the following simple Cobb-Douglas form, $u(c, G, \ell, p)$, of the utility function:

$$u(c, g, \ell, p) = B(\tau)\, c^{\alpha}\, G^{\beta}\, \ell^{\gamma} p^{\tau}, \qquad (6.1)$$

The multiplicative factor $B(\tau)$ (> 0) in the utility function depends on an exogenous factor, τ, which denotes a measure of the disruptive events of the past generating historical trauma. Trauma, of course, can be the result of past and ongoing events. As noted above, the focus is on past historical events and so we can take τ as a measure of the *intensity* of these past events, now exogenous. Higher τ implies greater trauma, and τ is scaled so that 0 denotes no trauma and 1 denotes the maximum possible trauma, that is $0 \leq \tau < 1$. This parameter may be informally taken to also represent the stock measure of unresolved historical trauma that scholars of disciplines outside economics speak of (e.g. Brave Heart and DeBruyn, 1998). I posit the derivative $B'(\tau) < 0$; greater historical trauma reduces an Indigenous community member's wellbeing, which is an uncontroversial claim. The other exogenous parameters in the exponents in (6.1) are presumed to satisfy the inequalities $0 < \alpha < 1, 0 < \beta < 1$, and $0 < \gamma < 1$—restrictions that ensure diminishing marginal utility.

Each person is assumed to have up to 1 unit of time endowment. Let t denote the amount of time they devote to food production, g that devoted to the group cultural activity, ℓ to the private leisure activity, and p the amount of time devoted to treating pain, which—for reasons given in the next paragraph—is taken to refer to pain- and anxiety-reducing substances. Note that the time spent managing pain is modelled here as a 'choice', as is done in rational choice models of utility maximization in economics. In some sense, it may be objectionable to couch the acquisition of pain-numbing substances as a voluntary 'choice' of an Indigenous person subjected to historical trauma. I am severely handicapped here by the paucity of the formal framework of economics, where such decisions are modelled as choices. However, in modelling it as such, I take my cue from Indigenous scholars. Brave Heart (2003), for example, has suggested that Indigenous members of the Lakota band take substances as a way of avoiding the pain of historical trauma.

There are many possible avenues for treating psychological pain. In Indigenous cultures, there were well-established collective mechanisms for addressing pain. These culturally-specific mechanisms were destroyed by colonialism and are no longer readily available. Access to western healthcare is well-known to be less available to Indigenous Peoples than to the rest of the population. There is chronic underfunding, limited access to counselling and rehabilitation, a scarcity of healthcare clinics in rural areas, and discrimination against Indigenous patients, among other factors that limit access to pain treatments.[7] In such circumstances, the use of substances to relieve pain should be seen as being forced to opt for poor substitutes for better (less available and, therefore, more expensive) ways of dealing with pain. This is important to bear in mind. In Chapter 9, we shall discuss traditional Indigenous ways of doing this that have positive effects.

When the parameter τ increases, the exogenous utility of an Indigenous community member declines, but by way of an endogenous response the person can consume substances as the only available pain treatment to alleviate the pain and anxiety associated with the trauma. The exponent τ of p also measures the efficacy with which this substance reduces pain and anxiety; for any given level of $B(\tau)$, an increase in τ

---

7   See CCR (2004) for the U.S. and Nguyen et al. (2020) and Yangsom, Masoud, and Hahmann (2023) for Canada.

raises the utility and marginal utility derived from the substance. In this model, pain-reducing substances consumed may be taken as an inverse measure of the health of an individual.[8] The utility related to trauma of a community member may be viewed informally as the sub-aggregate $B(\tau)\, p^{\tau}$, which combines the exogenous and the endogenous effects of trauma on health.

The adapted function in (6.1) will now be referred to as the 'egoistic' utility function of a typical community member in order to distinguish it from one that incorporates other-regarding preferences. The individual's time constraint may now be written as $t + g + \ell + p = 1$ in the absence of historical trauma. The psychological evidence on trauma and depression, especially PTSD, clearly suggests that they are disabling; they have numerous impacts that effectively reduce the productive capacity of the individual (Kessler and Frank, 1997; Berndt et al., 1998; Jellestad et al., 2021). This is modelled here as a reduction in the time endowment from 1 unit to a fraction $e(\tau)$ of 1 unit, consistent with the manner in which the World Health Organization computes effective loss of life due to disability.[9] I posit that $e(0) = 1, e(1) = 0$, and $e'(\tau) < 0$: the greater the trauma τ, the lower the fraction of time available for any and all activities including leisure. When the collective trauma of the band is τ, a fraction $1 - e(\tau)$ of productive time is lost. Thus, an individual's time constraint can be written as

$$t + g + \ell + p = e(\tau). \qquad (6.2)$$

I should note that positing the function $e(\tau)$ that declines with the degree of historical trauma τ is simply recognizing the empirical fact that trauma has a negative effect on productivity for *any* individual who has been seriously traumatized, not just for an Indigenous person. Therefore, this should not be read as a blanket suggestion that Indigenous Peoples are in any way 'damaged Peoples'. For the purposes of analysis, it is important to recognize the negative effects of colonialism that Indigenous writers and elders repeatedly emphasize if we are to understand the harm that

---

8   I do not incorporate the dynamic effects of the consumption of drugs and alcohol here because the technicalities will dominate the more substantive issues under consideration. In any case, including them will only strengthen the results of this paper and add little by way of insight.

9   https://www.who.int/data/gho/indicator-metadata-registry/imr-details/158

has been done. (However, the core results to follow do not depend on this empirically based assumption that $e(\tau)$ declines in τ.) Chapter 9 will discuss the manifest resilience and 'survivance' of North American Indigenous Peoples, a phenomenon that definitively repudiates any negative stereotypical view that uninformed people might entertain.

As before, I refer to the economic activity of the community (say, hunting/gathering/farming, but this is not by any means restricted to these) as food production. Assume there are n (≥ 2) people in the Indigenous band. I posit that the output, Q, of food is given by the production function

$$Q = A L^{1-\mu} T^{\mu}, \qquad (6.3)$$

where L and T denote, respectively, the land area and total effort applied, and A the total factor productivity of the technology, and $0 < \mu < 1$. As before, the total amount of land, L, in the economy is hereafter normalized to 1 unit.

The land of an Indigenous band is taken as communally owned and food production is jointly undertaken. Denoting the production effort of individual i by t_i, $i = 1,2,...,n$, the total effort may be written as $T = \sum_{i=1}^{n} t_i$. With an ethic of equal sharing, the consumption, c_i, of person i will be $c_i = Q/n$. (Consult Chapter 3 for evidence on this ethic.)

'Cultural production' is posited to be made up of each individual's contribution:

$$G = g_1 + g_2 + ...+ g_n. \qquad (6.4)$$

Recall that the cultural good G is a pure public good, and the importance of this good to Indigenous communities is captured in the preferences by the parameter β in the utility function in (6.1).

What prevents the standard free riding in teams from making the model's hypothetical Indigenous community dysfunctional is the attitude of the members towards land. This is the key cultural concept that Indigenous Peoples often speak of, stated as "The land does not belong to us; we belong to this land" (Akiwenzie-Damm, 1996, p. 21). It was argued in Chapters 2 and 3 that the very nature of Indigenous cultures implies that other-regarding preferences and altruism are important to an Indigenous community; Indigenous societies are relational societies (Trosper, 2022). A person is not concerned exclusively with their own consumption of various goods, as captured by the egoistic utility function in (6.1), but also places some importance on those of others in the group. Subscripting the individual-specific consumptions of person i by i, as before, we may now write the utility of this person with other-regarding preferences, $v_i(\vec{c}, G, \vec{\ell}, \vec{p})$, as given by

$$v_i(\vec{c}, G, \vec{\ell}, \vec{p}) = u_i(c_i, G, \ell_i, p_i) + \sigma \sum_{j \neq i}^{n} u_j(c_j, G, \ell_j, p_j), \qquad (6.5)$$

where $\vec{c}$, $\vec{\ell}$, and $\vec{p}$ denote the vectors of consumption levels of the production output, private leisure, and (private) substance consumption of the entire community, respectively. The functions $u_i(c_i, G, \ell_i, p_i)$ are assumed to retain the form given in (6.1). As before, the 'belongingness' parameter σ, with $0 \leq \sigma \leq 1$, captures the extent of a community member's culture of concern for all the others who also belong to and work on the same land. This would also include adult family members and, of course, one's spouse.[10] The magnitude of σ, which is assumed to be the same for all individuals in the community, will depend on the specific culture of the community.

The first term on the right-hand side of (6.5) captures person i's egoistic concern for oneself, and the remaining terms capture the person's concern for others in the community. As σ increases, preferences span the spectrum from $\sigma = 0$ (purely egoistic) to $\sigma = 1$ (the wellbeing of every other member is on par with one's own), and (6.5) with $\sigma = 1$ would be identical to the Benthamite welfare function. Free riding in the application of effort towards food and cultural good production is tempered when $\sigma > 0$ because each member of the community puts some weight on the utilities of other members.

An important implication of (6.5) for this and subsequent chapters is how traumatic events impinge on a person's wellbeing. Trauma from individual assaults like rape or battery will affect the 'me' component of the self. Collective assaults like dispossession, discrimination, and cultural denigration will affect not only the 'me' component but also the 'Us' component when $\sigma > 0$. This implication fits well with the view of traumatologists (e.g. Kira, 2010). We may also interpret the magnitude of σ as the extent to which community and kin are important

---

10 Typically, in economic models, spouse and children are all subsumed within an individual's utility function, but here it is important to draw a distinction.

to Indigenous identity (Maracle, 2021; Trosper, 2022). A decline in σ can also be interpreted as a fracturing of Indigenous kinship systems and identity.

The hypothetical model here is one of a self-governed Indigenous community. If it is not self-governed and is, say, overseen by *The Indian Act*, for example in Canada, the value of σ would be lower than it otherwise would be because the sense of 'I belong to the land' is diluted when the state exercises control over the land. So, a move towards self-determination can be modelled as an exogenous increase in the parameter σ. Also, Indigenous communities are understandably deeply distrustful of state governments, given the past history. As a result, self-government would also be accompanied by an increase in trust and, therefore, willingness to put oneself out on behalf of other community members: once again the parameter σ would increase.

6.3 The Nash Equilibrium

We will now work out the Nash equilibrium in an Indigenous community with historical trauma and the need for pain alleviation. Person i has control only over their own decisions, and so under Nash conjectures will maximize (6.5) by their choice of t_i, g_i, ℓ_i, and p_i subject to the time constraint $t_i + g_i + \ell_i + p_i = e(\tau)$.[11] This constraint can be used to eliminate ℓ_i and perform an unconstrained optimization with respect to t_i, g_i, and p_i. Taking the derivatives of (6.5) with respect to these three variables, simplifying the corresponding expressions after invoking symmetry and dropping the subscripts, solving the three first order conditions, and using the time constraint, we obtain the solution for the 'belonging equilibrium'—denoted by the quartet $\left(\tilde{t}^*, \tilde{g}^*, \tilde{\ell}^*, \tilde{p}^* \right)$, with details shown in the Appendix to this chapter—as

$$\tilde{t}^* = \frac{\alpha\mu\rho}{(\alpha\mu + \beta)\rho + n(\gamma + \tau)}e(\tau); \quad \tilde{g}^* = \frac{\beta\rho}{(\alpha\mu + \beta)\rho + n(\gamma + \tau)}e(\tau);$$

$$\tilde{\ell}^* = \frac{n\gamma}{(\alpha\mu + \beta)\rho + n(\gamma + \tau)}e(\tau); \quad \tilde{p}^* = \frac{n\tau}{(\alpha\mu + \beta)\rho + n(\gamma + \tau)}e(\tau), \quad (6.6)$$

where $\rho \equiv 1 + (n-1)\sigma$, and ρ varies from 1 when $\sigma = 0$ to n when $\sigma = 1$. The parameter ρ matters when $\sigma > 0$. An increase

---

11 As before, the Nash (non-cooperative) behaviour understates the effect of 'belongingness' on equilibrium wellbeing.

in group size, n, incentivizes a person to apply more effort towards the collective through ρ because the other-regarding preferences incorporate the wellbeing of more members into one's calculations when n increases. When belongingness, σ, increases, the associated increase in ρ is $(n - 1)$ times larger. Elsewhere in the expressions in (6.6), the appearance of n captures the standard incentive to free ride in the production of food and the cultural good—an incentive that gets magnified when n increases. This is because, in a larger team (higher n), the cost of free riding to oneself gets smaller for food and this encourages more free riding. (There is free riding in the contribution to the cultural good, too, but the shirker bears the full cost of the shirking, not $1/n$ of the decline in the cultural good.) In contrast, the effect through ρ of higher n works in the opposite direction when $\sigma > 0$: as n increases, because there are more people to be concerned about, a person would apply more effort. Nevertheless, the standard free riding problem of larger group sizes overwhelms the belongingness effect when $\sigma < 1$. When $\sigma = 1$, free riding is fully offset by ρ and the Benthamite welfare of the community is maximized for all n even in the Nash equilibrium. This is as expected because each member of the community puts the wellbeing of every other member on par with their own in their decision-making.

In the next chapter, we will discuss in detail the consequences of historical trauma for the Indigenous community in the short run and in the long run.

Before leaving this section, it must be emphasized that, although this derivation was for a typical member of the community, it was applied to *all* individuals in the community by invoking symmetry because the trauma parameter τ is common to all members. The commonness of τ is what separates historical trauma from other traumas like PTSD; the events that generate historical trauma are a *shared* experience for the community, and this will be important in subsequent chapters. An exogenous increase in τ increases the assumed historical trauma of all community members. This collective aspect is one of the hallmarks of historical trauma.

6.4 Summary

This chapter sought to incorporate into the economic model of a hypothetical Indigenous community the fact of historical trauma and the possibility of alleviating the psychological (and physical) pain that has been documented to accompany this type of trauma. Then, the Nash equilibrium outcome was derived. We are now ready to examine the details of this outcome and its implications in the following chapters.

6.5 Appendix

6.5.1 Derivation of the Nash Equilibrium

Consider the choices of a single individual, i. Holding the decisions of all other individuals $j \neq i$, we can take the derivatives of the objective function in (6.5) with respect to t_i, g_i, and p_i to obtain the respective first order conditions. Recognizing that the Nash equilibrium must be symmetric, we drop the subscripts on these variables. The three first order conditions obtained after symmetry is invoked are:

$$t_i: \quad \frac{\alpha \mu \rho}{nt} = \frac{\gamma}{1 - e(\tau) - g - p},$$

$$g_i: \quad \frac{\beta \rho}{ng} = \frac{\gamma}{1 - e(\tau) - g - p},$$

$$p_i: \quad \frac{\tau}{p} = \frac{\gamma}{1 - e(\tau) - g - p},$$

where $\rho = 1 + (n - 1)\sigma$.

Since the right-hand sides of all three first order conditions are the same, we may equate the left-hand sides. From this we obtain g and p in terms of t:

$$g = \frac{\beta}{\alpha \mu} t; \quad p = \frac{n\tau}{\alpha \mu \rho} t$$

Substituting these into the time constraint (6.2), we obtain the solution for $t, g,$ and p. Assuming the second order sufficient conditions for a maximum to hold, we obtain the Nash equilibrium allocations shown in (6.6) of the text.

7. Some Adverse Effects of Historical Trauma on Indigenous Communities

7.1 Introduction

In the previous chapter, based on Eswaran (2023b), we set up our economic model of a hypothetical Indigenous community to incorporate the effects of historical trauma in a simple way. In the model, this trauma directly reduces wellbeing but it also introduces the importance of pain alleviation measures as a response, and this was modelled as the resources (time) diverted to acquire substances that numb the pain of historical trauma. What the immediacy of psychological (and physical) pain universally does is that it increases the focus on the 'me' aspect of self at the expense of the 'Us' aspect. This shift in emphasis, we shall see, has a significant effect, because kinship and community ties are especially important in Indigenous cultures.

In the model, community solidarity is determined fundamentally by preferences for the cultural good, altruism towards other members of the community, and the intensity of historical trauma. We shall now see that, in the short run (where the sense of belongingness or the degree of altruism can be taken as given), historical trauma redirects resources toward individualistic activities and away from collective ones. This dismantles the community's solidarity and diminishes its community orientation. In the long run, this will be reflected in a lower degree of altruism displayed towards fellow members of the community as a result of historical trauma. This, in turn, heightens the effects of historical trauma in the long run compared to the short run. It is in this way, the model shows, that events from the past continue to exercise

    https://doi.org/10.11647/OBP.0477.07

their effects in the present. The effects, we shall see, are worse in the long run because the short-term behaviour that is induced by the trauma itself compounds the adverse effects of the trauma over the long haul.

This chapter is important because it shows how historical trauma can be incorporated into a model of a hypothetical Indigenous community— or any community with a similar culture. It then traces the mechanism through which the trauma does its pernicious work. It examines the effects in the short run and, after discussing what happens to community solidarity in the face of historical trauma, it goes on to examine the long-term effects. In short, it shows why the effects of colonialism, in which Indigenous culture was relentlessly assaulted, do not go away.

7.2 Short Run Effects of Historical Trauma

When the parameter τ denoting the intensity of events driving historical trauma changes, we shall soon see that it ultimately must also change the belongingness parameter, σ, in the long run. But, in the short run, we may take both as exogenous.

It is useful to draw a distinction between the absolute amount of time devoted to an activity and the relative amount of time devoted to it. The absolute amount refers to the total number of hours devoted to the activity per period. The relative amount of time is the fraction of the available productive time, $e(\tau)$, spent on the activity. This distinction between absolute and relative times matters because historical trauma changes the total amount of time available per period.

Taking the appropriate derivatives of the expressions in (6.6) of the previous chapter immediately yields the following proposition for the short run.

Proposition 7.1:
(a) An increase in the intensity of events, τ, inducing historical trauma for the community decreases the absolute and relative amounts of time devoted to food production, cultural production, and leisure, and increases the relative amount of time devoted to pain alleviation.
(b) An increase in cultural belongingness, σ, of the community increases the absolute and relative amounts of time devoted to food and cultural production, and reduces the absolute and relative amounts of time devoted to leisure and pain alleviation.

The intuition for part (a) of the above proposition is as follows. When the community's historical trauma becomes more severe, the attendant pain accompanying it is higher. To alleviate this, the endogenous response is to devote more resources (in this case, time) to pain reduction by the increased consumption of substances at the expense of other activities. The prediction of part (a) that higher trauma levels reduce food output and increase substance abuse is consistent with the observation of Bombay, Matheson, and Anisman (2009, p. 23). Furthermore, Spillane et al. (2022) in their recent review paper document evidence showing a positive correlation of substance use with historical trauma and also with lived (contemporary) trauma. The diversion of resources to numb pain, by itself, is rather mundane theoretically and is not the point. Rather, the point to note here is that the search for substances to alleviate pain detracts from the time devoted to all communal activities. The fact that leisure also declines in response to trauma exposes the lie in the offensive trope of 'lazy Indians'. This is important to note.

Pain, as we know from experience, has the unique ability to contract our attention to focus on the egoistic self at the expense of other people. There is empirical evidence for this general phenomenon, not specific to Indigenous Peoples.[1] Part (a) of the above proposition is consistent with these findings: historical trauma reduces food and cultural production and makes the community less functional.

The withdrawal of other-oriented effort as a result of historical trauma also impinges adversely on families—spouses, children, and extended family members. In general, the insight is that historical trauma compromises the *family- and community-orientation* within the Indigenous community. In particular, the decline in the cultural good will dilute the passing on of Indigenous culture to children, because culture is predominantly passed on across generations through the family and community.

Now consider part (b) of Proposition 7.1. When the cultural belongingness parameter, σ, exogenously increases, it induces greater concern for the wellbeing of other community members. The enhanced community orientation increases the time a member devotes to team

---

[1]   See Agerström et al. (2019) and Mancini et al. (2011) for evidence from two very different contexts. William James is said to have remarked "[D]isease makes you think of *yourself* all the time" (emphasis in original). Quoted in Leary (1990, p. 104).

activities (food and cultural production). This occurs despite the fact that I am invoking Nash (non-cooperative) behaviour in the equilibrium concept. The reason is that stronger other-regarding preferences indirectly induce more cooperation through altruism, thereby reducing the time devoted to leisure and pain reduction even when the level of pain is constant (because τ is held fixed in this exercise). The reduction in resources devoted to pain alleviation implies that *greater community orientation is a benign substitute for pain-numbing substances*. In other words, stronger community orientation counters pain's universal tendency to draw people into preoccupation with self. This explains part (b) of Proposition 7.1 and brings out an important benefit that Indigenous kinship relations confer on the communities. On the reverse side, it shows what was lost when kinship relations were undermined by colonialism.

Members of an Indigenous community that moves towards self-government would be predicted to display more engagement with the community's affairs because there is less interference from outside, and so belongingness should be higher. This is seen in the recent findings of Nikolakis and Nelson (2018), in which they compare the degree of trust that prevails in three First Nations in British Columbia, Canada. They find that trust in political institutions and social trust levels are highest in the First Nations that undertook the self-government reforms outside the *Indian Act*. This would correspond to an increase in the belongingness parameter σ which, according to Proposition 7.1 (b), will improve the equilibrium outcome due to the endogenous increased participation in collective activities; even the egoistic utility of a member will be higher in equilibrium. In the U.S., the *Indian Reorganization Act of 1934* allowed tribes to exercise more autonomy, within the Act or without the oversight of the Act. Frye and Parker (2021) find that the 2016 per capita income was 12–15% higher in tribes that opted to be more autonomous outside the Act. This is consistent with the claim in Proposition 7.1 (b) that greater self-determination elicits a higher degree of belongingness and, therefore, a higher food output, which may be taken here as a proxy for income.

7.3 Historical Trauma and Community Solidarity

The exogenous measure of belongingness in the model is the parameter σ. As we have seen, the sense of belongingness induces an endogenous response in the time devoted to collective activities, here food and cultural production. Let C denote this 'manifested' or 'empirical' measure of endogenous belonging or community orientation. We can quantify it by looking at the manifestation in the equilibrium of Chapter 6 and defining $C \equiv t^* + g^*$. Clearly, it must be the case that $0 < C < e(\tau)$. Let I denote the time devoted to individualistic activities (pain reduction and leisure) as manifested in the equilibrium, that is $I \equiv \ell^* + p^*$. It follows that $0 < I < e(\tau)$, with $I + C = e(\tau) \leq 1$. Using the expressions in (6.6), we can write down the expressions

$$C = \frac{(\alpha\mu + \beta)\rho}{(\alpha\mu + \beta)\rho + n(\gamma + \tau)}e(\tau); \quad I = \frac{n(\gamma + \tau)}{(\alpha\mu + \beta)\rho + n(\gamma + \tau)}e(\tau). \quad (7.1)$$

An increase in historical trauma τ has three distinct effects on outcomes: (1) it directly reduces a person's wellbeing exogenously through the multiplicative parameter B in the utility function (6.1), (2) it reduces the absolute amount of time devoted to collective activities by reducing the time endowment, $e(\tau)$, available to an individual,[2] and (3) it endogenously reduces the amount of time devoted to collective activities by diverting time to the acquisition of substances to relieve the pain of trauma. If individuals functioned in a world where all activities were privatized, effect (3) would be absent. In this view, it is the collective nature of Indigenous communities that makes them particularly vulnerable to historical trauma.

We may now identify the ways in which historical trauma impinges on the cohesiveness or solidarity of the hypothetical Indigenous community modelled here. The ratio C/I (dubbed 'community solidarity') may be construed as a measure of the equilibrium level of community strength relative to individual orientation. Using (7.1), 'community solidarity', denoted by S, may be written as

---

2   It is worth noting again that the main results of this chapter will go through even if, contrary to the evidence, historical trauma is not allowed to have adverse productivity effects—that is, if we let $e(\tau) = 1$. I allow $e(\tau) \leq 1$ so as to be consistent with the reality.

$$S \equiv \frac{C}{I} = \frac{(\alpha\mu + \beta)\rho}{n(\gamma + \tau)}.$$
(7.2)

Recalling that $\rho = 1 + (n-1)\sigma$, we see from (7.2) that the equilibrium group orientation relative to individual orientation is an increasing function of the exogenous component σ characterizing belongingness and a decreasing function of the historical trauma τ. If there were no endogenous responses to trauma (that is, if pain alleviation were not a possibility), the only effect of historical trauma would be to reduce the maximum productive time available for each member from 1 to the fraction $e(\tau)$, as noted. As we can see from (6.6), all activities would then be scaled down proportionately. This would reduce the absolute level of collective activities undertaken, which is damaging in itself, but the relative measure of community solidarity would be invariant with respect to the level of historical trauma. However, the inevitable endogenous response of pain alleviation reduces community solidarity by necessitating individual attention at the expense of the collective. This is an important route through which historical trauma has persistent and pervasive effects, consistent with the evidence: trauma attacks the collective activities (especially cultural) that are at the heart of Indigenous societies.

Taking the logarithm of S in (7.2) and then differentiating totally with respect to σ, we can verify that the elasticity of community solidarity with respect to σ is increasing in n. That is, a marginal increase in belongingness increases the community solidarity more steeply for larger groups. This brings out the importance of belongingness for larger groups as a counter to the usual moral hazard in teams. Furthermore, taking the cross partial of (7.2) we can verify that $\frac{\partial^2 S}{\partial \tau \partial \sigma} < 0$; that is, trauma dilutes the marginal benefit of belongingness. It does so by reducing the resources available for belongingness to produce its salutary effects.

Encounters with various forms of violence can result in extreme trauma, but not always. However, the effects of historical trauma resulting from extended assaults on the Indigenous Peoples have been shown to be very persistent (Matheson et al., 2022). These assaults were on the very fabric of the collective cultures. Eswaran (2023a) has shown, and we have seen in Chapter 2, that when the preference for the cultural good is high, privatizing the communal land of the Indigenous Peoples reduces the equilibrium level of wellbeing. We see here that historical trauma accomplishes the same end in an even more damaging manner because it also undermines the social fabric of the community.

Apart from the effects of historical trauma, the model can also offer insight on the effects of current discrimination against Indigenous Peoples. There is a long and ongoing history of discrimination against Indigenous Peoples; persistent discrimination is likely to have an adverse effect on the targeted groups if it is internalized (Shaw, 2001; Loppie, Reading, and de Leeuw, 2014; Harding, 2006; Allan and Smylie, 2015). Even minor acts of day-to-day prejudice or discrimination (called 'micro-aggressions') can lead to what has been dubbed 'racial battle fatigue' in targeted individuals over time, which dissipates a person's mental and emotional resources (see Smith, Allen, and Danly (2007) on African American students in the U.S. and Currie et al. (2012) on Indigenous students in Canada). Furthermore, the effect of current trauma is magnified by historical trauma, as shown empirically by Bombay, Matheson, and Anisman (2014).

Discrimination has three effects which can be broadly captured in the model: (1) it undermines the self-esteem of an Indigenous person and also their pride in Indigenous culture and practices. This will essentially reduce the parameter β that captures the importance of preferences for the cultural good. (2) Persistent derision of Indigenous culture would also lower the belongingness parameter σ due to the shame associated with it. (3) The dissipation of mental and emotional energy due to 'racial battle fatigue' will lower the productive time, $e(\tau)$, available to the individual.

It can readily be seen from the expressions in (6.6) and (7.1) that all these exogenous changes will reduce the time devoted to collective cultural activities. Even though (3) would merely scale down all activities proportionately, the overall result of the three effects will be to reduce the relative time devoted to the 'Us' component of Indigenous identity and raise that devoted to the 'me' component—thereby gradually contributing to the erosion of the community's cohesion; that is, community solidarity will decline.

Since public good externalities are built into community activities that constitute the cultural good, the communal orientation of Indigenous culture is very sensitive to the perceived importance of these activities (embodied in parameter β) and the shared sense of belonging (captured by parameter σ). As a result, discrimination and negative stereotyping can have sharply adverse effects on Indigenous communities in this model.[3] By reducing belongingness, racial discrimination thus affects the outcome for the Indigenous community in the model, but it also affects individual families. This is what Thibodeau and Peigan (2007) find. Based on interviews with social workers and health care workers in some First Nations communities, they report that members of First Nations communities lack trust at four levels: trust in oneself, trust in family, trust in community, and trust in outsiders.[4]

Due to the lack of available empirical evidence for the model's prediction regarding Indigenous families, I will cite some relevant findings for African Americans—another minority group that experiences considerable discrimination. Lavner et al. (2018) found that, among African American couples, men and women reported greater aggression towards each other after experiencing racial discrimination; men also reported greater relationship instability. Murry et al. (2001) found that increased racial discrimination magnified the effects of other stressors, which had damaging effects on parent-child and intimate relationships. Doyle and Molix (2014) found that discrimination perceived by African Americans strains their personal relationships through psychological and physiological routes. In light of this evidence, it would not be surprising to find that violence against one's own family members in Indigenous communities has causal origins in societal discrimination. Intimate partner violence, for example, is higher in Indigenous communities compared to the general population in North America.[5]

7.4 Long-Run Effect of Historical Trauma on Belongingness

When adverse conditions persist, we have seen that the manifested community orientation is negatively affected. Over time, this will affect the assumed or posited degree of belongingness, σ, within a community:

---

3   And this is so even though the negative stereotyping is without any basis in fact. Vowel (2016) shows that the stereotypical stories about Indigenous Peoples are uninformed and prejudiced myths.

4   A historical precedent from a different context is provided by the work of Nunn and Wantchekon (2011). They found that those countries in Africa that were more heavily raided during the slave trade era still exhibit lower trust levels today.

5   See the evidence in Rosay (2016) for the U.S. and Cotter (2021) in Canada.

it will become endogenous and cannot be taken as given. Assumptions cannot perpetually deviate from facts; persistent discrepancy between the two will bring forth an adjustment in the assumptions made. If the belongingness manifested in actuality persistently falls short, say, of that indicated by σ, the deficit in collective activity will induce a downward movement in σ. In the long run, the belongingness as *manifested* in the equilibrium must match the posited level of belongingness, σ.

We can formalize this idea quite easily. Suppose we spell out the determinants of the endogenously induced level of collective activity, C, defined earlier. We saw that C can be construed as the empirical or *manifested* measure of belongingness. Given what we have seen above, we may write this as the function $C(\sigma, \tau)$, with $\frac{\partial C(\sigma, \tau)}{\partial \sigma} > 0$ and $\frac{\partial C(\sigma, \tau)}{\partial \tau} < 0$, as can be verified using (7.1); all else constant, collective activity increases with belongingness and decreases with historical trauma. Over time, the endogenous and exogenous measures of belongingness must match. Therefore, in a steady-state equilibrium we would expect that this value of σ—call it $\sigma^*(\tau)$—will be determined by the equation:

$$C(\sigma, \tau) = \sigma. \tag{7.3}$$

Using the expression in (7.1) in equation (7.3), the relevant solution, σ^* (τ), is readily determined.[6] Thus, $\sigma^*(\tau)$ is the level of the belongingness parameter that the community will gravitate towards and settle at in the long run for a given level of historical trauma, τ. When $\sigma = \sigma^*(\tau)$, the belongingness manifested in the associated equilibrium level of collective activity, $C(\sigma^*(\tau), \tau)$, coincides with $\sigma^*(\tau)$. Taking the total derivative of equation (7.3) with respect to τ at the solution and rearranging, we obtain

$$\left(1 - \frac{\partial C(\sigma, \tau)}{\partial \sigma}\right)\frac{d\sigma^*}{d\tau} = \frac{\partial C(\sigma, \tau)}{\partial \tau}. \tag{7.4}$$

Assuming the long-run steady state solution is interior and stable, the bracket on the left-hand side of (7.4) must be positive, and so it follows that

---

6   Standard adjustment equations would specify that σ would change over time at a rate proportional to the difference $(C(\sigma, \tau) - \sigma)$. The steady state is determined by the fixed point of $C(\sigma, \tau)$, as in (7.3). Since $C(0, \tau) > 0, C(1, \tau) < 1$, and $C(\sigma, \tau)$ is increasing and strictly concave in σ, it follows that there exists a unique solution, $\sigma^*(\tau)$.

$$\frac{d\,\sigma^*(\tau)}{d\tau} < 0. \qquad\qquad (7.5)$$

Thus, we have this chapter's second theoretical result:

Proposition 7.2: When events induce a higher level of historical trauma, the steady state level of belongingness in an Indigenous community will be lower in the long run.

The nature of the steady state solution is intuitively seen by consulting Figure 7.1. In the Figure, as functions of σ, the left-hand side of (7.3) is shown as the schedule AB for a given level of trauma ('low') and the right-hand side as the 45° line, OP.

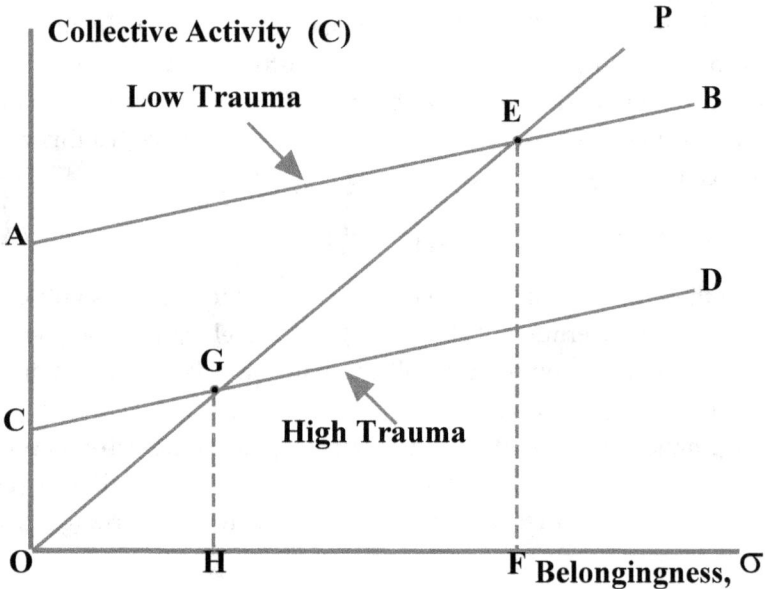

Fig. 7.1. Illustration of how the intensity of historical trauma determines the steady-state (long run) degree of Belongingness.

The schedule AB is increasing because the time devoted to collective activities increases with belongingness.[7] The steady state solution to

---

7   The fact the slope of AB must be less than 1 (that of OP) stems from the assumption that the steady state be dynamically stable—that is, the tendency will be to reestablish the steady state value after small deviations from it.

(7.3) occurs at the intersection E and the steady state value of σ is given by OF. When the given trauma level is 'high', the left-hand side shifts down to the position CD because less time is devoted to collective effort for each value of σ. The steady-state value of σ is now given by OH, where OH is clearly less than OF.

Proposition 7.2 reveals the central mechanism in the model through which historical trauma serves to further dismantle the cohesiveness of Indigenous families and communities in the long run. *It demonstrates that the effects of historical trauma are persistent.* By diverting attention and resources to addressing the immediacy of pain and further incapacitating the abilities of community members, trauma undermines the core collective activities that constitute the social organizations. Collective activities that are in the nature of public goods, of course, are undersupplied unless offset by a sense of belongingness that facilitates cooperation. In this model, historical trauma undermines the sense of belongingness, which is the unique feature of Indigenous identities and communities that ensures success in collective action.

Proposition 7.1 (a) tells us that, even when belongingness is held constant, historical trauma undermines communal activities. Proposition 7.2 tells us that events generating historical trauma also undermine belongingness in the long run, when it is endogenous. Thus, historical trauma has a double-barrelled effect on communal living over the long haul. The durability of unresolved trauma persistently exerts its influence (by diverting resources away from communal activities), undermining belongingness in the community. This is how historical trauma erodes culture and identity, according to this model. It confirms that historical trauma is responsible for the current ills of Indigenous Peoples in North America, as proposed by Brave Heart and Debruyn (1998) and Duran and Duran (1995). The model spelled out here reveals precisely how this pernicious mechanism operates.

A decline in σ would also reduce concern for one's spouse, too, which implies that in the new equilibrium, family ties will be loosened. The investment in children that would otherwise have been forthcoming through the cultural good will not take place to the same extent, and this neglect clearly will have consequences for subsequent generations. This is suggestive of one way in which the family becomes a vehicle for intergenerational trauma. Evans-Campbell (2008, p. 325) notes, "[S]cholars have suggested that among historically oppressed peoples, intergenerational trauma can become an organizing concept for family systems". She also points out that an important issue that has been neglected in discussions of historical trauma is the effect at the community level. It is precisely the importance of community that the economic model here brings out. In fact, the rendition of historical trauma in the model shows that the functioning of the *individual*, the *family*, and the *community* all get disrupted in proportion to the intensity of the trauma.

Proposition 7.2 also helps us understand an insight of C. Murray Sinclair (1998), who later chaired Canada's Truth and Reconciliation Commission. Writing about the effect of racist attitudes of colonialism and the perpetration of cultural genocide through policies based on the presumed inferiority of Indigenous Peoples, he wrote "In a strange sort of way, this state of affairs—an almost direct result of the ethnocidal policies mentioned—reinforced the unspoken belief that Indian people were inherently inferior. The result of the practice confirmed its premise—*a true self-fulfilling prophesy*" (Sinclair, C.M., 1998, p. 174, emphasis added).

In communities where the events were not very traumatic, the Indigenous sense of identity and belongingness—which can be viewed as engendering social capital—will show greater cooperativeness and collective action. This may be dubbed a 'good' equilibrium, as at point E in Figure 7.1 On the other hand, after events that were highly disruptive, relentless, and traumatic, have taken effect, the community would show a low level of belongingness and a greater degree of fragmentation at the individual, family, and community levels. The low level of belongingness and fractured identity will result in low levels of cooperativeness and collective action. Such an outcome can be deemed to be a 'bad' equilibrium, as at point G in Figure 7.1.[8] Being stuck in this equilibrium is one reason—arguably the main reason—why the "past is not the past" for Indigenous Peoples, as per *The Lancet* quotation at the beginning of Chapter 6. This

---

8   As Methot (2019, p. 2) succinctly put it in her description of the condition of contemporary Indigenous communities, "The social structures that hold families and communities together —trust, common ground, shared purpose and direction, a vibrant ceremonial and civic life, co-operative networks and associations —have broken down, and in many families and communities, there are only a few people working for the common good."

theoretical result is a formal rendition, couched in terms of economics, of the claims of many Indigenous and non-Indigenous scholars.

Unresolved trauma resulting from colonization, then, can lead to an Indigenous community being stuck or trapped in a bad equilibrium which can be difficult to escape. We may construe the pre-colonial state as a 'good' equilibrium and post-colonialism as a 'bad' equilibrium.

Before ending this chapter, I draw out an illustration of Proposition 7.2 that may be relevant to a recent and important finding. Feir, Gillezeau, and Jones (2024) investigated the effects of the near-extinction of the bison in the late nineteenth century on the wellbeing of the bison-reliant Indigenous nations in the plains of North America. They found that nations which were bison-reliant had adverse long-term health consequences and still have income levels that are 25% below the average of other nations that were not so reliant on bisons. The entire trajectory of economic development was seen to be different for the bison-reliant nations. Also, the marginal effect on income of a bank failure during the Great Depression was higher in regions exposed to more bison slaughter. The authors provide an economic explanation, backed by evidence, based on access to capital. Proposition 7.2 of this chapter offers a complementary explanation by suggesting that nations which saw greater destruction of the 10,000-year bison-reliant livelihoods with little or no alternative means for subsistence would have experienced more trauma and a more drastic unravelling of functionality at the individual, family, and community levels. This would have made it more difficult to recover on the path of economic development, even without any changes to access to credit. In other words, this would have exacerbated the effect on Indigenous wellbeing based on differential access to credit.

7.5 Summary

This chapter introduced into an economic model of a hypothetical Indigenous community the phenomenon of historical trauma and worked out some of the implications for family and community ties. We saw that historical trauma loosens these ties by diverting resources to pain alleviation at the expense of community activities. Even the short-run effects are detrimental, but in the long run the effects are worse because the diversion of resources from collective activities gradually leads to a decline in the sense of belongingness, which further dismantles community ties. This chapter has set the stage to consider the role of historical trauma in contemporary Indigenous health and deaths of despair—which is the topic of the next chapter.

8. The Consequences for Indigenous Deaths of Despair

8.1 Introduction

The reader may wish to review Chapter 5 again for a brief and focused outline of Indigenous history in the past 150 years that has been deemed by scholars to have contributed to historical trauma. It provides context for the historical trauma stemming from the Indigenous residential schools and the child welfare system which led the pre-colonial 'good' equilibrium to deteriorate to the post-colonial 'bad' equilibrium, as I claim in the previous chapter. This chapter spells out how this deterioration translates to Indigenous deaths of despair. The model also offers plausible reasons for many related empirical observations.

High levels of substances ingested to numb the pain that accompanies historical trauma may be reasonably construed in the static model of this book as synonymous with greater substance abuse. Given the well-documented evidence of the much higher levels of trauma experienced by Indigenous Peoples relative to non-Indigenous people, the results of the previous chapter offer a theoretical step towards one explanation for the poor health conditions and deaths of despair of Indigenous Peoples. These conditions are documented in the literature. In a recent study of mortality among First Nations Peoples in Canada, Park (2021) found that the age-standardized suicide rate per 100,000 person years at risk was 33.1, 17.4, and 8.0 for on-reserve, off-reserve, and non-Indigenous individuals, respectively.[1] The rates of death from chronic liver disease

---

[1] The suicide rate expressed in this manner is a ratio used in epidemiology. The numerator of the ratio is the number of people who have succumbed to suicide. The denominator is the sum of the total number of years for which all the people at

 https://doi.org/10.11647/OBP.0477.08

or cirrhosis were 22.3, 17.3, and 3.8, respectively. These dramatic differences in death rates are qualitatively analogous to the overall mortality rates documented by Feir and Akee (2019) and by Akee et al. (2024). For Indigenous Americans, Spillane et al. (2020) document excessive alcohol-related deaths relative to other groups during the period of 2000–2016; Barnes et al. (2010) document poorer health and higher levels of risky behaviour; and Espey et al. (2014) document higher rates of mortality and risky behaviours. Blanchflower and Feir (2023) found that Indigenous Americans experienced significantly more physical pain and depression than other races. Friedman, Hansen, and Gone (2023) have shown that the deaths of despair of middle-aged Indigenous Americans exceed those of middle-aged, non-Hispanic whites without college education who were the focus of Case and Deaton (2015, 2020).

8.2 Implications for Indigenous Deaths of Despair

A theory in psychology attributes very important roles in suicide to 'thwarted belongingness' and 'perceived burdensomeness' (the perception that one is a burden to one's family and others) in general populations (Joiner, 2005; Van Orden et al., 2010).[2] The idea of belongingness draws on the well-established need to belong as a fundamental human drive (Baumeister and Leary, 1995). When this need is thwarted, it can lead to suicidal thoughts and sometimes to actual suicide. Shneidman (1993) viewed the pain from unmet psychological needs as the prime cause of suicide. Meta-analyses of many studies in the literature provide evidence for this theory (Chu et al., 2017; Hatcher and Stubbersfield, 2013). The applicability of this theory to Indigenous Peoples specifically has not yet been formally tested in the literature (see O'Keefe et al. (2014) for some weak and tentative evidence), but there is good reason to believe that since belongingness is so crucial to Indigenous cultures, the effect would be much stronger in Indigenous

---

risk have been observed. One interpretation of the first number in the text would be that, on average, 33.1 Indigenous people die per year out of 100,000 people on reserves.

2   Joiner (2005) argues that attempted suicides facilitate the completion of suicides later. Among the Indigenous Peoples, attempted suicides, too, are much higher than among the rest of the population in North America.

societies. I argue that the effect runs far deeper in Indigenous Peoples of settler colonies because they have suffered far greater losses. However, belongingness at the *individual level* does not apply straightforwardly to Indigenous communities. When the community that one wants to belong to is itself fragmented and its culture is being eroded, what is an Indigenous person to identify with? This is why suicide is a *collective* issue in this context. The loss of identity is seen by Indigenous elders as crucial to the phenomenon of the Indigenous suicide crisis.[3]

Why does the undermining of identity have ill effects on health, the most drastic of which is suicide? In their landmark research on Indigenous suicides, Chandler and Lalonde (1998) attribute suicides to disruptions in the development of the self-concept.[4] For adolescents to develop a sense of self, they argue, there needs to be a stable cultural background that forms the support during the inevitable upheavals in this difficult process (Chandler and Ball, 1990; Chandler and Proulx, 2006). When this process is blocked or fails, suicide can result. When cultural continuity is undermined, as in the case of Indigenous Peoples, the generally traumatic process of self-development can become even more traumatic. This, the authors argue, is why Indigenous youth are at disproportionate risk of suicide.

The Sami, for example—who are Indigenous people of Scandinavia— exhibit elevated levels of suicide relative to the general Danish, Swedish, and Norwegian populations. Silviken, Haldorsen, and Kvernmo (2006) investigate suicides among the Sami in artic Norway in the last three decades of the twentieth century—a period during which there was a spurt in Indigenous suicides. Interestingly, they found that there was no increased risk among the Sami who engaged in the traditional practice of reindeer herding, from which they derived a sense of identity. This gives some credence to the claim that it is deviation from tradition and the attendant loss of identity that are correlated with the risk of suicide. In an

---

3   C. Murray Sinclair, while speaking on the issue of youth suicides, attributed the tragedy to lack of identity. "Part of the problem of suicide among young people is the loss of hope they feel because they do not know who they are. We are responding to the suicide rate by giving them drugs, but this won't give them a sense of who they are." (First Nations Health Authority, 26 April 2019).

4   The importance given to the self-concept or identity is in line with a long tradition in psychology, starting with William James (1890), who made it the central concept of his classic work. Identity was introduced into economics first by Akerlof and Kranton (2000) in a very different context than what is under consideration here.

investigation into the reasons for Sami suicides in Scandinavia, Stoor et al. (2015) suggest that when the traditional occupation of herding reindeer began to decline, the Sami saw suicide as a way out of the 'existential void' following the loss of identity. Given the far more egregious offences against Indigenous Peoples in Canada and the United States, where expunging Indigenous identities was colonial policy, there can be little doubt that this erosion of identity and the subsequent compounding and perpetuation of historical trauma are factors contributing to Indigenous suicides.

Case, Deaton, and Cutler (2017) find that suicide rates are inconsistently correlated with subjective wellbeing measures (Layard, 2005; Helliwell, 2007). They find that, even after controlling for income inequality and religious denomination, *pain* is strongly correlated with suicide rates.[5] This underlines the importance of accounting for pain, as I have done here and in Eswaran (2023b). The results of my model can be seen as being consistent with the findings on Indigenous suicides.

Durkheim (1897/1951) posited that the greater the strength of social integration within a society, the lower the suicide rate should be.[6] The definition of belongingness here, as in Eswaran (2023a) and the earlier chapters of this book, is precisely this notion of social integration, so Durkheim's theory is directly relevant. May and Van Winkle (1994) applied the theory to Indigenous bands in the southwestern United States and found that the suicide rates were inversely correlated with the level of social integration. Although Chandler and Lalonde (1998) do not link their work to Durkheim's, my model bridges their theories by providing a theoretical link between historical trauma and the dismantling of collective activities of Indigenous communities. It may be noted that the relational nature of Indigenous societies that Trosper (2022) emphasizes is what facilitates the sense of community. When relationality is disrupted, the social capital it engenders will be eroded, and the sense of community will inevitably be undermined.

---

5   Duran and Duran (1995, p. 180) point out that, in their clinical experience with Indigenous Americans, suicidal patients' common theme is "I don't want to hurt anymore."

6   Durkheim referred to this type of suicide as 'egoistic'. He also posited that there could be what he called 'altruistic' suicide if the degree of social integration is very high, where people commit suicide for others. This latter type is less relevant to the context of Indigenous Peoples because suicide was historically not a tradition among the First Nations and Inuit Peoples (Kirmayer et al., 2007, p. 59; RCAP, 1996, p. 10).

One of the clinically established features of Indigenous trauma is PTSD (Basset et al., 2014), which is known to be associated with chronic pain, anxiety, depression, suicidal thoughts, and inability to sustain relationships, among other traits. It has also been found that PTSD reduces the time horizon of interest—that is, it increases the discount rate of the person (Bryan and Bryan, 2021). The discount rate describes how much a person prefers present benefits over future benefits. If one were to construct an intertemporal version of my model, the higher discount rate would readily be seen to result in higher alcohol and drug consumption, increasing the chances of death due to drug overdoses and alcohol poisoning. Since drugs show diminishing returns in suppressing pain, sensitivity to pain ultimately increases with drug use (Nakajima and al'Absi, 2016), which would tend to increase drug use and the possibility of overdosing in turn. More generally, in a dynamic framework, it would be inferred that any investment in one's human capital (not just health but also education and work experience) in general will be undermined by historical trauma. Short-term pain relief will be traded off against the long-term wellbeing that would have been feasible through greater accumulation of human capital.

In the absence of evidence supporting purely economic models of suicide in the literature,[7] Case, Deaton, and Cutler (2017) propose that suicide may be impulsive and may depend on how one feels in the moment, without future considerations. This claim fits well with a theory from psychology that views suicide as basically an escape from a suffering sense of self (Baumeister, 1990; Shneidman, 1993). It also accords well with my claim that, at least for Indigenous Peoples, historical trauma increases the discount rate and narrows a person's focus to their suffering in the present. This would be an economic interpretation of Chandler and Lalonde's (1998) psychological insight that disruptions in the continuity of the self-concept promote Indigenous suicides.

One may ask: why do people not alleviate pain by choosing healthy and character-building habits rather than maladaptive ones like imbibing alcohol and consuming drugs? It is certainly true that there can be scenarios where pain is managed through various practices—like land-based activities, counselling, engaging with self-help groups, etc.—which

---

7   See Hammermesh and Soss (1974). Chen et al. (2012) offer a review of the literature in economics and sociology.

do not have dire consequences and, in fact, have positive outcomes. The general answer to this question can only come from the field of psychology, not from economics, but one suspects that positive pain responses are only feasible for trauma that, in some sense, is not 'excessive'. In the face of overwhelming trauma, immediate relief from pain is sought, and that is usually obtained via maladaptive habits when more positive avenues are unavailable. Positive, life-affirming projects tend to generate benefits only in the long run whilst offering limited pain relief in the present. A traumatized person will have difficulty committing to positive programs without help from other people in the community—which is precisely what is unavailable when the sense of community has been eroded. We must bear in mind that detrimental means of pain relief are chosen because more healthful treatments have been made unavailable to Indigenous Peoples. This point cannot be emphasized enough.

Chapter 9 offers a tentative theory from economics for why some communities are more resilient to collective trauma than others. There we shall encounter some positive Indigenous ways of dealing with trauma. In the next section of this chapter, I investigate what the model suggests about Indigenous deaths of despair.

8.3 A Formal Statement of the Implications for Deaths of Despair

Let us now relate the model of Chapter 7 to Indigenous deaths of despair more formally. Suppose we denote the rate of deaths of despair in an Indigenous community of given size by D. On the basis of what we have seen in this book thus far, we may claim that D is given by a mortality function, say $M(\tau, \sigma, p, C)$, with four arguments: τ, historical trauma; σ, belongingness; p, the time each individual devotes to acquiring pain- and anxiety-reducing substances; and C, the time each individual devotes to collective activities—either food production or cultural activities. Individuals in the community are, for simplicity, considered to be identical, though in reality there is a wide variation in the level of pain experienced, pain-avoidance behaviours, and resilience of individuals.

We may posit the following partial derivatives, denoted here by subscripts:
(1) $M_\tau > 0$, capturing the direct effect of trauma on deaths of despair;
(2) $M_\sigma < 0$, since belongingness reduces deaths of despair by cementing

community ties; (3) $M_p > 0$, since pain-reducing substances increase deaths indirectly through overdoses, etc.; and (4) $M_C < 0$, since collective activity reduces deaths of despair by increasing community support. Of the four arguments of $M(\tau, \sigma, p, C)$, only the first—historical trauma—is truly exogenous in my model. The second is exogenous in the short run but not in the long run; belongingness ultimately responds to the level of trauma (see Proposition 7.2). The remaining two variables are endogenous in both the short run and the long run. Substance use is endogenous at the individual level whereas the collective communal activity, C, is exogenous to the individual but endogenous to the community in aggregate.

Consider the effect of historical trauma on deaths of despair, D. Taking the total derivative of D with respect to τ, and evaluating the function $M(\tau, \sigma, p, C)$ at the steady state equilibrium of the community, we obtain

$$\frac{d}{d\tau} D = \left\{ M_\tau + M_p \frac{dp}{d\tau} + M_C \frac{dC}{d\tau} \right\} + \left\{ \left[M_\sigma + M_p \frac{dp}{d\sigma} + M_C \frac{dC}{d\sigma} \right] \frac{d\sigma}{d\tau} \right\}, \quad (8.1)$$

where the terms in the first set of curly braces capture the effects in the short run (when σ is constant) and the terms in the second set of curly braces must be added for the long run, when σ responds to τ. Using the results of Propositions 7.1 and 7.2, expression (7.1) for C, and the posited partials of $M(\tau, \sigma, p, C)$ above, we obtain the signs of the various terms on the right hand side as follows:

$$\frac{d}{d\tau} D = \{(+) + (+)(+) + (-)(-)\} + \{[(-) + (+)(-) + (-)(+)] \\ (-)\} > 0.$$

The signs of all the terms in both sets of curly braces are unambiguously positive. It follows that the deaths of despair increase with historical trauma, but more so in the long run since the positive terms in the second set of braces (capturing the long-run effects) add to the positive terms in first set of braces (capturing the short-run effects). I record this result below.

Proposition 8.1: An increase in the severity of historical trauma,
(a) increases the rate of Indigenous deaths of despair in the short and long runs, and
(b) the rate of Indigenous deaths of despair is higher in the long run than in the short run.

It must be noted that Proposition 8.1 applies not only to Indigenous deaths of despair; it would also apply to deaths of despair in other communities in which culture is critical to identity, and where historical trauma has undermined the culture. Deaths of despair occur in Indigenous communities because colonization has led to the destruction of Indigenous cultures that are very important to them.

The first two terms in the curly braces for the short run in expression (8.1) capture the deaths by deliberate suicide and, indirectly, through overdoses. This response to trauma would hold for Indigenous Peoples as well as for the rest of the population. What is different for Indigenous communities and other communal societies in the short run is the third term, which compounds the effect through a decline in social support by the dismantling of communal activities. In the long run, as shown by the additional second set of curly braces in (8.1), matters are worse. The steady undermining of communal bonds results in a decline in the sense of belongingness in the steady state, and this erosion of Indigenous identity further increases substance abuse and fragmentation of the community. I suggest that this additional feature—a consequence of high levels of historical trauma—is an important reason why the rates of Indigenous deaths of despair in the data are so much higher than those for the rest of the population, as documented by Akee et al. (2024) and by Friedman, Hansen, and Gone (2023). Proposition 8.1 brings out the core mechanism that reveals what long-term impact the destruction of Indigenous identity has on deaths of despair.

One thing must be clarified regarding the above proposition. One may wonder why we might observe more deaths of despair in Indigenous communities than in non-Indigenous ones when the former culturally provide a stronger support system. To be sure, if all else were constant (especially historical trauma), the theory suggests that Indigenous communities should experience fewer deaths of despair. But all else most definitely is *not* constant. Rarely have societies been subjected to such unrelenting and comprehensive cultural assaults for centuries as have North American Indigenous Peoples. Furthermore, the proposition is a comparative static result that investigates the effect of the level of historical trauma on deaths of despair. When historical trauma increases, Indigenous deaths of despair increase not only for the same reasons they would for non-Indigenous societies, but also for additional reasons pertaining to the dismantling of culture.

At the centre of the effect of exogenous changes to belongingness on Indigenous wellbeing is the fact that the most important production activities (food and culture) are communal and, therefore, entail teamwork. The nature of both of these activities is that the action of one member impinges on others and their incentives. Since historical trauma is a shared community phenomenon, an induced reduction in team effort across the board can have a very deleterious effect on the equilibrium outcome. This belongingness aspect of identity makes Indigenous communities simultaneously stronger than organizations based on purely egoistic cultures, but also more vulnerable to negative shocks to culture. Thus, the compounded effect of a series of shocks—the loss of loved ones due to European diseases, the loss of land, traditional customs, language, identity, self-determination, kinship system, and spirituality, to name a few—would exacerbate the adverse impact on the wellbeing of Indigenous Peoples. This offers some insight from economics into why the net effect of what Indigenous and non-Indigenous scholars and psychologists have labelled as 'historical trauma' is so detrimental.

We may ask whether the same results would be obtained if historical trauma directly reduced the weight on culture in preferences, as captured by the parameter β in the utility function in (6.1). The answer is no. First it should be clarified that the reduction in the time constraint, $1 - e$ (τ), due to historical trauma has been used here for consistency with empirical evidence. We would obtain the same qualitative results even if the time constraint were invariant to the intensity of historical trauma, as already noted. What is crucial for our result, however, is that the *time diversion* to pain alleviation is an endogenous response to the trauma. This is the reason for the grave consequences of historical trauma, such as substance abuse and deaths of despair. A mere reduction in the cultural parameter β would not deliver the results of this chapter.

We may also wonder how the effects of historical trauma may differ from the direct effects of institutional changes intended to divide communities. Theoretically, institutional change and historical trauma can be conceptually distinguished. In practice, however, this distinction is not clear-cut in the case of Indigenous Peoples. The reason is that Indigenous institutions are deeply embedded in Indigenous culture, as we have seen earlier. (This is true of all societies to some extent, but it is particularly so in Indigenous societies.) One such institutional change that we studied in Part I of this book is the *Dawes Act*, which broke up communally-owned land into individually-owned plots. One may reasonably speculate that the effects of the division of land into individual lots would be milder than those of historical trauma (which entailed the loss of family members, loss of land through colonial appropriations and relocations, etc.), because the former is a less comprehensive an assault on culture. So, *if* we could isolate the institutional change from historical trauma, we would expect deaths of despair to be fewer in the former case. However, the communities facing the *Dawes Act* would have experienced institutional change *as well as* historical trauma. From this reasoning it would follow that, holding historical trauma constant across Indigenous communities, those communities that were additionally subjected to the *Dawes Act* would exhibit higher rates of deaths of despair. This is potentially an empirically testable prediction—potentially, because it is contingent on finding Indigenous communities for which the distinction between institutional change and trauma can be credibly made.

In the introductory chapter of this book, I alluded to the fact that ethnic group size—which proves to be a protective factor for immigrant groups in Canada—does not necessarily protect Indigenous communities. We now have an explanation for this fact. Historical trauma, by Propositions 7.1 and 7.2, reduces the extent of social integration and support within an Indigenous community in the short run and reduces them even further in the long run. The fact of historical trauma is what separates Indigenous Peoples of North America from most other ethnic and demographic groups that immigrated to Canada and the United States.

8.4 Explanations for Some Observed Patterns

After demonstrating the cascading effects of historical trauma at the individual, family, and community levels, the theoretical model also contributes towards an understanding of why the effects of this trauma are so all-encompassing.

My argument may be seen as possibly providing a theoretical underpinning for some recent empirical findings. Using contemporary data, Akee et al. (2024) unearth some very startling facts. They find that, in contrast to the deaths of despair of non-Hispanic white males which correspond counter-cyclically with local economic conditions, those of Native Americans males seem relatively impervious to economic conditions. The deaths of despair of Native American women, they find, can be procyclical with economic conditions: more deaths in good economic times and fewer deaths in bad times. Recognizing that Indigenous deaths of despair in the U.S. may be unrelated to economics, they venture that these deaths may instead be attributed to the "legacy of centuries of racism and deprivation" (p. 7)—a view that is endorsed by my theory. Furthermore, Akee et al. (2024) find that the modal age of suicides is very different for non-Hispanic whites and Indigenous Americans: it is in the mid-fifties for the former and in the late teens and early twenties for the latter. Both of these facts are consistent with the proposition that Native American deaths of despair are driven by historical trauma which, as shown by my theory, undermines the cultural support that protects adolescents, in line with Chandler et al. (2003).

The theoretical framework provided in this book may also go some distance in explaining an important difference in suicide rates between Canadian and American Indigenous communities. Indigenous suicide rates in Canada are higher than those in the United States, which themselves are elevated relative to the rest of the population. During the period 2010–2016, the suicide rate among First Nations Peoples in Canada was 24.3 deaths per 100,000 of the population compared to 8.0 deaths for the rest of the population (Kumar and Tjepkema, 2019). The corresponding figures for 2020 for American Indian and Alaskan Natives were 16.9 deaths compared to 12.1 for non-Hispanic whites (Center for Disease Control and Prevention, 2022). In fact, the real difference between suicide rates would be even higher if we recognize— as Raifman, Sampson, and Galea (2020) have—that if gun ownership in the U.S. was hypothetically reduced to the same level as in Canada, U.S. suicide rates for the general population would fall by as much as a quarter (even after accounting for the fact that guns can be substituted with other methods of suicide). If the difference is not entirely explained by socioeconomic variables, the higher Indigenous suicide rate in Canada requires an explanation.

One reason for the higher Indigenous suicide rates in Canada may be the difference in the *intensity* of historical trauma. The federal residential schools in the U.S. were shut down in the 1960s. In Canada, the residential schools were not reformed till the 1970s and the last school closed its doors only in the mid-1990s. The fact that residential schools were operating as colonial institutions for assimilation for several more decades in Canada seems relevant, considering how these schools contributed to historical trauma (Bombay, Matheson, and Anisman, 2014).

A second reason for the Canada-U.S. difference in suicide rates could be the child welfare system (CWS). For reasons given in Chapter 5, the disproportionate representation of Indigenous children in the child welfare system has been far higher in Canada. The removal of children from a household by the CWS naturally has an extremely traumatic effect on all parents, but more so for Indigenous parents (Evans-Campbell, 2008). Using data from the province of Manitoba in Canada, Wall-Wieler et al. (2018) found that mothers who had a child taken away by the CWS had twice the rates of attempted and completed suicides compared to mothers who did not. Thumath et al. (2021) found that, compared to non-Indigenous women in Canada who did not have a child taken away, women whose children were removed experienced increased risks of unintended overdose of substances, but this increase was more pronounced for Indigenous women—even after controlling for other potential contributory factors. In a study of young Indigenous women in British Columbia who use drugs, Ritland et al. (2021) found that women who experienced child apprehension by the CWS were more likely to attempt suicide than women who did not have a child removed.

We would expect that, given the strength of the maternal bond, mothers who use drugs would be extremely motivated to break the habit in order to regain custody of their children. However, the evidence suggests that the trauma of separation may actually lead some mothers to attempt suicide. This is but one example of the child removal policy of the CWS aggravating the existing dysfunction caused by historical trauma. As Sinha et al. (2021, p. 2) say, "The removal of children by the child welfare system has, in many ways, perpetuated the destruction of Indigenous community ties and local decision-making." We may reasonably conjecture that the traumatic effects of residential schools and the CWS were more extensive in Canada than in the U.S. Propositions

7.1, 7.2, and 8.1 would then explain the higher Indigenous suicide rates in Canada relative to those in the U.S.

The theory in this book may also tentatively suggest why there are gender differences in suicide rates and mental health statistics between Indigenous men and women. A formal analysis is outside the scope of this book, but an intuitive and informal hypothesis is possible given what the model captures. May and Van Winkle (1994) pointed out that men's suicide rates exceeded women's in almost all Indigenous communities. They argued that Indigenous men are less well adapted to American society than Indigenous women because the former's traditional roles are less available to them than the latter's.[8] This is also the perspective of Indigenous psychologists Duran and Duran (1995). If we accept this view, which does not seem unreasonable given the limited scope of jobs available on reserves, then it would follow that the impact of historical trauma should be greater on Indigenous men than Indigenous women. The intuitive logic of Chapter 7's Proposition 7.1 (a)—though not the formal analysis, because the model does not permit heterogeneity within a community—would imply greater dysfunction among Indigenous men. This seems to be supported by contemporary data. For example, between 2011 and 2016, the age-adjusted suicide rate per 100,000 First Nations persons in Canada was 29.6 for men and 19.5 for women (Kumar and Tjepkema, 2019).[9]

Note that these health consequences prevail even in a simple static model that does not incorporate the addictive behaviour which frequently co-occurs with PTSD and chronic pain. In reality, matters would likely be much worse because many of the affected individuals

---

8   Specifically, they say "The warrior, farmer, hunter, and protector role of the male is no longer as viable in traditional or modern Indian societies, while the child-bearer and home-maker role of the female has changed less. Further, Indian females are more likely than males to enter the modern wage work labour system in education, clerical, administrative, social service, and other service sector jobs, jobs which are quite dominant on and around most Indian reservations in the West". May and Van Winkle (1994, pp. 308–309).

9   The ratios of Indigenous to non-Indigenous suicide rates were 2.4 for men and 5.0 for women. Indigenous women seem to face harsher current environments compared to non-Indigenous women than do Indigenous men compared to non-Indigenous men. The number of missing and murdered Indigenous women is a case in point (see McDiarmid, 2020), as Akee et al. (2024) have suggested. This is an issue that warrants more research. Burnette (2015) suggests that additional trauma for women can come from intimate partner violence.

are compelled by addictions. To consider issues of addiction, one would of course need a dynamic model, which would take us outside the scope of this book.

Historical trauma disrupts a person's sense of self, as discussed earlier. The most suggestive evidence on the connection between the strength of self and suicide risk is provided by the work of Chandler and Lalonde (1998), alluded to earlier. They use data from the 196 Indigenous bands in British Columbia, aggregated into few tribal groupings because many of the bands had very small populations. For each aggregate group they computed six binary variables that measured cultural continuity (initiation of land claims, initiation of self-government, control over education, control over police, control over healthcare, and cultural centres) and summed them to produce an index number ranging from 0 to 6. They found that this aggregate measure was inversely correlated with the suicide rate in each group—a correlation that is very noteworthy.

In their review of the literature on the risk and protective factors pertaining to Indigenous youth suicides, Harder et al. (2012) find that some activities (e.g. spiritual ones) are protective but the factors with the most pronounced protective effect are those characterized as a 'group process', as in Chandler and Lalonde (1998, 2008). It is noteworthy, in my view, that the pertinent institutions and activities of Indigenous Peoples (making land claims, Indigenous education, demanding self-government, etc.) were not individual efforts but required collective action. In this book's model, investment in the cultural good denoted by the variable G—which can be viewed as the relational good that Uhlaner (1989) and Trosper (2002) have emphasized—would facilitate cooperation.

Indigenous communities are not the only groups subject to deaths of despair, as noted earlier. When the phenomenon was first brought to light by Case and Deaton (2015, 2020) for non-Hispanic, middle-aged whites without college education in the United States, they attributed these deaths to a sense of hopelessness in the lower class of American society. More specifically, they argued that the causes have to do with unemployment, family breakups, decline in social capital, etc.[10] King,

---

10   Ruhm (2019) contends that the triggering cause was the opioid drug crisis in the U.S.

Scheiring, and Nosrati (2022) offer a survey of the evidence to date on these particular deaths of despair and also those which occurred in Eastern Europe following the breakup of the Soviet Union in 1989.

Interestingly, some indirect, suggestive evidence on the role of culture as a determinant of Indigenous deaths of despair comes from this non-Indigenous group of middle-aged, non-Hispanic whites without college education. As alluded to in Chapter 1 of this book, Giles, Hungerman, and Oostrom (2023) examined the role of religion in deaths of despair in this group of Americans. They found that an exogenous event (the repeal of blue laws) led to lower religious participation by non-Hispanic, middle-aged whites without college education, which drove them to deaths of despair. If a voluntary reduction in religious participation following a cultural shock can ultimately lead to deaths of despair in non-Indigenous groups, we can reasonably infer that the wilful attempt to expunge Indigenous religions and religious practices for decades in the United States and Canada would have had at least as large an impact. And this was only *one* of many concerted approaches to erasing Indigenous cultures. The greater severity of the problem in these communities compared to non-Hispanic, middle-aged whites without college education—as seen in the evidence of Friedman, Hansen, and Gone (2023)—may reasonably be attributed to the comprehensive erosion of Indigenous cultures.[11]

Before leaving this section it is important to note that, since the model is focused on investigating the effects of the erosion of culture, it downplays other important factors that influence deaths of despair. Two such factors are poverty and adverse social conditions. In their empirical work, Akee et al. (2024) found that general economic conditions do not seem to be correlated with Indigenous deaths of despair. This is not to say that the economic and social conditions faced by Indigenous Peoples are irrelevant to the phenomenon. In fact, Blanchflower and Feir (2023), who examine the incidence of chronic stress in Indigenous Americans, found that much of the gap in chronic stress between Indigenous Americans and whites is explained by differences in the economic and social circumstances confronting the two aggregate groups. While

---

11   It is conceivable that the assault on Indigenous cultures may have been greater on the more functional communities in order to hasten assimilation with mainstream society in North America.

chronic stress is different from deaths of despair, a positive correlation can be expected between the two (Case and Deaton, 2020).

Employment, which is clearly related to income, is another factor that can lead to deaths of despair. Richards (2023) argues that low levels of Indigenous employment in the Canadian prairies have a lot to do with Indigenous deaths of despair. In subjective wellbeing studies, it has been well-established that unemployment is one of the most important factors that impinges adversely on subjective wellbeing (see e.g. Helliwell and Huang, 2014). A meta-analysis by Milner, Page, and LaMontagne (2013) reveals that long-term unemployment is associated with a greater risk of suicide and suicide attempts. The effect of employment goes beyond the mere earning of income because it can also give meaning to life, which directly relates to will to live.

8.5 On the Role of Settler Colonialism

The specific role of settler colonialism in the outcomes being discussed needs to be emphasized. The elevated suicide rates of Indigenous Peoples relative to the rest of the population are seen not only in Canada and the United States but also in Australia and New Zealand (see Dudgeon et al., 2018). By collating the sparse extant evidence from across the world, Pollock (2018) has shown, however, that Indigenous suicide rates are not uniformly elevated in all countries.

Hatcher (2016) attributes the high suicide rates of Canadian Indigenous Peoples to being colonized. It is not merely colonialism but, rather, *settler colonialism* that is very likely to be partly responsible for these elevated rates of Indigenous suicides, because settler colonialism is tied to the loss of land. Economists have largely been silent on this subject, but this hypothesis is assumed to be true in the literature that exists in disciplines outside economics (e.g. Czyzewski, 2011; RCAP, 1996).

The model of this chapter suggests reasons why settler colonization is intimately linked to elevated Indigenous suicide rates. Settlers desired land that could be converted to private, fee simple property. This necessitated the erasure of Indigenous communal culture (Wolfe, 2006). It is this desire for land and resources that ultimately drove the repeated efforts to erase Indigenous culture—relegation to reserves, inducements for enfranchisement, residential schools, bans on Indigenous languages, and attempts to purge Indigenous spirituality, to name a few.[12] In terms of the model, settlers' desire for land was ultimately responsible for inflicting historical trauma (increasing the parameter τ) and loosening the bonds of belongingness (lowering the parameter σ). And unresolved trauma, as we have seen, perpetuates the adverse impact on belongingness into the present. Had the colony merely been, in the terminology of Acemoglu, Johnson and Robinson (2001), an 'extractive' colony—one from which resources were extracted without changing land ownership and with no significant settlement by people from the colonizing country—there would have been little need for a sustained assault on Indigenous cultures and identities. For example, the cultures of India during British colonialism were not assaulted like those of Indigenous Peoples of North America, Australia, and New Zealand.

8.6 Summary

This chapter dealt with the implications of the economic model of this book for the grave phenomenon of Indigenous deaths of despair. It traced the effects of historical trauma, the individual responses to it, and the consequences for families and communities. By increasing the need for pain alleviation, historical trauma undermines the family and the community and, in the long run, the sense of belonging. This, in turn, undermines the capacity of a community to buffer pain and offer support, resulting in an increase in deaths of despair. This chapter isolated the cause of the disparity between Indigenous and non-Indigenous deaths of despair. The model was then used to explain many documented facts pertaining to Indigenous suicides and to identify the role played by settler colonialism.

---

12   While these attempts severely undermined the identities of Indigenous peoples, they failed to expunge them. In a different context, Fouka (2020) showed that when some states in the U.S. banned the teaching of German after WWI, the bans actually hardened the identity of German Americans.

9. Indigenous Survivance

9.1 Introduction

Indigenous Peoples of North America have been under assault for 500 years, and yet Indigenous populations have survived. This would not have been possible were it not for their formidable strength of spirit to resist and to endure. Despite being murdered, robbed of land, and faced with persistent discrimination and concerted efforts to erase their religions, traditions, languages, and identities, Indigenous Peoples of North America are still here, still visible, still resisting oppression, and still fighting to preserve traditional ways of life. What is it that has led to endurance under such conditions? What cultural aspects of Indigenous ways of life have enabled the surmounting of such incredible odds? This chapter is an attempt to offer a limited answer to these questions in the context of the admittedly narrow economic model of this book—narrow because economics is only one field among many (such as sociology, psychology, history, Indigenous studies, and others) that are relevant to the phenomenon of resilience.

In the previous chapter, I attributed Indigenous deaths of despair to the unravelling of Indigenous cultures. We may envisage culture as the shared human and social capital of a society. The erosion of this form of capital is far more destructive than the loss of physical capital through wars and environmental disasters. The latter can be quickly replaced when the human capital that embodies knowledge and skill and the social capital that facilitates cooperation are intact. However, when human and social capitals at the level of culture are diminished, a process of further deterioration could be set in motion, and this is the mechanism revealed by the economic model of the three previous chapters.

 https://doi.org/10.11647/OBP.0477.09

When, as we have done thus far, we focus on the pathological conditions brought about by colonialism—which Indigenous scholars argue is still ongoing in many ways—we may be left with the impression that Indigenous Peoples are 'damaged' in some ways. In this chapter, we shall see that this is hardly so.

It is very important to recognize the harm that colonialism has inflicted on Indigenous Peoples, because in order to right the wrongs, we need to understand the root causes of contemporary Indigenous conditions and behaviours. But to stop there would be to stop too early. It is equally important to recognize the strength of spirit and the resilience that has enabled Indigenous survival, and to build on that.[1] This is a point that has been increasingly insisted upon by Indigenous scholars in recent decades following Vizenor's (2008) concept of survivance (to be discussed in the next section), which speaks of more than just survival. In this chapter, I argue that the collective aspect of Indigenous ways of life can contribute substantively to survivance, and I use the economic model of this book to outline how this is the case.

In the study of historical trauma, psychologists encounter many of its adverse effects (like PTSD and intergenerational persistence). However, they also encounter resilience to trauma and, in some cases, even psychological growth where the people affected have in some ways benefitted from trauma in the long run. The previous two chapters have focused only on adverse responses to historical trauma. This is no ordinary trauma, as we have seen. The myriad attacks—physical, psychological, and cultural—over an extended duration of centuries mark historical trauma out for special consideration. Its effects are glaringly visible from the socioeconomic statistics and deaths of despair in Indigenous communities compared to the rest of the population in North America. It is important, therefore, to first focus on the negative effects of historical trauma to understand the mechanisms through which it functions. This is what we have done in the previous three chapters. But now it is time to examine the very uplifting phenomenon of Indigenous resilience.

Indigenous deaths of despair are most certainly not uniformly spread out across all or even most Indigenous communities, as we shall see in the next section of this chapter. So, when we focus on deaths of despair, we are

---

1   Kirmayer et al. (2009a) offer a good overview of the concept of resilience in the field of psychology.

inevitably sampling a selection of communities for theoretical analysis—which may give the mistaken impression that all Indigenous communities are affected. What separates communities that exhibit survivance from those that are badly affected by the legacies of colonialism? This is an important question to ask. In this chapter, I briefly address how this question may be approached using the model of Part II.

9.2 Survivance

The term that is usually applied to a positive response to trauma is resilience. It refers to the fact that an individual who has been traumatized overcomes the shock of the trauma and recovers their original stance towards life. Indigenous scholars have discussed the drawbacks of the concept of resilience in the phenomenon of historical trauma (Vizenor, 2008; Kirmayer et al., 2011). As we have seen, historical trauma is not merely an individual shock but also a family and community one, and so the focus cannot be merely on individuals. Furthermore, there is a somewhat static aspect to the concept of resilience, whereas Indigenous scholars emphasize a more dynamic aspect focusing on the positive features of the response. In the Indigenous context, the concept that scholars now apply is 'survivance' instead of resilience, following Vizenor (2008), who first coined the term.[2] Loosely, survivance is a combination of survival and resistance that emphasizes spirit, vitality, and courage. It is an exercise of autonomy, an assertion of identity and an attempt to force recognition of Indigenous presence through actions, imagination, and narratives. Wilbur and Gone (2023, p. 1) helpfully summarize how the concept is invoked in the recent health literature: "[*A*]*s resilience is to trauma, so survivance is to historical trauma*" (emphasis in the original).[3]

A good contemporary example of the concept of survivance in action is provided by the 2016 Indigenous collective action at Standing Rock reservation in North Dakota, United States (Hedlund, 2020). An energy company, Energy Transfer Partners, was building a pipeline to ship oil from North Dakota to southern Illinois, with a 1-mile stretch of the pipeline going below Lake Oahe, the sole water supply of Standing Rock reservation. Standing Rock Sioux

---

2   Wilbur and Gone (2023) provide a good overview of the concept of survivance.

3   Hartmann et al. (2019) discuss the various approaches to historical trauma in the literature.

Tribe, joined by other Indigenous groups, protested against construction of the pipeline due to the possibility of water contamination from leaks in the pipeline. In a show of unity, Indigenous Peoples from many communities—including Canadian ones—participated. The pipeline was built anyway, and oil started being shipped in June 2017. Even in 2023, however, Indigenous and environmental groups protested that the pipeline was built without a careful assessment of possible environmental impacts.[4] Over a period of seven years, Indigenous groups made their presence felt, seeking to hold the government and private enterprises accountable for violations of Indigenous rights. This is a demonstration of Indigenous survivance.

Another example of survivance—and this one from Canada—pertains to the Wet'suwet'en territory in the northern part of the province of British Columbia.[5] A commercial enterprise called Coastal GasLink was building a 670-kilometer pipe line for natural gas over the unceded territory of Wet'suwet'en. This was done after getting the support of twenty First Nations band councils, which also included five out of the six (elected) Indigenous councils in the Wet'suwet'en nation. The hereditary Indigenous chiefs, however, asserted that the elected band councils have no authority outside their reserves; the territory in question was unceded and, therefore, fell within the jurisdiction of the hereditary Indigenous chiefs who had authority over these lands before the *Indian Act*. The protests by Indigenous groups over the intended pipeline began in 2010 but came to a head in 2019–2020 when they blocked access to the area for building the pipeline, which led to the arrest of some protestors by the Royal Canadian Mounted Police. Indigenous protests spread across Canada, which shut down Canada's national transportation system for some weeks. The courts supported Coastal GasLink, so the pipeline was ultimately built and became operational in November 2024. Nevertheless, the protests of the Indigenous Peoples of Wet'suwet'en led to greater awareness of Indigenous rights, brought about increased involvement by the provincial and federal governments and the courts.[6] A refusal to

---

4   See e.g. https://www.sierraclub.org/press-releases/2023/12/indigenous-tribes-congressional-leaders-and-allies-demand-biden

5   For more details, see "What you need to know about the Coastal GasLink pipeline conflict," *CBC News*, 5 February 2020, https://www.cbc.ca/news/indigenous/wet-suwet-en-coastal-gaslink-pipeline-1.5448363

6   In February 2025, the Supreme Court of British Columbia ruled in favour of three Indigenous women who were criminalized for protesting against Coastal GasLink

have hereditary rights annulled by the laws of colonizers extended over unceded land and to stand up for these rights in the face of unpromising odds is an illustration of what is meant by Indigenous survivance.

On the basis of case studies of Indigenous communities in Canada, Kirmayer et al. (2011) emphasize the communal aspect of Indigenous responses to historical trauma and argue that Indigenous narratives play an important role, as emphasized in Vizenor's (2008) notion of survivance. Even in the study of non-Indigenous trauma, in fact, scholars have recently been emphasizing the importance of community and social identity (Muldoon et al., 2019; Haslam et al., 2018). The basic idea is that one's social group determines the risk of exposure to traumatic experiences and also determines the response to trauma.

The theoretical model in Part II of this book emphasizing the role of the community is exactly in line with these arguments from psychologists. As an economist, I am not equipped to offer a full-blown theory of why some Indigenous communities may be very adversely affected by historical trauma while others exhibit strong survivance and even thrive. That would require input from anthropologists, sociologists, social and clinical psychologists, and also from scholars in Indigenous studies. However, based on my model, I attempt below to offer at least an impressionistic view of when we might observe these divergent effects.

Recall the egoistic utility function, $u(c, G, \ell, p)$, of Chapter 6 used in this part of the book, which is reproduced below:

$$u(c, g, \ell, p) = B(\tau)\, c^{\alpha}\, G^{\beta}\, \ell^{\gamma}\, p^{\tau}, \tag{9.1}$$

where all the parameters in Greek occurring as exponents are exogenous. For the discussion below, note that the exponent β captures the importance of culture in the community. In response to historical trauma, τ, it has been assumed all along that the individual will devote resources denoted by p to pain relief. This implies that the individual opts for a negative response to the trauma, because it alleviates immediate pain. It might be objected that perhaps the individual could respond positively to the trauma by, say, devoting more resources to the cultural good G. That is not possible in the Nash equilibrium (nor even in the best outcome of the Benthamite social planner) in the static model. The reason for this is that when the marginal

in 2019. See https://www.frontlinedefenders.org/en/case/court-rules-rcmp-abused-its-power-criminalisation-three-wetsuweten-defenders#

utility of pain relief increases due to historical trauma, that option will necessarily draw more resources, and these must come from other uses of the resource (that is, from agricultural and cultural activities and leisure).

Nevertheless, the model can help us distinguish those communities that will be destabilized by historical trauma from those that could show survivance. The outcome that is most relevant to this discussion is the community solidarity variable that was introduced in Chapter 7. Recall that C denoted the total community-oriented time invested and I the total individually-oriented time invested, and that community solidarity, S, was defined as the ratio C/I. The equilibrium value of this is given in (7.2) and is reproduced below:

$$S \equiv \frac{C}{I} = \frac{(\alpha\mu + \beta)\rho}{n(\gamma + \tau)}, \tag{9.2}$$

where $\rho = 1 + (n-1)\sigma$ and σ is the strength of other-regarding preferences. We may argue that this solidarity variable would tend to cement culture in a dynamic scenario if it is large enough. From (9.2), we may intuitively conjecture that large values of the cultural parameter, β, and of altruism, σ, would facilitate a positive response to trauma while large values of τ—that is, high intensity traumas—would do the opposite.

Is it possible that, over time, the importance of culture itself in the community could change in response to the trauma? To answer this, we need a theory of how the cultural parameter, β, that has been assumed to be exogenous thus far, might change. A suggestive theory might work as follows. For the cultural parameter to change, the equilibrium outcome has to persist long enough to initiate a change in the preferences. In such a scenario, the community solidarity variable will likely determine how the cultural parameter β will change.

If community solidarity is not high enough in the Nash equilibrium, culture is likely to unravel because the individualistic orientation induced by pain will undermine the necessary 'glue' to sustain the community's culture. Suppose we denote by $\hat{S}$ the minimum value of the community solidarity at which culture can be sustained. If the community solidarity S falls below $\hat{S}$, we can posit that culture unravels; if the community solidarity S is above $\hat{S}$, it strengthens. If $\dot{\beta}$ denotes the time rate of change in the parameter β that captures the importance of culture in the preferences, we may posit that

$$\dot{\beta} = f(S - \hat{S}), \tag{9.3}$$

where f is a function that is positive when its argument is positive and negative when its argument is negative, with $f(0) = 0$. It is reasonable to posit that the function $f(\cdot)$ is nonlinear in its argument and asymptotically goes to 0 as β reaches some finite upper limit—say $\bar{\beta} < 1$—and as β approaches the lower limit 0.

This would suggest that, as long as the initial value of the community solidarity exceeds $\hat{S}$, culture would become more entrenched over time (β would increase). On the other hand, if the initial value falls short of $\hat{S}$, the cultural parameter β would continuously decline until it ultimately becomes 0. We would see the community's culture completely unravel in this case because individuals place no value on the cultural good in this outcome. Holding all other parameters constant, there is a critical knife-edge value of β, call it β_c, at which value the right-hand side of (9.3) vanishes. At this critical value, which can be computed using (9.2), the cultural parameter β will be stable over time. For $\beta > \beta_c$ the cultural parameter will increase, and for $\beta < \beta_c$ it will decline to 0 over time. This is illustrated in Figure 9.1, which is drawn on the simplifying assumption that the trauma strikes the community at a single point in time, say 0.

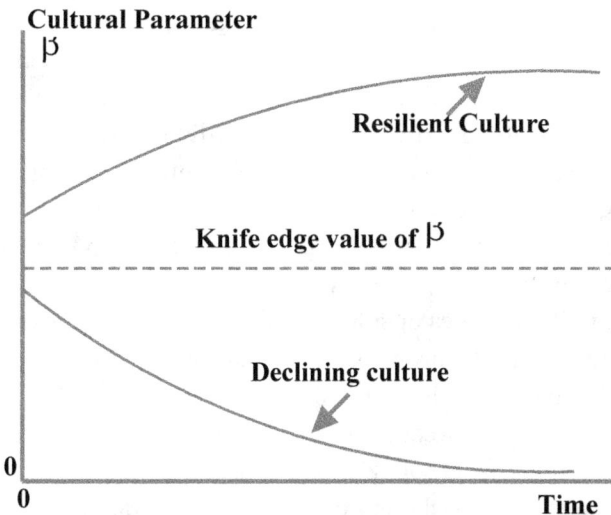

Fig. 9.1. The enhancement and decline of culture over time after trauma.

When would we expect the cultural parameter β to increase over time in response to historical trauma and when would we expect it to decrease? Expression (9.2) gives us an idea. Community solidarity will tend to be high and exceed $\hat{S}$ when β and σ are high. Thus, communities that are initially very community-oriented, which have stronger relational ties, are more likely to exhibit survivance in the face of historical trauma. On the other hand, communities with weak community orientation or relational ties are more likely to unravel in the face of historical trauma. Furthermore, from (9.2) we see that, for given β and σ, the higher the value of τ the more likely is it that the community's culture will unravel because pain-alleviation absorbs resources. Even the culture of strongly bound communities could start dismantling if the historical trauma is intense enough.

In the previous chapters, the parameter β was taken as exogenously given. The theoretical results, however, remain true at every value of β even when we allow this parameter to change over time. The discussion on deaths of despair, however, was implicitly dealing with Indigenous communities that roughly speaking would fall in the *lower panel* of Figure 9.1, below the horizontal dashed line.

The theoretical rendition here complements the theory proposed in the field of psychology by Chandler and Ball (1990), Chandler and Lalonde (1998), Chandler and Lalonde (2008), Chandler and Proulx (2006), and Lalonde (2013). They argue that preserving a sense of continuity in identity is crucial as a preventative measure against suicide in adolescents, as is a sense of collective identity for communities. In reviewing this body of seminal work, Lalonde (2013, p. 367) says, "Just as threats to personal continuity are associated with individual acts of suicide, our research has shown that threats to cultural continuity are associated with rates of suicide within cultural communities. More importantly, efforts to promote culture are associated with increased resilience". The unravelling of culture when β declines is what, in my model, brings about a weakening and discontinuity of cultural identity. And to anticipate what follows in this chapter, we note that anything which bolsters β would therefore strengthen cultural identity.

An example of how Indigenous communities can disintegrate following European colonization is provided by the communities in the San Francisco Bay Area during the period 1769–1810, chronicled by Milliken (1995). During this period, the Spanish sought to establish property rights over land along the coast with their superior military force. Indigenous lands were appropriated and given to Christian missionaries. Intimidation and killings were used by the Spanish to establish missions, and Indigenous Peoples were encouraged to join the missions and proselytize. Indigenous kinship systems comprising extended families were replaced by nuclear families. Indigenous communities lost their previous zest for life and carried out their daily duties with a "mechanical, lifeless, careless indifference" (Milliken, 1995, p. 4). The author goes on to say, "Limited by their cultural chauvinism, the missionaries failed to see that they had undermined the peoples' sense of mastery, choice, and efficacy, important prerequisites for human health and happiness" (p. 4). Indigenous religions lost their hold. Faced with massive mortality rates from epidemics of diseases brought by the Spanish and their animals, the Indigenous communities were left with little choice but to join the missionaries to survive. Indigenous communities that flourished before contact with the Spanish, who arrived in the Bay region in 1769, had all but disintegrated by 1810.

It is worth exploring evidence in favour of the view that loss of culture plays a primary role, because this casts light on the differences between Indigenous communities that exhibit survivance and ones that languish and experience deaths of despair. The results of this section also speak to the issue of self-determination and Indigenous wellbeing. In their examination of the youth suicide rate in 196 bands in British Columbia, Chandler and Lalonde (1998)—whom we alluded to in Chapter 8— found great variation in the suicide statistics; some had suicide rates that were 800 times the national average while others had no suicides at all. Based on data updated to the year 2000, Lalonde (2013) reports that, over the fourteen-year period 1987–2000, more than half the Indigenous communities in British Columbia had zero deaths by suicide.

To explain the variation, the authors hypothesized that communities which maintain cultural continuity experience fewer suicides. To test this hypothesis, they looked for the presence or absence of six different indicators of autonomy and self-government and aggregated the measures to construct an index that goes from a minimum of 0 to a maximum of 6. They observed a negative correlation between this index and the number of suicides.

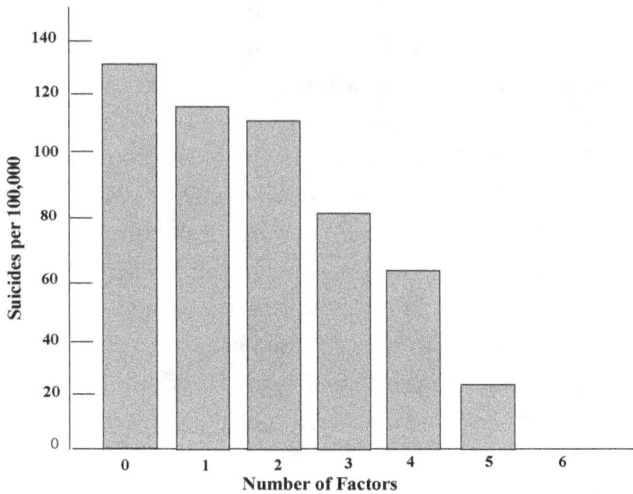

Fig. 9.2. Youth suicide rates by number of self-government indicators present. Lalonde (2013), Fig. 29.3.

Figure 9.2 shows the results, with the number of self-government indicators present in a band on the horizontal axis and the average number of youth suicides per 100,000 on the vertical. This Figure starkly brings home the importance of community cultural engagement to the phenomenon of youth deaths of despair in Indigenous communities. Communities exhibiting the maximum community engagement of 6 on this index had no suicides, while communities showing no engagement on this index had the maximum youth suicide rate. Indigenous communities that are strongly relational in the sense of Trosper (2022) perform the best because they are the most able to mobilize collective action.

There is a question that is as yet unanswered in the literature but which may be answered by the results of the model presented here. The variables used by Chandler and Lalonde (1998), Chandler et al. (2003), and Lalonde (2013) to test their hypothesis are actually endogenous, and depend on the community's ability to organize collective action. The question then is: 'Why do Indigenous communities differ in their organizing ability?' The literature is silent on the exogenous features that would induce such collective actions in the first place.[7] We can plausibly

---

7   There are, however, a few hints in the literature (e.g. see Kirmayer, Brass, and Tait,

supply an answer by demonstrating why Indigenous communities vary in their *capacities* for self-government in terms of the exogenous parameters of the model.

In terms of the simple model in this section, community engagement would be measured by the equilibrium value of community solidarity shown in (9.2). Inspecting this expression, and recalling that $\rho = 1 + (n - 1)\sigma$, we arrive at the last theoretical proposition of this book:

Proposition 9.1:
(a) The higher the initial value of the cultural variable, β, and the level of altruism, σ, between community members, the more likely an Indigenous community is to exhibit survivance and to thrive.
(b) The greater the intensity of the historical trauma, τ, that has been experienced, the greater the chances that the community will have deaths of despair.

Communities with high values of β and σ and low values of τ are precisely those that would actively engage in the survivance factors that are included in the index of Chandler and Lalonde (1998) and Lalonde (2013). We may identify the communities with no (or few) suicides as the ones that fall in the region above the critical knife-edge line in Figure 9.1, and the ones with large numbers of suicides as those that fall below this critical line. The above proposition would then suggest a way to understand the empirical findings.

The level of historical trauma is very likely to be *community-specific* due to the very different geographical environments, histories, treaties, provincial treatments, territorial encroachments, etc. of different communities. My model suggests that variation in the intensity of historical trauma across different communities would be an important factor to explain their variation in suicide rates. To my knowledge, Jacklin (2009) is the only piece of research (albeit based on a very small sample) suggesting on empirical grounds that differences in colonial exposure matter. Future empirical research could fruitfully identify common measures of historical trauma for each of the over 1000 Indigenous communities in North America, along the lines of the indices suggested by Whitbeck et al. (2004) and Walters et al. (2011).

2000, p. 611; Bombay, Matheson, and Anisman, 2014, p. 332).

This discussion brings home three important points. Firstly, the considerable effort that psychologists and Indigenous and non-Indigenous scholars have devoted to studying the psychopathological effects of historical trauma has not been wasted. This has led to important insights into the reasons for serious problems, such as deaths of despair, in many Indigenous communities. Secondly, the communities that still experience such serious effects of historical trauma cannot be taken as the majority of Indigenous communities by any means. If the communities studied by Chandler, Lalonde, and their co-authors are anything to go by, the majority of Indigenous communities did not lose even a single youth to suicide during the period 1987–2000. As Lalonde (2013, p. 373) puts it:

> [A]lthough all Aboriginal cultures have suffered and had much of their culture stolen from them, they have not all responded to these assaults in identical ways. Some communities have been able to rebuild or rehabilitate a connection to their own cultural past with more success than others. Perhaps differences in suicide rates between communities are associated with differing levels of success in their struggles to resist the sustained history of acculturative practices that threaten their very cultural existence.

The third important point that emerges from the theoretical analysis, bolstered by the landmark empirical work of Chandler and Lalonde, is that the success stories can offer lessons for less successful communities. In terms of policies the latter can pursue, these lessons may prove invaluable.

9.3 Indigenous Practices Relevant to Survivance

According to the economic theory in this chapter, Indigenous communities that were less exposed to events which led to historical trauma would retain more functionality. Of the members' time and attention, more would be devoted to the 'Us' aspect of self and less to the 'me' aspect—that is, more time would be invested in collective activities. These communities are thus better able to organize, govern, plan, offer community support, and pass on cultural values to youth. In general, such communities would display greater survivance in the face of contemporary adversities and have fewer deaths of despair than communities with more historical trauma.

The models presented in this book suggest that Indigenous communities which flourished as a result of collective activities—which were facilitated by cultural values sustained over millennia—also became vulnerable when these underlying cultural edifices were destroyed. But, on the upside, Indigenous communities are more amenable to positive measures to restore these cultural values. Any boost to communal capacities from tempering the effects of historical trauma will have a salutary effect on the collective equilibrium. This is what the theory suggests and the empirical findings in the literature demonstrate. Thus, there is strong reason from economics to believe that it is possible for collective endeavours to undo the damage of historical trauma, at least partly, and promote survivance. This view is consistent with the work of Indigenous scholars (Walters, Simoni, and Evans-Campbell, 2002; Evans-Campbell, 2008; Walls and Whitbeck, 2012; Gone, 2013).

It is well-understood by Indigenous scholars that western approaches to reducing Indigenous suicide rates based on egoistic perspectives—such as individual therapy sessions—do not work (White and Mushquash, 2016). In an exhaustive survey of the outcomes of approaches in place at the time, Kirmayer et al. (2009b) found that none of them were particularly effective. Chandler and Dunbar (2018) persuasively argue that cultural wounds warrant cultural solutions. Though pain is individually felt—we are programmed to feel pain in the same way—the damage inflicted has been collective in nature, so the solutions also have to be collective. The effects of collective remedies, they claim, are multiplicative not additive. Presumably this is because of synergies that arise from collective participation. Ansloos (2018) has sharply criticized western methods of dealing with Indigenous suicides. He asserts, "[S]ubstantial investments have gone into national efforts for youth suicide prevention research, at times often to the exclusion of critical Indigenous knowledge holders, traditional elders, and dynamic kinship networks, communities and families" (p. 15). In a similar vein, Lawson-Te Aho and Liu (2010) have emphasized the role of the collective in the context of Maori suicides in New Zealand.

Community building warrants collective action, and a sufficient degree of belongingness and cultural orientation to begin with is required to overcome the problem of free riding in teams. In short, it requires a restoration of the relational society. If recovery from historical trauma requires community development, as it seems to, then for reasons provided by my model, a highly traumatized community may not be able to internally mobilize the initiative needed. Thus, there is a natural role for dedicated effort on the part of allies to help Indigenous communities build up to the necessary capacity. Seen through the lens of economics, the case for public funding of Indigenous collective healing traditions is very strong. This is in sharp contrast to the neoliberal view dominant in western countries, which emphasizes the role of the individual while minimizing that of the government.

Numerous policy recommendations have been offered in the literature for ameliorating the problem of Indigenous suicides (see e.g. RCAP, 1996; Sinclair, C.M., 2015). I restrict myself here to briefly discussing policy lessons that are supported by the limited economic model in this book. In particular, the focus below is on policies that promote Indigenous collective activities. Gone et al. (2019) have argued that more research is needed on what contributes to survivance. My theoretical framework suggests that the very domains that were weakened by historical trauma (cultural institutions, self-determination, and spirituality, among others) would facilitate survivance if reconstituted. The question is how. There are at least three potential areas, which are consistent with a few of the '94 Calls to Action' listed by the *Report of Canada's Truth and Reconciliation Commission* (2015). These are briefly discussed below.

9.3.1 Language Revitalization

Of the many uses of language, an important one is that it is instrumental in enabling individuals to form a robust self-concept, a notion of who they are. As many Indigenous scholars have affirmed, Indigenous languages are intimately tied to the land (Shaw, 2001; Ferguson and Weaselboy, 2020) and land is intimately tied to Indigenous identity (Akiwenzie-Damm, 1996; Noble, 2008). When an Indigenous language is lost, one of the core features of Indigenous culture and identity is erased, as Indigenous Peoples insist. In terms of the economic model in this book, the cultural parameter β and the belongingness parameter σ are dramatically reduced by language loss, which will have a deleterious effect on the equilibrium outcome of the community.

Language also proves to be a powerful buffer against the effects of historical trauma. Hallett, Chandler, and Lalonde (2007) examined data from 152 Aboriginal bands in British Columbia, Canada, in which youth suicide rates varied considerably across bands as we saw. The authors found that, relative to other markers of identity, knowledge of the heritage language had the most predictive power with regard to the suicide rate in the band. Bands in which only a minority of the people spoke the heritage language had six times the suicide rate of those in which the majority spoke the language. The findings strongly suggest that being embedded in Indigenous culture through language is associated with lower youth suicide rates among Indigenous Peoples. Ritland et al. (2021) found that that knowing an Indigenous language is a protective factor against suicide for Indigenous women using substances. It is likely that the higher suicide rate generally among First Nations, Métis, and Inuit youths (Kumar and Tjepkema, 2019; Park, 2021) and among Native Americans (Akee et al., 2024; Friedman, Hansen, and Gone, 2023) is related to the rapid language loss among the Indigenous Peoples.[8]

A policy which may not be obvious to economists but which would improve the health of Indigenous Peoples would be to reinstate and revitalize Indigenous languages. What is special here is that there is an important externality: the language of an Indigenous community reinforces identity and improves wellbeing for oneself and others. So, the revitalization of Indigenous languages cannot be left to individual initiatives or to market forces—it requires a coordinating agent with funding, and that agent is clearly the government. The health implications of language revitalization are now recognized even by health professionals (see the reviews in *Lancet* by Gracey and King, 2009; King, Smith, and Gracey, 2009). This book's model offers, to my knowledge, the first theoretical justification for it from economics—by bringing out the importance of the Indigenous sense of belongingness and the role of language in restoring it.

---

8   Krauss (1992, p. 5) reports that children are no longer learning 149 of the 187 languages in the U.S. and Canada together—that is, 80% of the languages are heading for certain extinction unless reversed.

9.3.2 Self-Determination

We have already discussed some evidence on the importance of self-determination for suicide prevention in the work of Chandler and Lalonde in the previous section. However, there is also evidence from non-Indigenous settings. Guiso, Sapienza, and Zingales (2016) have shown that those cities in Italy that were independent city-states (communes) in medieval times exhibit more civic or social capital today. Culture is seen to be the source of persistence even when—pace Acemoglu, Johnson, and Robinson (2001, 2002)—the intervening institutions have long disappeared. This, they argue, is due to greater self-efficacy generated in independent city-states, whereby people come to rely on their own effort and are prone to less free riding and greater trust. This culture is passed down through generations within families through socialization. These findings are clearly in line with the empowerment of self-determination sought by Indigenous Peoples, especially given the importance of Indigenous cultures.

Self-determination requires commitment and effort. When historical trauma undermines belongingness, as noted earlier the teamwork needed for self-determination will not be forthcoming, and so the trauma needs to be addressed first or, at least, simultaneously. In my economic model, self-determination will enhance belongingness because the land will not be seen as being controlled by the government. It is through effects of this kind that, based on the results in Chapters 2, 3, and 8, we can expect greater self-determination to reduce deaths of despair.

9.3.3 Indigenous Healing Practices

The economic model also offers some support for collective Indigenous practices that deal with healing trauma and substance abuse. While an economist cannot speak much to these healing practices per se, it does seem that the core feature singling out Indigenous healing programs is *interconnectivity* between members of the community (see Fleming and Ledogar (2008) for a review of the literature). McCormick (2000) offers a clear outline of the philosophy behind the Indigenous treatments of substance abuse. Dependence on substances such as alcohol is seen to arise as a coping mechanism in the face of the powerlessness felt when traditional cultural and spiritual values have been abandoned. The Indigenous solution is to restore adherence to these values, which in

Indigenous spirituality is described in terms of "getting beyond the self" (McCormick, 2000, p. 26). This ties in with my claim that suffering focuses attention on the 'me' aspect of self (to the detriment of belongingness), and the shift to cultural values broadens the focus. Lester (1999) found that, around the 1970s in the U.S., Indigenous communities exhibiting a higher degree of enculturation (traditional integration) were associated with lower suicide rates than those with more acculturation (assimilation with the dominant culture). The former acts as a buffer against stress, whereas the latter causes greater stress.[9]

Indigenous healing procedures may be seen as increasing the belongingness parameter σ in the model, which then predicts less diversion of resources to pain-relieving substances, in accordance with Proposition 7.1(b). The model, therefore, is consistent with the view espoused by psychiatrists and Indigenous scholars that collective Indigenous healing procedures are efficacious in curbing substance abuse (Duran and Duran, 1995; Katz, 2017).[10] My economic model of Indigenous communities is thus in alignment with 'culture as treatment' as one of the approaches to resolving Indigenous historical trauma espoused by scholars (Brave Heart, 1998; Walters, Simoni, and Evans-Campbell, 2002; Gone, 2009; Matheson, Bombay, and Anisman, 2018; Wexler and Gone, 2012). Since culture is a collective phenomenon, this treatment necessarily takes a collective approach as opposed to individual therapy which is more appropriate in individualistic western cultures. There is some evidence to date for the efficacy of cultural treatments (e.g. Rowan, 2014). That said, however, it must be noted that, for various nontrivial reasons, there is an absence of randomized control trials demonstrating causality regarding the efficacy of Indigenous treatments for substance abuse.[11]

---

9   A graphic illustration of the success of communal action accompanied by enculturation is illustrated by the Shuswap band on the Alkali Lake Reserve in British Columbia, Canada. Within a span of a decade, starting from the early 1970s, the community reduced its rate of alcoholism from 97% to 5% (Guillory, Willie, and Duran, 1988).

10 Alcoholics Anonymous (AA) shares some of these characteristics such as invoking a 'higher power', as noted by Guillory, Willie, and Duran (1988). I interpret this as AA, one of the most successful organizations for dealing with alcoholism, also attempting to make the individual 'go beyond self' by relinquishing the control exercised by the 'me'.

11 There are many reasons for the paucity of randomized control trials (RCTs) conducted

9.4 Summary

This chapter addressed the resilience or survivance exhibited by Indigenous communities. It identified what factors are likely to be conducive to survivance. If these factors are absent or only weakly present, we are more likely to find that intense historical trauma induces a serious disruption of Indigenous culture. It is these more disrupted communities—which may well be the minority—that are likely to witness large numbers of deaths of despair. The economic model presented in this chapter is shown to be consistent with the evidence of Chandler and Lalonde (1998) and Lalonde (2013) for Indigenous communities in British Columbia, Canada. Finally, the chapter discussed why, from the viewpoint of economics, some Indigenous activities and healing practices are particularly efficacious in promoting survivance.

---

in Indigenous populations. Here are some in brief. Research funding for Indigenous research is relatively scarce. Performing RCTs with Indigenous participants requires a fair amount of Indigenous trust in western scientific methods, which is lacking because western methodologies have usually undermined Indigenous knowledge. Given the history of treatment of Indigenous Peoples by the colonizers, there are also issues pertaining to who should own and have control over the Indigenous data generated. Furthermore, for statistical tests to yield results with any precision, the sample sizes have to be sufficiently large, and Indigenous groups are often too small in number. There are several other reasons.

10. Some Concluding Thoughts

Culture perpetually functions in the background of every society, so much so that we are usually too preoccupied with our day-to-day lives to question what would happen if the culture were badly fractured. This book examines through the lens of economics the effects of colonial and post-colonial assaults on Indigenous cultures in North America for over 500 years. The theory proposed shows that the erosion of culture has very grave consequences, and it explains a substantial number of empirical findings regarding the Indigenous Peoples of North America. These consequences cover a wide spectrum, going from a decline in wellbeing at one end to deaths of despair from drug abuse and suicide at the other. Although the focus of this book has been North America, the theory is very likely to be applicable to other settler colonies, too, like Australia and New Zealand.

The kinship system that prevails in a society is strongly correlated with the nature of the culture in which it evolves. The attempted destruction of Indigenous extended family systems through colonialism by Europeans in North America was undertaken to acquire Indigenous land. The Indian residential schools and the child welfare system unhinged Indigenous cultures, thus disabling embedded buffering mechanisms against external shocks. Much of the destruction seems to have been by design, although some of it was probably unintended. Nevertheless, the Indigenous Peoples of North America are still experiencing the consequences because the resulting historical trauma continues to perpetuate the harm.

From a theoretical point of view, the innovations of the models in Parts I and II of this book are simple but are based on evidence that is in plain sight. Part I incorporates the role of Indigenous culture in Indigenous economic activity, in recognition of the fact that the two are inseparable. Part II is premised on the importance of communal culture

 https://doi.org/10.11647/OBP.0477.10

to Indigenous societies and the stark reality of pain as a consequence of historical trauma. The implications, which are important, follow from the model in a straightforward way. They explain a fair amount of the evidentiary patterns pertaining to Indigenous substance abuse and deaths of despair.

The facts modelled here are well-known to Indigenous scholars and elders. As a non-Indigenous academic with no lived experience of the subject, my limited contribution in this book comes only from reading, observing, and translating into the language of mainstream economics what I think I 'heard' or what I have understood.[1] This attempt, I submit, may not be entirely misguided, for the theoretical analysis leads to a conclusion that echoes that of the 1996 *Royal Commission on Aboriginal Peoples*, which was based on extensive empirical observations: "The evidence before the Commission has led us to conclude that high rates of suicide among Aboriginal people are primarily the result of severe social and cultural disorganization" (RCAP, 1996, p. 76).

In the past few decades, the literature on economic development has established that good institutions are paramount for economic growth (North, 1981). Acemoglu, Johnson, and Robinson (2001, 2002) demonstrated that European colonizers installed good institutions that protected private property rights in settler colonies while implementing exploitative institutions in colonies that were intended merely for extractive purposes, and this resulted in a 'reversal of fortunes' over time. Feir, Gillezeau, and Jones (2024) have recently demonstrated compellingly that a reversal of fortunes took place in the bison-dependent Indigenous communities in the plains of North America. The virtual extinction of the bison reduced the communities from being the richest on the continent, with standards of living at least as high as those of Europeans, to being the poorest after the demise of the bison.

Carlos, Feir, and Redish (2022) have documented how, while the property rights of the United States in increasing amounts of land were being cemented, the property rights of the Indigenous Peoples were being eroded. The Indigenous Peoples experienced a dramatic reversal of fortunes in terms of income and wealth. This book suggests that the

---

1   I have tried somewhat to heed the advice of Huston Smith, who used to urge his (non-Indigenous) audience to learn to listen to Indigenous Peoples, saying, "Listen, or your tongue will keep you deaf". Smith, H. (2005, p. xiv).

reversal of fortunes which worked to the benefit of European settlers and to the detriment of Indigenous Peoples is even more general, covering other domains besides wealth. In at least four settler colonies—namely, Canada, the United States, Australia, and New Zealand—colonization has wrought devastation on Indigenous Peoples. Given that suicide was not a traditional occurrence amongst Indigenous Peoples (Kirmayer et al., 2007, p. 59; RCAP, 1996, p. 10), the elevated rates of Indigenous deaths of despair in current times are one such manifestation of this reversal in wellbeing.[2]

The fact that Indigenous Peoples of North America have sustained a 500-year-long assault and have refused to fade into oblivion points to the fact that the survivance of Indigenous societies has come from some bedrock strengths. The findings of this book are consonant with the views of scholars and Indigenous elders in suggesting that the effects of historical trauma are best countered by fostering the original strengths and focusing on the survivance of Indigenous societies rather than focusing on the deficits.[3]

Indigenous scholar Lyons (2010, p. 40) claimed that "Indigenous identity is something they do, not what they are", a view seconded by Maracle (2021). We may interpret this as saying that Indigenous identity tends to be a *verb*, not a noun—an interpretation that fits well with Trosper's (2022) notion of relational identity. If we accept this, non-Indigenous people can appreciate the importance of communal activities to Indigenous cultures and perhaps glimpse the profound consequences of the disruption of these activities.

Fostering Indigenous survivance, as Indigenous scholars emphasize (Evans-Campbell, 2008; Wilbur and Gone, 2023), requires coordinated effort to facilitate the rebuilding of Indigenous identities with community-oriented cultural practices. These activities will promote survivance while also healing unresolved historical trauma. The model in this book

---

2 To economize on space, I have not discussed the contribution of the rise in neoliberalism in the last decades, which coincides with the rise of Indigenous suicide rates. Because neoliberal ideology emphasizes individualism and private property, it represents the very antithesis of Indigenous cultures. As neoliberalism swept across the developed world, governments further encroached on Indigenous territories and ways of life. It is still ongoing.

3 See e.g. Red Horse (1997), van Uchelen et al. (1997), Evans-Campbell (2008), NNAPF (2011), FNIGC (2020), Wilbur and Gone (2023).

offers support for this view from economics. It also offers a plausible theory to predict when a community may settle into a bad equilibrium following historical trauma and when it would tend to overcome adversities, exhibit survivance, and flourish. In other words, it offers a theory for the considerable variation that is observed in socioeconomic and health conditions across the Indigenous communities of North America. This variation, it is proposed, could be partly explained by the variation in severity of the historical trauma experienced.

Finally, I end this book by noting that I have applied the standard neoclassical tools of mainstream economics, but not its standard assumptions. Rather, the assumptions that are built into the models are those that reflect the lived experience of Indigenous Peoples. The book shows that it is not necessary to discard the entire framework of mainstream economics in order to understand Indigenous issues and obtain insights that have consequential implications for policy. We only need to drop the presumption that the typical assumptions used in mainstream economics are, by any stretch of imagination, universal. They are not; they may be relevant for western cultures, but not necessarily for others. When we shed the tacit Eurocentric approach and pay attention to what is actually relevant and important to Indigenous Peoples, neoclassical economics—as an efficient and reliable framework—delivers the insights that Indigenous elders and scholars have intuited for a long time.

References

Abramitzky, D. (2011) "Lessons from the Kibbutz on the Equality-Incentives Trade-off," *Journal of Economic Perspectives*, 25(1), pp. 185–208, https://doi.org/10.1257/jep.25.1.185

Acemoglu, D., S. Johnson, and J.A. Robinson (2001), "The Colonial Origins of Comparative Development: An Empirical Investigation," American Economic Review, 91, pp. 1369–1401, https://doi.org/10.1257/aer.91.5.1369

Acemoglu, D., S. Johnson, and J.A. Robinson (2002), "Reversal of Fortune: Geography and Institutions in the Making of the Modern World Income Distribution," *Quarterly Journal of Economics*, 117, pp. 1231–1294, https://doi.org/10.1162/003355302320935025

Acemoglu, D. and J.A. Robinson (2012), *Why Nations Fail: The Origins of Power, Prosperity, and Poverty*, Crown Publishers, New York.

Adams, D.W. (1995), *Education for Extinction: American Indians and the Boarding School Experience, 1875-1928*, University Press of Kansas, Lawrence, Kansas.

Agerström, J. et al. (2019), "Pain Here and Now: Physical Pain Impairs Transcendence of Psychological Distance," *Journal of Pain Research*, 12, pp. 961–968, https://doi.org/10.2147/JPR.S194114

Aguiar, W. and R. Halseth (2015), "Aboriginal Peoples and Historic Trauma: The Process of Intergenerational Transmission," National Collaborating Center for Aboriginal Health, Prince George, B.C.

Ahedo V., J. Caro et al. (2019), "Quantifying the Relationship between Food Sharing Practices and Socio-Ecological Variables in Small-Scale Societies: A Cross-Cultural Multi-Methodological Approach," *PLoS ONE*, 14(5), e0216302. https://doi.org/10.1371/journal.pone.0216302

Akee, R.K. (2020), "Land Titles and Dispossession: Allotment on American Indian Reservations," *Journal of Economics, Race, and Policy*, 3, pp. 123–143, https://doi.org/10.1007/s41996-019-00035-z

Akee, R. and D. Feir (2016), "Excess Mortality, Institutionalization and Homelessness Among Status Indians in Canada," IZA Institute of Labor Economics, IZA DP No. 10416, https://www.iza.org/publications/dp/10416/excess-mortality-institutionalization-and-homelessness-among-status-indians-in-canada

Akee, R. et al. (2024), "Native American 'Deaths of Despair' and Economic Conditions," *Research in Social Stratification and Mobility*, 89, https://doi.org/10.1016/j.rssm.2023.100880

Akerlof, G.A. and R. Kranton (2000), "Economics and identity," *Quarterly Journal of Economics*, 115, pp. 715–753, https://doi.org/10.1162/003355300554881

Akesaka, M. (2019), "Change in Time Preferences: Evidence from the Great East Japan Earthquake," *Journal of Economic Behavior and Organization*, 166, pp. 239–245, https://doi.org/10.1016/j.jebo.2019.08.013

Akiwenzie-Damm, K. (1996), "We Belong to This Land: A View of 'Cultural Difference'," *Journal of Canadian Studies*, 31(3), pp. 21–28, https://doi.org/10.3138/jcs.31.3.21

Alcantara, C. (2003), "Individual Property Rights on Canadian Indian Reserves: The Historical Emergence and Jurisprudence of Certificates of Possession", *Canadian Journal of Native Studies*, 23(2), pp. 391–424, https://scholars.wlu.ca/poli_faculty/6

Alcantara, C. (2007), "Reduce Transaction Costs? Yes. Strengthen Property Rights? Maybe: The First Nations Land Management Act and Economic Development on Canadian Indian Reserves," *Public Choice*, 132, pp. 421–432, https://doi.org/10.1007/s11127-007-9168-7

Alchian, A.A. and H. Demsetz (1972), "Production, Information Costs, and Economic Organization," *American Economic Review*, 62(5), pp. 777–795, https://www.jstor.org/stable/1815199

Alesina, A. and P. Giuliano (2015), "Culture and Institutions," *Journal of Economic Literature*, 53(4), pp. 898–944, https://doi.org/10.1257/jel.53.4.898

Allan, B. and J. Smylie (2015), "First Peoples, Second Class Treatment: The Role of Racism in the Health and Well-being of Indigenous Peoples in Canada," Wellesley Institute, Toronto.

Allen, D.W. (1991), "Homesteading and Property Rights; Or, "How the West Was Really Won," *The Journal of Law & Economics*, 34(1), pp. 1–23, https://www.jstor.org/stable/725412

Anderson, T.L. (ed. 1992), *Property Rights and Indigenous Economies*, Rowman & Littlefield, Lanham.

Anderson, T.L. and Lueck (1992), "Land Tenure and Agricultural Productivity on Indian Reservations," *Journal of Law & Economics*, 35(2), pp. 427–454, https://doi.org/10.1086/467261

Anderson, T.L. and F.S. McChesney (1994). "Raid or Trade? An Economic Model of Indian-White Relations." *Journal of Law and Economics*, 37(1), pp. 39–74, https://doi.org/10.1086/467306

Ansloos, J. (2018), "Rethinking Indigenous Suicide," *International Journal of Indigenous Health*, 13(2), pp. 8–28, https://doi.org/10.32799/ijih.v13i2.32061

Aragòn, F.M. (2015), "Do Better Property Rights Improve Local Income? Evidence from First Nations' Treaties," *Journal of Development Economics*, 116, pp. 43–56, https://doi.org/10.1016/j.jdeveco.2015.03.004

Aragòn, F.M. and A.S. Kessler (2020), "Property Rights on First Nations Reserve Land," *Canadian Journal of Economics*, 53(2), pp. 460–495, https://doi.org/10.1111/caje.12434

Arneil, B. (1996), "The Wild Indian's Venison: Locke's Theory of Property and English Colonialism in America," *Political Studies*, 44, pp. 60–74, https://doi.org/10.1111/j.1467-9248.1996.tb00764.x

Bailey, M.J. (1992), "Approximate Optimality of Aboriginal Property Rights," *Journal of Law & Economics*, 35(1), pp. 183–198, https://www.jstor.org/stable/725559

Bagley, C. (1991), "Adoption of Native Children in Canada: A Policy Analysis and a Research Report," in *Adoption: A Multinational Perspective*, H. Altstein & J.J. Simon (eds), Praeger, New York, pp. 55–79.

Bakht, N. and L. Collins (2017), "'The Earth is Our Mother': Freedom of Religion and the Preservation of Indigenous Sacred Sites in Canada," *McGill Law Journal*, 62(3), pp. 779–812, http://dx.doi.org/10.2139/ssrn.2802262

Barnes, P.M. et al. (2010), "Health Characteristics of the American Indian or Alaska Native Adult Population: United States, 2004-2008," National Essential Health Statistics Reports, No. 20, 9 March, https://web.p.ebscohost.com/ehost/pdfviewer/pdfviewer?vid=1&sid=67ba2e37-075d-4d04-8da0-84ea7705e65b%40redis

Barocas, H.A. and C.B. Barocas (1973), "Manifestations of Concentration Camp Effects on the Second Generation," *American Journal of Psychiatry*, 130(7), pp. 820–821, https://doi.org/10.1176/ajp.130.7.820

Baragwanath, K. and E. Bayi (2020), "Collective Property Rights Reduce Deforestation in the Brazilian Amazon," *Proceedings of the National Academy of Sciences*, 117(34), pp. 20495–20502, https://doi.org/10.1073/pnas.1917874117

Barrington-Leigh, C. and S. Sloman (2016), "Life Satisfaction among Aboriginal Peoples in the Canadian Prairies: Evidence from the Equality, Security and Community Survey," *The International Indigenous Policy Journal*, 7(2), Article 2, https://www.jstor.org/stable/48767188

Bassett, D. et al. (2014), "Post Traumatic Stress Disorder and Symptoms Among American Indians and Alaska Natives: a Review of the Literature," *Social Psychiatry Psychiatric Epidemiology*, 49, pp. 417–433, https://doi.org/10.1007/s00127-013-0759-y

Bateman, R.B. (1996), "Talking with the Plow: Agricultural Policy and Indian Farming in the Canadian and US Prairies," *Canadian Journal of Native Studies*, 16(2), pp. 211–228, https://cjns.brandonu.ca/wp-content/uploads/16-2-bateman.pdf

Batson, C.D., D.A. Lishner, and E.L. Stocks (2015), "The Empathy-Altruism Hypothesis," in *The Oxford Handbook of Prosocial Behavior*, D.A. Schroeder and W.G. Graziano (eds), Oxford University Press, New York, pp. 259–281.

Baumeister, R.F. (1990), "Suicide as Escape from Self," *Psychological Review*, 97(1), pp. 90–113, https://doi.org/10.1037/0033-295X.97.1.90

Baumeister, R.F. and M.R. Leary (1995), "The Need to Belong: Desire for Interpersonal Attachments as a Fundamental Human Motivation," *Psychological Bulletin*, 117(3), pp. 497–529, https://doi.org/10.1037/0033-2909.117.3.497

Beals, J. et al. (2013), "Lifetime Prevalence of Post Traumatic Stress Disorder in Two American Indian Reservation Populations," *Journal of Traumatic Stress*, 26, pp. 512–520, https://doi.org/10.1002/jts.21835

Belanger, Y.D. et al. (2013), "Homelessness, Urban Aboriginal People, and the Need for a National Enumeration," *Aboriginal Policy Studies*, 2(2), https://doi.org/10.5663/aps.v2i2.19006

Bellamy, S. and C. Hardy (2015), "Post-Traumatic Stress Disorder in Aboriginal People in Canada: Review of Risk Factors, the Current State of Knowledge and Directions for Further Research," National Collaborating Centre for Aboriginal Health, Prince George, B.C., https://canadacommons.ca/artifacts/1190658/post-traumatic-stress-disorder-in-aboriginal-people-in-canada/1743782/view/

Bentham, J. (1789), *An Introduction to the Principles of Morals and Legislation*, Clarendon Press, Oxford.

Berndt, E.R. et al. (1998), "Workplace Performance Effects from Chronic Depression and its Treatment," *Journal of Health Economics*, 17, pp. 511–535, https://doi.org/10.1016/S0167-6296(97)00043-X

Blackstock, C. (2007), "Residential Schools: Did They Really Close or Just Morph into Child Welfare?" *Indigenous Law Journal*, 6(1), pp. 71–78, https://jps.library.utoronto.ca/index.php/ilj/article/view/27665

Blanchflower, D.G. and D. Feir (2023), "Native Americans' Experience of Chronic Distress in the USA," *Journal of Population Economics*, 36(2), pp. 885–909, https://doi.org/10.1007/s00148-022-00910-4

Blomley, N. (2010), "Cuts, Flows, and the Geographies of Property," *Law, Culture and the Humanities*, 7(2), pp. 203–216, https://doi.org/10.1177/1743872109355583

Bodenhorn, B. (2000), "It's Good to Know Who Your Relatives Are but We Were Taught to Share with Everybody: Shares and Sharing among Inupiaq Households," *Senri Ethnological Studies*, 53, pp. 27–60.

Bombay, A., K. Matheson, and H. Anisman (2009), "Intergenerational Trauma: Convergence of Multiple Processes among First Nations Peoples in Canada," *Journal of Aboriginal Health*, November, pp. 6–47, https://jps.library.utoronto.ca/index.php/ijih/article/view/28987

Bombay, A., K. Matheson, and H. Anisman (2014), "The Intergenerational Effects of Indian Residential Schools: Implications for the Concept of Historical Trauma," *Transcultural Psychiatry*, 51(3), pp. 320–338, https://doi.org/10.1177/1363461513503380

Bombay, A. et al. (2020), "Familial Attendance at Indian Residential School and Subsequent Involvement in the Child Welfare System Among Indigenous Adults Born During the Sixties Scoop Era," *First Peoples Child & Family Review*, 15(1), pp. 62–79, https://doi.org/10.7202/1068363ar

Booth, A.L. (2003), "We are the Land: Native American Views of Nature," in H. Selin (ed.), *Nature Across Cultures: Views of Nature and the Environment in Non-Western Cultures*, Kluwer Academic Publishers, New York, pp. 329–349.

Borowsky, I.W. et al. (1999), "Suicide Attempts Among American Indian and Alaska Native Youth: Risk and Protective Factors," *Archives of Pediatrics & Adolescent Medicine*, 153(6), pp. 573–580, https://doi.org/10.1001/archpedi.153.6.573

Brave Heart, M.Y.H. (1998), "The Return to the Sacred Path: Healing the Historical Trauma and Historical Unresolved Grief Response among the Lakota through a Psychoeducational Group Intervention," *Smith College Studies in Social Work*, 68(3), pp. 287–305, https://doi.org/10.1080/00377319809517532

Brave Heart, M.Y.H. (2003), "The Historical Trauma Response Among Natives and Its Relationship with Substance Abuse: A Lakota Illustration," *Journal of Psychoactive Drugs*, 35(1), pp. 7–13, https://doi.org/10.1080/02791072.2003.10399988

Brave Heart, M.Y., and L. M. DeBruyn (1998), "The American Indian Holocaust: Healing Historical Unresolved Grief," *American Indian Alaska Native Mental Health Research*, 8(2), pp. 56–78, PMID: 9842066

Brennstuhl, M.-J. et al. (2015), "Chronic Pain and PTSD: Evolving Views on Their Comorbidity," *Perspectives in Psychiatric Care*, 51, pp. 295–304, https://doi.org/10.1111/ppc.12093

Bryan, B. (2000), "Property as Ontology: On Aboriginal and English Understandings of Ownership," *Canadian Journal of Law and Jurisprudence*, 13(1), pp. 3–32, https://doi.org/10.1017/S0841820900002290

Bryan, C.J. and A.O. Bryan (2021), "Delayed reward discounting and increased risk for suicide attempts among U.S. adults with probable PTSD," *Journal of Anxiety Disorders*, 81, 102414, https://doi.org/10.1016/j.janxdis.2021.102414

Burnette, C. (2015), "Historical Oppression and Intimate Partner Violence Experienced by Indigenous Women in the United States: Understanding Connections," *Social Service Review*, 89(3), pp. 531–563, https://doi.org/10.1086/683336

Canadian Encyclopedia (2020), "Indian Act," https://www.thecanadianencyclopedia.ca/en/article/indian-act (accessed 7 August 2021).

Carlos, A.M. and F.D. Lewis (1999), "Property Rights, Competition, and Depletion in the Eighteenth-Century Canadian Fur Trade: The Role of the European Market," *The Canadian Journal of Economics*, 32(3), pp. 705–728, https://doi.org/10.2307/136445

Carlos, A.M., D.L. Feir, and A, Redish (2022), "Indigenous Nations and the Development of the U.S. Economy: Land, Resources, and Dispossession," *Journal of Economic History*, 82(2), pp. 516–555, https://doi.org/10.1017/S0022050722000080

Carlson, L.A. (1981a), "Land Allotment and the Decline of American Indian Farming," *Explorations in Economic History*, 18, pp. 128–154, https://doi.org/10.1016/0014-4983(81)90023-1

Carlson, L.A. (1981b), *Indians, Bureaucrats, and Land: The Dawes Act and the Decline of Indian Farming*, Greenwood Press, Westport, Connecticut.

Carriere, J. (2005), "Connectedness and Health for First Nation Adoptees," *Pediatrics & Child Health*, 10(9), pp. 545–548, https://doi.org/10.1093/pch/10.9.545

Carter, S. (1991), "Two Acres and a Cow: 'Peasant' Farming for the Indians of the Northwest, 1889-1897," in *Sweet Promises: A Reader in Indian-White Relations in Canada*, J.R. Miller (ed.), University of Toronto Press, Toronto, pp. 353–377.

Carter, S. (2019), *Lost Harvests: Prairie Indian Reserve Farmers and Government Policy*, 2nd edn, McGill-Queen's University Press, Montreal, https://doi.org/10.1515/9780773557697

Carter, S. and N. Kermoal (2020), "Property Rights on Reserves: 'New' Ideas from the Nineteenth Century," in *Creating Indigenous Property: Power, Rights and Relationships*, A. Cameron, S. Graben, and V. Napoleon (eds), University of Toronto Press, Toronto, pp. 163–183, https://doi.org/10.3138/9781487532116

Case, A. and A. Deaton (2015), "Rising Morbidity and Mortality in Midlife Among White Non-Hispanic Americans in the 21st century," *Proceedings of the National Academy of Sciences*, 112(49), pp. 15078–15083, https://doi.org/10.1073/pnas.1518393112

Case, A. and A. Deaton (2017), "Mortality and Morbidity in the 21st century," *Brookings Papers on Economic Activity*, Spring, pp. 397–476, https://www.jstor.org/stable/90013177

Case, A. and A. Deaton (2020), *Deaths of Despair and the Future of Capitalism*, Princeton University Press, Princeton, N.J.

Case, A., A. Deaton, and D.M. Cutler (2017), "Suicide, Age, and Well-Being: An Empirical Investigation," in *Insights into the Economics of Aging*, D.A. Wise (ed.), University of Chicago Press, Chicago, pp. 307–338, https://doi.org/10.7208/chicago/9780226426709.001.0001

Castenello, M.B. (2002), "Aboriginal Family Trends: Extended Families, Nuclear Families, and Families of the Heart," The Vanier Institute of the Family.

Castro-Rea, J. and I. Altamirano-Jimenez (2008), "North American First Peoples: Self-Determination or Economic Development?" in *Politics in North America: Redefining Continental Relations*, Y. Abu-Laban et al. (eds), Broadwiew Press, Peterborough, pp. 225–250, https://doi.org/10.3138/9781442689794

CCR (2004), *Broken Promises: Evaluating the Native American Health Care System*, U.S. Commission on Civil Rights, Washington D.C..

Center for Disease Control and Prevention (2022), "Suicide Data and Statistics," https://www.cdc.gov/suicide/suicide-data-statistics.html (accessed 12 December 2022).

Chandler, M. and L. Ball (1990), "Continuity and Commitment: A Developmental Analysis of the Identity Formation Process in Suicidal and Non-Suicidal Youth," in *Coping and Self-Concept in Adolescence*, H.A. Bosma and A.E.S. Jackson (eds), Springer-Verlag, Berlin, pp. 149–166, https://doi.org/10.1007/978-3-642-75222-3

Chandler, M.J. and C. Lalonde (1998), "Cultural Continuity as a Hedge Against Suicide in Canada's First Nations," *Transcultural Psychiatry*, 35(2), pp. 191–219, https://doi.org/10.1177/136346159803500202

Chandler, M.J. and C. Lalonde (2008), "Cultural Continuity as a Protective Factor Against Suicide in First Nations Youth," *Horizons, A Special Issue on Aboriginal Youth, Hope or Heartbreak: Aboriginal Youth and Canada's Future*, 10(1), pp. 68–72.

Chandler, M.J. et al. (2003), "Personal Persistence, Identity Development, and Suicide: A Study of Native and Non-Native North American Adolescents," *Monographs of the Society for Research in Child Development*, 68(2), pp. 1–130.

Chandler, M.J. and W. Dunlop (2018), "Cultural wounds demand cultural medicine," in *Determinants of Indigenous Peoples' Health in Canada: Beyond the Social*, M. Greenwood et al. (eds), Canadian Scholars Press, Toronto, pp. 78–89.

Chandler, M.J. and T. Proulx (2006), "Changing Selves in Changing Worlds: Youth Suicide on the Fault-Lines of Colliding Cultures," *Archives of Suicide Research*, 10(2), pp. 125–140, https://doi.org/10.1080/13811110600556707

Chansonneuve, D. (2007), "Addictive Behaviours Among Aboriginal People in Canada," Aboriginal Healing Foundation, Ottawa, https://nctr.ca/wp-content/uploads/2021/01/addictive-behaviours.pdf

Chen, J. et al. (2012), "Socio-Economic Studies on Suicide A Survey," *Journal of Economic Surveys*, 26(2), pp. 271–306, https://doi.org/10.1111/j.1467-6419.2010.00645.x

Chernoff, A. and C. Cheung (2024), "An Overview of Indigenous Economies within Canada," *Canadian Public Policy*, 50(4), pp. 364–390, https://doi.org/10.3138/cpp.2023-053

Child, B. J. (2014), "The Boarding School as Metaphor," in *Indian Subjects: Hemispheric Perspectives on the History of Indigenous Education*, B. J. Child and B. Klopotek (eds), SAR Press, Santa Fe, N.M., pp. 267–284.

Chu, C. et al. (2017), "The Interpersonal Theory of Suicide: A Systematic Review and Meta-Analysis of a Decade of Cross-National Research," *Psychological Bulletin*, 143(12), pp. 1313–1345, https://doi.org/10.1037/bul0000123

Coates, K. and B. Baumann (2023), "Beyond the Indian Act: Lessons Learned from Independent Land Management by First Nations," Macdonald-Laurier Institute, Ottawa, https://macdonaldlaurier.ca/wp-content/uploads/2023/04/20230424_FN_land_management_Coates_Baumann_PAPER_FWeb.pdf

Collings,P., G. Wenzel and R.G. Gordon (1998), "Modern Food Sharing Networks and Community Integration in the Central Canadian Arctic," *Arctic*, 51(4), pp. 301–314, https://doi.org/10.14430/arctic1073

Conching, A.K.S. and Z, Thayer (2019), "Biological Pathways for Historical Trauma to Affect Health: A Conceptual Model Focusing on Epigenetic Modifications," *Social Science & Medicine*, 230, pp. 74–82, https://doi.org/10.1016/j.socscimed.2019.04.001

Cooke, M. (2019), "Application of the United Nations Human Development Index to Registered Indians in Canada, 2006-2016," Indigenous Services Canada, https://publications.gc.ca/site/eng/9.895951/publication.html

Cotter, A. (2021), "Intimate Partner Violence in Canada, 2018: An Overview," *Juristat*, Statistics Canada, Catalogue no. 85-002-X ISSN 1209-6393, https://www150.statcan.gc.ca/n1/pub/85-002-x/2021001/article/00003-eng.pdf

Crawford, J. (1995), "Endangered Native American Languages: What is to be Done, and Why?" *The Bilingual Research Journal*, 19(1), pp. 17–38, https://doi.org/10.1080/15235882.1995.10668589

Currie, C.L. et al. (2012), "Racial Discrimination Experienced by Aboriginal University Students in Canada," *Canadian Journal of Psychiatry*, 57(10), pp. 617–625, https://doi.org/10.1177/070674371205701006

Czyzewski, K. (2011), "Colonialism as a Broader Social Determinant of Health," *International Indigenous Policy Journal*, 2(1), Article 5, https://www.jstor.org/stable/48766922

Daes, E.-I.A. (2001), "Prevention of Discrimination and Protection of Indigenous Peoples and Minorities: Indigenous Peoples and their Relationship to Land," Final working paper, UN Economic and Social Council, https://digitallibrary.un.org/record/445803?v=pdf

Diempsey, J., K. Gould, and J. Sundberg (2011), "Changing Land Tenure, Defining Subjects: Neo-Liberalism and Property Regimes on Native Reserves," in *Rethinking the Great White North: Race, Nature, and the Historical Geographies of Whiteness in Canada*, A. Baldwin, L. Cameron, and A. Kobayashi (eds), University of British Columbia Press, Vancouver, pp. 233–256, https://doi.org/10.59962/9780774820158

Denevan, W.M. (1992), "The Pristine Myth: The Landscape of the Americas in 1492," *Annals of the Association of American Geographers*, 82(3), The Americas before and after 1492: Current Geographical Research, pp. 369–385, https://www.jstor.org/stable/2563351

De Soto, H. (2003), *The Mystery of Capital: Why Capitalism Triumphs in the West and Fails Everywhere Else*, Basic Books, New York.

Dippel, C. and D. Frye (2021), "The Effect of Land Allotment on Native American Households During the Assimilation Era," Working Paper, https://dustinfrye.github.io/research/

Doyle, M.D. and L. Molix (2014), "Perceived Discrimination as a Stressor for Close Relationships: Identifying Psychological and Physiological Pathways," *Journal of Behavioral Medicine*, 37, pp. 1134–1144, https://doi.org/10.1007/s10865-014-9563-8

Dudgeon et al. (2018), *Global Overview: Indigenous Suicide Rates*, University of Western Australia, Perth, WA.

Dunbar-Ortiz, R. (2014), *An Indigenous Peoples' History of the United States*, Beacon Press, Boston.

Duran, E. and B. Duran (1995), *Native American Postcolonial Psychology*, State University of New York Press, Albany.

Durkheim, E. (1897/1951), *Suicide: A Study in Sociology*, J.A. Spaulding and G. Simpson (trans.), The Free Press, Glencoe, Illinois.

Eaton, B.C., M. Eswaran, and R. Oxoby (2011), "'Us' and 'Them': Origin of Identity, and its Economic Implications," *Canadian Journal of Economics*, 44, pp. 719–748, https://www.jstor.org/stable/41336384

Egan, B. and J. Place (2013), "Minding the Gaps: Property, Geography, and Indigenous Peoples in Canada," *Geoforum*, 44, pp. 129–138, https://doi.org/10.1016/j.geoforum.2012.10.003

Enloe, J.G. (2003), "Food Sharing Past and Present: Archaeological Evidence for Economic and Social Interactions," *Before Farming: The Archaeology and Anthropology of Hunter-Gatherers*, 1(1), pp. 1–23, https://doi.org/10.3828/bfarm.2003.1.1

Espey, D.K. et al. (2014), "Leading Causes of Death and All-Cause Mortality in American Indians and Alaska Natives," *Research and Practice*, Supplement 3, 104, No. S3, pp. S303–S313, https://doi.org/10.2105/AJPH.2013.301798

Eswaran, M. (2023a), "The Wrongs of Property Rights: The Erosion of Indigenous Communal Land Rights and its Welfare Consequences," *Canadian Public Policy*, 49(3), pp. 267–292, https://www.jstor.org/stable/27343264

Eswaran, M. (2023b), "Historical Trauma and Indigenous 'Deaths of Despair': A Link Seen by the Lens of Economics," University of British Columbia, Unpublished, https://papers.ssrn.com/sol3/papers.cfm?abstract_id=4677715

Eswaran, M. and H.M. Neary (2014), "An Economic Theory of the Evolution of Property Rights," *American Economic Journal: Microeconomics*, 6(3), pp. 203–226, https://www.jstor.org/stable/725249

Evans-Campbell, T. (2006) "Indian Child Welfare Practice Within Urban American Indian/Native American Communities," in *Mental Health Care for Urban Indians: Clinical Insights from Native Practitioners*, T.M. Witko (ed.), American Psychological Association, Washington D.C., pp. 33–53.

Evans-Campbell, T. (2008), "Historical Trauma in American Indian/Native Alaska Communities: A Multilevel Framework for Exploring Impacts on Individuals, Families, and Communities," *Journal of Interpersonal Violence*, 23(3), pp. 316–338, https://doi.org/10.1177/0886260507312290

Fabris, M. (2017), "Decolonizing neoliberalism? First Nations reserves, private property rights, and the legislation of Indigenous dispossession in Canada," in *Contested Property Claims: What Disagreement Tells Us About Ownership*, Bruun, M.H. (ed.), Routledge, New York, https://doi.org/10.4324/9780203712153

Farrell, J. et al. (2021), "Effects of land dispossession and forced migration of Indigenous peoples in North America," *Science*, 374, https://doi.org/10.1126/science.abe4943

Feir, D.L. (2016a), "The Long-Term Effects of Forcible Assimilation Policy: The Case of Indian Boarding Schools," *Canadian Journal of Economics*, 49(2), pp. 433–480, https://doi.org/10.1111/caje.12203

Feir, D.L. (2016b), "The Intergenerational Effects of Residential Schools on Children's Educational Experiences in Ontario and Canada's Western Provinces," *International Indigenous Policy Journal*, 7(3), https://doi.org/10.18584/iipj.2016.7.3.5

Feir, D.L. (2024), "Policies for Other People: Reflections from an Economist on Research and Federal Policy Regarding Indigenous Nations in Canada after 1975," *Canadian Public Policy*, 50(1), pp. 36–61, https://doi.org/10.3138/cpp.2023-051

Feir, D.L. and R. Akee (2019), "First Peoples Lost: Determining the State of Status First Nations Mortality in Canada Using Administrative Data," *Canadian Journal of Economics*, 52(2), pp. 490–525, https://doi.org/10.1111/caje.12387

Feir, D.L., R. Gillezeau, and E.C.M. Jones (2024), "The Slaughter of the Bison and Reversal of Fortunes on the Great Plains," *The Review of Economic Studies*, 91(3), pp. 1634–1670, https://doi.org/10.1093/restud/rdad060

Felsen, I. and H.S. Erlich (1990), "Identification Patterns of Offspring of Holocaust Survivors with Their Parents," *American Journal of Orthopsychiatry*, 60(4), pp. 506–520, https://doi.org/10.1037/h0079205

Ferguson, J. and M. Weaselboy (2020), "Indigenous sustainable relations: considering land in language and language in land," *Current Opinion in Environmental Sustainability*, 43, pp. 1–7, https://doi.org/10.1016/j.cosust.2019.11.006

Field, M. (2022) "Decolonizing Healing Through Indigenous Ways of Knowing," in *Reimagining Science Education in the Anthropocene*, Palgrave Studies in Education and the Environment, M.F.G. Wallace et al. (eds), Palgrave Macmillan Cham, London, pp. 121–134, https://doi.org/10.1007/978-3-030-79622-8_8

Field, E. and M. Torero (2006), "Do Property Titles Increase Credit Access Among the Urban Poor? Evidence from a Nationwide Titling Program," Harvard University, Mass.

First Nations Health Authority (2019), "The Honourable Senator Murray Sinclair speaks with the FNHA Family and Shares Residential School Survivors' Stories to Make Canada better," https://www.fnha.ca/about/news-and-events/news/the-honourable-senator-murray-sinclair-speaks-with-the-fnha-family-and-shares-residential-school-survivors-stories-to-make-canada-better

Flanagan, T., C. Alcantara, A. Le Dressay (2010), *Beyond the Indian Act: Restoring Aboriginal Property Rights*, McGill-Queen's University Press, Montreal, Quebec, https://doi.org/10.1515/9780773581838

Fleming, J., and R.J. Ledogar (2008), "Resilience and Indigenous Spirituality: A Literature Review," *Pimatisiwin*, 6(2), pp. 47–64, https://pmc.ncbi.nlm.nih.gov/articles/PMC2956755/

Fligg, R.A. and D.T. Robinson (2020), "Reviewing First Nation Land Management Regimes in Canada and Exploring their Relationship to Community Well-being," *Land Use Policy*, 90, https://doi.org/10.1016/j.landusepol.2019.104245

FNIGC (2020), Strengths-Based Approaches to Indigenous Research and the Development of Well-Being Indicators, First Nations Information Governance Centre, Ottawa, https://fnigc.ca/wp-content/uploads/2021/05/FNIGC-Research-Series-SBA_v04.pdf

Fouka, V. (2020), "Backlash: The Unintended Effects of Language Prohibition in U.S. Schools after World War I," *Review of Economic Studies*, 87, pp. 204–239, https://doi.org/10.1093/restud/rdz024

Fournier, S. and E. Crey (1997), *Stolen from our Embrace: The Abduction of First Nations Children and the Restoration of Aboriginal Communities*, Douglas & McIntyre, Vancouver.

Friedman, J., H. Hansen, and J.P. Gone (2023), "Deaths of Despair and Indigenous Data Genocide,' *The Lancet*, 401, pp. 874–876, https://doi.org/10.1016/S0140-6736(22)02404-7

Fruehwirth, J., S. Iyer, and A. Zhang (2019), "Religion and Depression in Adolescence," *Journal of Political Economy*, 127(3), pp. 1178–1209, https://doi.org/10.1086/701425

Frye, D. and D.P. Parker (2021), "Indigenous Self-Governance and Development on American Indian Reservations," *AEA Papers and Proceedings*, 111, pp. 233–237, https://doi.org/10.1257/pandp.20211099

Galiani, S. and E. Schargrodsky (2010), "Property rights for the Poor: Effects of Land Titling," *Journal of Public Economics*, 94, pp. 700–729, https://doi.org/10.1016/j.jpubeco.2010.06.002

George, L.J. (1997), "Why the Need for the Indian Child Welfare Act?" *Journal of Multicultural Social Work*, 5(3/4), pp. 165–175, https://doi.org/10.1300/J285v05n03_04

Giles, T., D.M. Hungerman, and T. Oostrom (2023), "Opiates of the Masses? Deaths of Despair and the Decline of American Religion," NBER, Working Paper 30840, Washington D.C., https://www.nber.org/papers/w30840

Godon-Decoteau, D. and P.G. Ramsey (2018), "Positive and Negative Aspects of Transracial Adoption: An Exploratory Study from Korean Transracial Adoptees' Perspectives," *Adoption Quarterly*, 21(1), pp. 17–40, https://doi.org/10.1080/10926755.2017.1387209

Gone, J.P. (2009), "A Community-Based Treatment for Native American Historical Trauma: Prospects for Evidence-Based Practice," *Journal of Consulting and Clinical Psychology*, 77(4), pp. 751–762, https://doi.org/10.1037/a0015390

Gone, J.P. (2013), "Redressing First Nations Historical Trauma: Theorizing Mechanisms for Indigenous Culture as Mental Health Treatment," *Transcultural Psychiatry*, 50(5), pp. 683–706, https://doi.org/10.1177/1363461513487669

Gone, J.P. et al. (2019), "The Impact of Historical Trauma on Health Outcomes for Indigenous Populations in the USA and Canada: A Systematic Review," *American Psychologist*, 74(1), pp. 20–35, https://doi.org/0.1037/amp0000338

Gone, J.P. (2023), "Indigenous Historical Trauma: Alter-Native Explanations for Mental Health Inequities," *Daedalus*, 152(4), pp. 130–150, https://doi.org/10.1162/daed_a_02035

Gone, J.P. (2025), "Trauma, Coloniality and Survivance among Indigenous Peoples in the US," *World Psychiatry*, 24(1), pp. 85–86, https://doi.org/10.1002/wps.21273

Gracey, M. and M. King (2009), "Indigenous Health Part 1: Determinants and Disease Patterns," *Lancet*, 374, pp. 65–75, https://doi.org/10.1016/S0140-6736(09)60914-4

Granovetter, M. (1985), "Economic Action and Social Structure: The Problem of Embeddedness," *American Journal of Sociology*, 91(3), pp. 481–510, https://www.jstor.org/stable/2780199

Green, P., F. Gino, and B.R. Staats (2017), "Seeking to Belong: How the Words of Internal and External Beneficiaries Influence Performance," Harvard Business School, Working Paper 17-073, https://www.hbs.edu/ris/Publication%20Files/17-073_9e2b9c23-cac0-4dcc-86ae-aaa2d32698d1.pdf

Greenland, F. and F.M. Gocek (2020), *Cultural Violence and the Destruction of Communities: New Theoretical Perspectives*, Routledge, New York, https://doi.org/10.4324/9781351267083

Gregg, M.T. (2018), "The Long-term Effects of American Indian Boarding Schools," *Journal of Development Economics*, 130, pp. 17–32, https://doi.org/10.1016/j.jdeveco.2017.09.003

Greif, A. (1994), "Cultural Beliefs and the Organization of Society: A Historical and Theoretical Reflection on Collectivist and Individualist Societies," *Journal of Political Economy*, 102(5), pp. 912–950, https://doi.org/10.1086/261959

Guillory, B., E. Willie, and E. Duran (1988), "Analysis of a Community Organizing Case Study: Alkali Lake," *Journal of Rural Community Psychology*, 9(1), pp. 27–35, https://www.researchgate.net/publication/306451427_Analysis_of_a_community_organizing_case_study_Alkali_Lake

Guiso, L., P. Sapienza, and L. Zingales (2006), "Does Culture Affect Economic Outcomes?" *Journal of Economic Perspectives*, 20(2), pp. 23–48, https://doi.org/10.1257/jep.20.2.23

Guiso, L., P. Sapienza, and L. Zingales (2016), "Long-term Persistence," *Journal of the European Economic Association*, 14(6), pp. 1401–1436, https://doi.org/10.1111/jeea.12177

Hageman, A. and P. Galoustian (2024), *Economic Aspects of the Indigenous Experience in Canada*, 2nd edn, https://doi.org/10.24908/b0a67ddbac0f

Hallett, D., M.J. Chandler, and C.E. Lalonde (2007), "Aboriginal Language Knowledge and Youth Suicide," *Cognitive Development*, 22, pp. 392–399, https://doi.org/10.1016/j.cogdev.2007.02.001

Hames, R. (2007), "The Ecologically Noble Savage Debate," *Annual Review of Anthropology*, 36, pp. 177–190, https://doi.org/10.1146/annurev. anthro.35.081705.123321

Hammermesh, D.S. and N.M. Soss (1974), "An Economic Theory of Suicide," *Journal of Political Economy*, 82(1), pp. 83–98, https://doi.org/10.1086/260171

Harder, H.G. et al. (2012), "Indigenous Youth Suicide: A Systematic Review of the Literature," *Pimatisiwin: A Journal of Aboriginal and Indigenous Community Health*, 10(1), pp. 125–142, https://www.taylorfrancis.com/chapters/edit/10.4324/9780203795583-47/indigenous-youth-suicide-henry-harder-joshua-rash-travis-holyk-eduardo-jovel-kari-harder

Harding, R. (2006), "Historical Representations of Aboriginal People in the Canadian News Media," *Discourse & Society*, 17(2), pp. 205–235, https://doi.org/10.1177/0957926506058059

Harris, C. (2004), "How Did Colonialism Dispossess? Comments from an Edge of Empire," *Annals of the Association of American Geographers*, 94(1), pp. 165–182, https://doi.org/10.1111/j.1467-8306.2004.09401009.x

Hartmann, W.E. et al. (2019), "American Indian Historical Trauma: Anti-Colonial Prescriptions for Healing, Resilience, and Survivance," *American Psychologist*, 74(1), pp. 6–19, https://doi.org/10.1037/amp0000326

Haslam, C. et al. (2018), *The New Psychology of Health: Unlocking the Social Cure*, Routledge, London, https://doi.org/10.4324/9781315648569

Hatcher, S. and O. Stubbersfield (2013), "Sense of Belonging and Suicide: A Systematic Review," *Canadian Journal of Psychiatry*, 58(7), pp. 432–436, https://doi.org/10.1177/070674371305800709

Hatcher, S. (2016), "Indigenous Suicide: A Global Perspective with a New Zealand Focus," *Canadian Journal of Psychiatry*, 61(11), pp. 684–687, https://doi.org/10.1177/0706743716644147

Hayes, S.C., P. Atkins, and D.S. Wilson (2021), "Prosocial: Using an Evolutionary Approach to Modify Cooperation in Small Groups," in *Applied Behavior Science in Organizations: Consilience of Historical and Emerging Trends in Organizational Behavior Management*, R.A. Houmanfar et al. (eds), Routledge, New York, pp. 193–220, https://doi.org/10.4324/9781003198949

Hedlund, S. (2020), "Medicines at Standing Rock: Stories of Native Healing Through Survivance," *American Indian Culture and Research Journal*, 44(4), pp. 59–78, https://doi.org/10.17953/aicrj.44.4.hedlund

Heid, O. et al. (2022), "Indigenous Youth and Resilience in Canada and the USA: A Scoping Review," *Adversity and Resilience Science*, 3, pp. 113–147, https://doi.org/10.1007/s42844-022-00060-2

Helliwell, J.F. (2007), "Well-Being and Social Capital: Does Suicide Pose a Puzzle?" *Social Indicators Research*, 81, pp. 455–496, https://doi.org/10.1007/s11205-006-0022-y

Helliwell, J.F. and H. Huang (2008), "How's Your Government? International Evidence Linking Good Government and Well-Being," *British Journal of Political Science*, 38(4), pp. 595–619, https://doi.org/10.1017/S0007123408000306

Helliwell, J.F. and H. Huang (2014), "New Measures of the Costs of Unemployment: Evidence from the Subjective Well-Being of 3.3 million Americans," *Economic Inquiry*, 52(4), pp. 1485–1502, https://doi.org/10.1111/ecin.12093

Herman, J. (1992), "Complex PTSD: A Syndrome in Survivors of Prolonged and Repeated Trauma," *Journal of Traumatic Stress*, 5(3), pp. 377–391, https://doi.org/10.1007/BF00977235

Hoelle, J.C. (2011), "Re-Evaluating Tribal Customs of Land Use Rights," *University of Colorado Law Review*, 82, pp. 551–594, https://scholar.law.colorado.edu/lawreview/vol82/iss2/5

Hudson, P. and B. McKenzie (1981), "Child Welfare and Native People: The Extension of Colonialism," *The Social Worker*, 49(2), pp. 63–88, https://doi.org/10.59962/9780774857109-009

Hurt, R.D. (1987), *Indian Agriculture in America: Prehistory to Present*, University Press of Kansas, Lawrence.

Hyden, G. (2012), "The Economy of Affection," in *African Politics in Comparative Perspective*, Cambridge University Press, Cambridge, pp. 74–96, https://doi.org/10.1017/CBO9781139343756

Iannaccone, L. R. (1992), "Sacrifice and Stigma: Reducing Free Riding in Cults, Communes, and Other Collectives," *Journal of Political Economy*, 100, pp. 271–92, https://doi.org/10.1086/261818

Indian Chiefs of Alberta (1970/2011), "Citizens Plus," *Aboriginal Policy Studies*, 1(2), pp. 181–281, https://doi.org/10.5663/aps.v1i2.11690

Innis, H.A. (1962), *The Fur Trade in Canada: An Introduction to Canadian Economic History*, University of Toronto Press, Toronto.

Jacklin, K. (2009), "Diversity Within: Deconstructing Aboriginal Community Health in Wikwemikong Unceded Indian Reserve," *Social Science & Medicine*, 68, pp. 980–989, https://doi.org/10.1016/j.socscimed.2008.12.035

James, W. (1890), "The Consciousness of Self," *The Principles of Psychology*, Henry Holt & Co., New York.

Jellestad, L. et al. (2021), "Functional impairment in Posttraumatic Stress Disorder: A Systematic Review and Meta-Analysis," *Journal of Psychiatric Research*, 136, pp. 14–22, https://doi.org/10.1016/j.jpsychires.2021.01.039

Jobin, S. (2020), "Market Citizenship and Indigeneity," in *Creating Indigenous Property: Power, Rights and Relationships*, A. Cameron, S. Graben, and V. Napoleon (eds), University of Toronto Press, Toronto, pp. 94–119, https://doi.org/10.3138/9781487532116

Johnsen, D.B (1986), "The Formation and Protection of Property Rights among the Southern Kwakiutl Indians," *Journal of Legal Studies*, 15, pp. 41–67, https://www.jstor.org/stable/724361

Johnson, P. (1983), *Native Children and the Welfare System*, Canadian Council on Social Development, James Lorimer & Co., Ottawa.

Joiner, T. (2005), *Why People Die by Suicide*, Harvard University Press, Boston.

Jones, L.E. (2016), "Missionary Boarding Schools: The Long-Term Cultural, Health and Social Impacts of Integration Policy on Indigenous Peoples," Department of Human Sciences Working Paper, Ohio State University.

Kades, E. (2000), "The Dark Side of Efficiency: Johnson v. M'Intosh and the Expropriation of American Indian Lands," *University of Pennsylvania Law Review*, April, 148(4), pp. 1065–1190, https://scholarship.law.upenn.edu/penn_law_review/vol148/iss4/2

Kahneman, D., J.L. Knetsch, and R.H. Thaler (1990), "Experimental Tests of the Endowment Effect and the Coase Theorem," *Journal of Political Economy*, 98(6), pp. 1325–1348, https://doi.org/10.1086/261737

Kant, S., I. Vertinsky, and B. Zheng (2016), "Valuation of First Nations Peoples' Social, Cultural, and Land Use Activities Using Life Satisfaction Approach," *Forest Policy and Economics*, 72, pp. 46–55, https://doi.org/10.1016/j.forpol.2016.06.014

Kaspar, V. (2014a), "Long-term Depression and Suicidal Ideation Outcomes Subsequent to Emancipation from Foster Care: Pathways to Psychiatric Risk in the Métis Population," *Psychiatry Research*, 215, pp. 347–354, https://doi.org/10.1016/j.psychres.2013.09.003

Kaspar, V. (2014b), "The Lifetime Effect of Residential School Attendance on Indigenous Health Status," *American Journal of Public Health: Research and Practice*, 104(11), pp. 2184–2190, https://doi.org/10.2105/AJPH.2013.301479

Katz, R. (2017), *Indigenous Healing Psychology: Honoring the Wisdom of the First Peoples*, Healing Arts Press, Toronto.

Kelly, D. (2017), "Feed the People and You Will Never go Hungry: Illuminating Coast Salish Economy of Affection," University of Auckland, Auckland, https://www.researchgate.net/publication/322702552_Feed_the_people_and_you_will_never_go_hungry_Illuminating_Coast_Salish_economy_of_affection

Keller, H. and N. Chaudhary (2017), "Is the Mother Essential for Attachment? Models of Care in Different Cultures," in *The Cultural Nature of Attachment: Contextualizing Relationships and Development*, H. Keller and K.A. Bard (eds), MIT Press, Cambridge, Mass., https://doi.org/10.7551/mitpress/9780262036900.001.0001

Kessler, R.C. and R.G. Frank (1997), "The Impact of Psychiatric Disorders on Work Loss Days," *Psychological Medicine,* 27, pp. 861–873, https://doi.org/10.1017/S0033291797004807

Khawaja, M. (2021), "Consequences and Remedies of Indigenous Language Loss in Canada," *Societies,* 11, p. 89, https://doi.org/10.3390/soc11030089

Killsback, L.K. (2019), "A Nation of Families: Traditional Indigenous Kinship, the Foundation for Cheyenne Sovereignty," *Alter,* 15(1), pp. 34–43, https://doi.org/10.1177/1177180118822833

Kim, D.S. (1978), "Issues in Transracial and Transcultural Adoption," *Families in Society, The Journal of Contemporary Social Services,* 59(8), pp. 477–486, https://doi.org/10.1177/104438947805900804

King, L., G. Scheiring, and E. Nosrati (2022), "Deaths of Despair in Comparative Perspective," *Annual Review of Sociology,* 48, pp. 299–317, https://doi.org/10.1146/annurev-soc-030320-031757

King, M., A. Smith, and M. Gracey. (2009), "Indigenous Health Part 2: The Underlying Causes of the Health Gap," *Lancet,* 374, pp. 76–85, https://doi.org/10.1016/S0140-6736(09)60827-8

Kira, I.A. (2010), "Etiology and Treatment of Post-Cumulative Traumatic Stress Disorders in Different Cultures," *Traumatology,* 16(4), pp. 128–141, https://doi.org/10.1177/1534765610365914

Kirmayer, L.J. et al. (2007), "Suicide Among Aboriginal People in Canada," The Aboriginal Healing Foundation, Ottawa, http://www.douglas.qc.ca/uploads/File/2007-AHF-suicide.pdf

Kirmayer, L.J., M.E. Macdonald, and G.M. Brass (2001), "The Mental Health of Indigenous Peoples," Proceedings of the Advanced Study Institute, *The Mental Health of Indigenous Peoples,* McGill Summer Program in Social & Cultural Psychiatry and the Aboriginal Mental Health Research Team, 29–31 May, Montréal, Québec.

Kirmayer, L.J., G.M. Brass, and C.L. Tait (2000), "The Mental Health of Aboriginal Peoples: Transformations of Identity and Community," *Canadian Journal of Psychiatry,* 45, pp. 607–616, https://doi.org/10.1177/070674370004500702

Kirmayer, L.J. et al. (2009a), "Community Resilience: Models, Metaphors and Measures," *International Journal of Indigenous Health,* 5(1), pp. 62–117, https://www.proquest.com/scholarly-journals/community-resilience-models-metaphors-measures/docview/1138545030/se-2

Kirmayer, L. et al. (2009b), "Current Approaches to Aboriginal Youth Suicide Prevention," Institute of Community & Family Psychiatry Jewish General Hospital: Culture & Mental Health Research Unit, Quebec, http://www.mcgill.ca/tcpsych/files/tcpsych/Report14.pdf

Kirmayer, L.J. et al. (2011), "Rethinking Resilience from Indigenous Perspectives," *Canadian Journal of Psychiatry*, 56(2), pp. 84–91, https://doi.org/10.1177/070674371105600203

Krauss, M. (1992), "The World's Languages in Crisis," *Language*, 68(1), pp. 4–10, https://doi.org/10.1353/lan.1992.0075

Kumar, M.B. and M. Tjepkema (2019), "Suicide among First Nations people, Métis, and Inuit (2011-2016): Findings from the 2011 Canadian Census Health and Environment Cohort (CanCHEC)," Statistics Canada, Catalogue no. 99-011-X2019001, https://www.publications.gc.ca/site/eng/9.874824/publication.html

Lalonde, C.E. (2013), "Identity Formation and Cultural Resilience in Aboriginal Communities," in *Routledge International Handbook of Clinical Suicide Research*, J.R. Cutcliffe et al. (eds), Routledge, London, pp. 364–377.

Lavner, J.A. (2018), "Racial Discrimination and Relationship Functioning among African American Couples," *Journal of Family Psychology*, 32(5), pp. 686–691, https://doi.org/10.1037/fam0000415

Lavoie, M. (2016), "Why Restrain Alienation of Indigenous Lands," *U.B.C. Law Review*, 49(3), pp. 997–1060, https://canlii.ca/t/7nbxt

Lawson-Te Aho, K. and J.H. Liu (2010), "Indigenous Suicide and Colonization: The Legacy of Violence and the Necessity of Self-Determination," *International Journal of Conflict and Violence*, 4(1), pp. 124–133, https://doi.org/10.4119/ijcv-2819

Layard, R. (2005), *Happiness: Lessons from a New Science*, Penguin Press, New York.

Leary, D.E. (1990), "William James on the Self and Personality: Clearing the Ground for Subsequent Theorists, Researchers, and Practitioners," in *Reflections on The Principles of Psychology: William James after a Century*, (Eds). M.G. Johnson and T.B. Henley, Erlbaum Associates, Hillsdale, N.J., pp. 101–137.

Lemkin, R. (1944), *Axis Rule in Occupied Europe: Laws of Occupation, Analysis of Government, Proposals for Redress*, Columbia University Press, New York.

Lester, D. (1999), "Native American Suicide Rates, Acculturation Stress and Traditional Integration," *Psychological Reports*, 84, p. 398, https://doi.org/10.2466/pr0.1999.84.2.398

Liebmann, M.J. et al. (2016), "Native American Depopulation, Reforestation, and Fire Regimes in the Southwest United States, 1492–1900 CE," *Proceedings of the National Academy of Sciences*, 113(6), pp. E696–E704, https://doi.org/10.1073/pnas.1521744113

Lipsey, R.G. and K. Lancaster (1956), "The General Theory of Second Best," *Review of Economic Studies*, 24, pp. 11–32, https://doi.org/10.2307/2296233

Little Bear, L. (2000), "Jagged World Views Colliding," in *Reclaiming Indigenous Voice and Vision*, M. Battiste (ed.), University of British Columbia Press, Vancouver, pp. 77–85, https://doi.org/10.59962/9780774853170

Locke, J (1689/1967), *Two Treatises of Government*, 2nd edn, P. Laslett (ed.), Cambridge University Press, Cambridge.

Logan, T.E. (2006), "Lost Generations: The Silent Métis of the Residential School System," in *Métis History and Experience and Residential Schools in Canada*, Chartrand, Logan, and Daniels (eds), The Aboriginal Healing Foundation, Ottawa, pp. 57–89.

Loppie, S., C. Reading, and S. de Leeuw (2014), "Indigenous Experiences with Racism and its Impacts," National Collaborating Centre for Aboriginal Health, Prince George, B.C, https://www.nccih.ca/docs/determinants/FS-Racism2-Racism-Impacts-EN.pdf

Lyons, S.R. (2010), *X-Marks: Native Signatures of Assent*, University of Minnesota Press, Minneapolis, https://doi.org/10.5749/minnesota/9780816666768.001.0001

Mancini, A. et al. (2011), "Suffering Makes You Egoist: Acute Pain Increases Acceptance Rates and Reduces Fairness during a Bilateral Ultimatum Game," *PLoS ONE*, 6(10), e26008, https://doi.org/10.1371/journal.pone.0026008

Manuel, A. and R.M. Derrickson (2015), *Unsettling Canada: A National Wake-up Call*, Between the Lines, Toronto.

Maracle, G.K. (2021), "Connections and Processes: Indigenous Community and Identity's Place in the Healing Journey," *Turtle Island Journal of Indigenous Health*, 1(2), pp. 18–27, https://doi.org/10.33137/tijih.v1i2.36052

Matheson, K., A. Bombay, and H. Anisman (2018), "Culture as an Ingredient of Personalized Medicine," *Journal of Psychiatry and Neuroscience*, 43(1), pp. 3–6, https://doi.org/10.1503/jpn.170234

Matheson, K. et al. (2022), "Canada's Colonial Genocide of Indigenous Peoples: A Review of the Psychosocial and Neurobiological Processes Linking Trauma and Intergenerational Outcomes," *International Journal of Environmental Research and Public Health*, 19, p. 6455, https://doi.org/10.3390/ijerph19116455

May, P.A. and N.W. Van Winkle (1994), "Durkheim's Suicide Theory and Its Applicability to Contemporary American Indians and Alaska Natives," in *Emile Durkheim, Le Suicide: Once Hundred Years Later*, D. Lester (ed.), The Charles Press, Philadelphia, pp. 296–318.

Mazumdar, S. and S. Mazumdar (2004), "Religion and Place Attachment: A Study of Sacred Places," *Journal of Environmental Psychology*, 24, pp. 385–397, https://doi.org/10.1016/j.jenvp.2004.08.005

McChesney, F.S. (1990), "Government as Definer of Property Rights: Indian Lands, Ethnic Externalities, and Bureaucratic Budgets," *The Journal of Legal Studies*, 19(2), pp. 297–335, https://www.jstor.org/stable/724423

McCormick, R.M. (2000), "Aboriginal Traditions in the Treatment of Substance Abuse," *Canadian Journal of Counselling*, 34(1), pp. 25–32, https://cjc-rcc.ucalgary.ca/article/view/58635

McDiarmid, J. (2020), *Highway of Tears: A True Story of Racism, Indifference and the Pursuit of Justice for Missing and Murdered Indigenous Women and Girls*, Random House, Canada.

Mcdonnell, M.A. and A.D. Moses (2005), "Raphael Lemkin as Historian of Genocide in the Americas," *Journal of Genocide Research*, 7(4), pp. 501–529, https://doi.org/10.1080/14623520500349951

McQuaid, R.J. et al. (2022) "Parent-Child Separations and Mental Health among First Nations and Métis Peoples in Canada: Links to Intergenerational Residential School Attendance," *International Journal of Environmental Research and Public Health*, 19, p. 6877, https://doi.org/10.3390/ijerph19116877

Methot, S. (2019), *Legacy: Trauma, Story, and Indigenous Healing*, ECW Press, Toronto.

Milliken, R. (1995), *A Time of Little Choice: The Disintegration of Tribal Culture in the San Francisco Bay Area, 1769-1810*, Ballena Press Publishers' Service, Menlo Park, California.

Milloy, J.S. (2017), *A National Crime: The Canadian Government and the Residential School System, 1879 to 1986*, University of Manitoba Press, Winnipeg, Manitoba, https://doi.org/10.1515/9780887553035

Mills, A. (2010), "Aki, Anishinaabek, kaye tahsh Crown," *Indigenous Law Journal*, 9(1), pp. 107–166, https://ilj.law.utoronto.ca/sites/ilj.law.utoronto.ca/files/media/Aaron_Mills_-_C2_0.pdf

Milner A., A. Page, and A.D. LaMontagne (2013), "Long-Term Unemployment and Suicide: A Systematic Review and Meta-Analysis," *PLoS ONE*, 8(1), e51333, https://doi.org/10.1371/journal.pone.0051333

Mignone, J. and J. O'Neil (2005), "Social Capital and Youth Suicide Risk Factors in First Nations Communities," *Canadian Journal of Public Health*, 96, Suppl. 1, pp. S51–S54, https://doi.org/10.1007/BF03405317

Morales, S. and B. Thom (2020), "The Principle of Sharing and the Shadow of Canadian Property Law," in *Creating Indigenous Property: Power, Rights, and Relationships*, A. Cameron, S. Graben, and V. Napoleon (eds), University of Toronto Press, Toronto, pp. 120–162, https://doi.org/10.3138/9781487532116

Muldoon, O.T. et al. (2019), "The Social Psychology of Responses to Trauma: Social Identity Pathways Associated with Divergent Traumatic Responses," *European Review of Social Psychology*, 30(1), pp. 311–348, https://doi.org/10.1080/10463283.2020.1711628

Murry, V.M. et al. (2001), "Racial Discrimination as a Moderator of the Links Among Stress, Maternal Psychological Functioning, and Family Relationships," *Journal of Marriage and Family*, 63, pp. 915–926, https://doi.org/10.1111/j.1741-3737.2001.00915.x

Nakajima, N. and M. al'Absi (2016), "Addiction, Pain, and Stress Response," in *The Neuroscience of Pain, Stress, and Emotion: Psychological and Clinical Implications*, M. al'Absi and M.A. Flaten (eds), Elsevier/Academic Press, Amsterdam.

Natcher, D.C. (2009), "Subsistence and the Social Economy of Canada's Aboriginal North," *The Northern Review*, 30 (Spring), pp. 83–98, https://thenorthernreview.ca/index.php/nr/article/view/6#:

NCJFCJ (2017), "Disproportionality Rates for Children of Color in Foster Care," National Council of Juvenile and Family Court Judges, Reno, Nevada, https://www.ncjfcj.org/wp-content/uploads/2017/09/NCJFCJ-Disproportionality-TAB-2015_0.pdf

Nikolakis, W. and H. Nelson (2018), "Trust, Institutions, and Indigenous Self-governance: An Exploratory study," *Governance*, pp. 1–17, https://doi.org/10.1111/gove.12374

Nedelsky, J. (1993), "Reconceiving Rights as Relationship," *Review of Constitutional Studies*, 1(1), pp. 1–26, https://go.gale.com/ps/i.do?p=LT&u=ubcolumbia&id=GALE%7CA238352907&v=2.1&it=r&sid=summon&asid=099e5864.

Newland, B. (2022), *Federal Indian Boarding School Initiative Investigative Report*, United States Department of the Interior, Washington D.C., https://www.bia.gov/sites/default/files/media_document/doi_federal_indian_boarding_school_initiative_investigative_report_vii_final_508_compliant.pdf

Nguyen, N.N. et al. (2020), "Barriers and Mitigating Strategies to Healthcare Access Among Indigenous Communities in Canada: A Narrative Review," *Healthcare*, 8, p. 112, https://doi.org/10.3390/healthcare8020112

Niezen, R. (2000), *Spirit Wars: Native North American Religions in the Age of Nation Building*, University of California Press, Berkeley, https://doi.org/10.1525/9780520923430

NNAPF (2011), "Honouring Our Strengths: A Renewed Framework to Address Substance Use Issues Among First Nations People in Canada", https://thunderbirdpf.org/?resources=honouring-our-strengths-a-renewed-framework-to-address-substance-use-issues-among-first-nations-people-in-canada

Noble, B. (2008), "Owning as Belonging/Owning as Property: The Crisis of Power and Respect in First Nations Heritage Transactions with Canada," in *First Nations Cultural Heritage and Law*, vol. I, C. Bell and V. Napoleon (eds), University of British Columbia Press, Vancouver, pp. 465–488.

North, D.C (1981), *Structure and Change in Economic History*, W. W. Norton & Co., New York.

Nunn N. (2009), "The Importance of History for Economic Development," *Annual Review of Economics*, 1, pp. 65–92, https://doi.org/10.1146/annurev. economics.050708.143336

Nunn, N. and L. Wantchekon (2011), "The Slave Trade and the Origins of Mistrust in Africa," *American Economic Review*, 101(7), pp. 3221–3252, https://doi.org/10.1257/aer.101.7.3221

O'Keefe, V.M. et al. (2014), "Interpersonal Suicide Risk for American Indians: Investigating Thwarted Belongingness and Perceived Burdensomeness," *Cultural Diversity and Ethnic Minority Psychology*, 20(1), pp. 61–67, https://doi.org/10.1037/a0033540

O'Fallon, B.D. and L. Fehren-Schmitz (2011), "Native Americans Experienced a Strong Population Bottleneck Coincident with European Contact," *Proceedings of the National Academy of Sciences*, 108(51), pp. 20444–20448, https://doi.org/10.1073/pnas.1112563108

Ostrom, E. (1990). *Governing the Commons: The Evolution of Institutions for Collective Action*, Cambridge University Press, Cambridge.

Ostrom, E. and C. Hess (2008), "Private and Common Property Rights," *Encyclopedia of Law & Economics*, Edward Elgar, Northampton, Mass.

Otis, D.S. (1973), *The Dawes Act and the Allotment of Indian Lands*, The University of Oklahoma Press, Norman, Oklahoma.

Ozbay, F. et al. (2007), "Social Support and Resilience to Stress: From Neurobiology to Clinical Practice," *Psychiatry*, 4(5), pp. 35–40, https://pmc. ncbi.nlm.nih.gov/articles/PMC2921311/

Park, J. (2021), "Mortality among First Nations People, 2006 to 2016," Statistics Canada, Health Reports, 32(10), Catalogue no. 82-003-X, https://doi.org/10.25318/82-003-x202101000001-eng

Pasternak, S. (2015), "How Capitalism Will Save Colonialism: The Privatization of Reserve Lands in Canada," *Antipode*, 47(1), pp. 179–196, https://doi.org/10.1111/anti.12094

Pendakur, K. and R. Pendakur (2018), "The Effects of Modern Treaties and Opt-In Legislation on Household Incomes in Aboriginal Communities," *Social Indicators Research*, 137(1), pp. 139–165, https://doi.org/10.1007/s11205-017-1593-5

Pendakur, K. and R. Pendakur (2021), "The Impact of Self-Government, Comprehensive Land Claims, and Opt-In Arrangements on Income Inequality in Indigenous Communities in Canada," *Canadian Public Policy*, 47(2), pp. 180–201, https://www.jstor.org/stable/27034150

Penner, J. E. (1997), *The Idea of Property in Law*, Clarendon Press, Oxford.

Phinney, J.S. (1991), "Ethnic Identity and Self-Esteem: A Review and Integration," *Hispanic Journal of Behavioral Sciences*, 13(2), pp. 193–208, https://doi.org/10.1177/07399863910132005

Pollock, N.J. et al. (2018), "Global incidence of suicide among Indigenous peoples: a systematic review," *BMC Medicine*, 16, p. 145, https://doi.org/10.1186/s12916-018-1115-6

Public Health Agency of Canada (2018), "Key Health Inequalities in Canada: A National Portrait, Statistics Canada," https://www150.statcan.gc.ca/n1/daily-quotidien/180528/dq180528e-info-eng.htm

Qikiqtani Truth Commission (2014), *Thematic Reports & Special Studies, 1950-1975*, Qikiqtani Inuit Association, https://www.qtcommission.ca/sites/default/files/public/thematic_reports/thematic_reports_english_final_report.pdf

Raifman, J., L. Sampson, and S. Galea (2020), "Suicide Fatalities in the US Compared to Canada: Potential suicides Averted with Lower Firearm Ownership in the US," *PLoS ONE*, 15(4), e0232252, https://doi.org/10.1371/journal.pone.0232252

Red Horse, J.G. et al. (1978), "Family Behavior of Urban American Indians," *Social Casework: The Journal of Contemporary Social Work*, 59(2), pp. 67–72, https://doi.org/10.1177/104438947805900201

Red Horse, J. (1997), "Traditional American Indian Family Systems," *Families, Systems & Health*, 15(3), pp. 243–250, https://doi.org/10.1037/h0089828

Richards, J. (2023), "Low Indigenous Employment and 'Deaths of Despair' in the Canadian Prairies," Policy Brief, Johnson Shoyama Graduate School, www.schoolofpublicpolicy.sk.ca

Ritland, L. et al. (2021). "The Cedar Project: Relationship between Child Apprehension and Attempted Suicide among Young Indigenous Mothers Impacted by Substance Use in Two Canadian Cities," *PLoS ONE*, 16(6), e0252993, https://doi.org/10.1371/journal.pone.0252993

Roback, J. (1992), "Exchange, Sovereignty, and Indian-Anglo Relations," in *Property Rights and Indian Economies*, T. L. Anderson (ed.), Rowman & Littlefield, Lanham, pp. 5–26.

Rocha Beardall, T. and F. Edwards (2021), "Abolition, Settler Colonialism, and the Persistent Threat of Indian Child Welfare," *Columbia Journal of Race and Law*, 11(3), pp. 533–573, https://doi.org/10.52214/cjrl.v11i3.8744

Rosay, A.B. (2016), "Violence Against American Indian and Alaska Native Women and Men, 2010: Findings from the National Intimate Partner and Sexual Violence Survey," U.S. Department of Justice, Washington D.C., https://nij.ojp.gov/library/publications/violence-against-american-indian-and-alaska-native-women-and-men-2010-findings

Rose, D.C. (2018), *Why Culture Matters Most*, Oxford University Press, New York, https://doi.org/10.1093/oso/9780199330720.001.0001

Rowan, M. et al. (2014), "Cultural Interventions to Treat Addictions in Indigenous Populations: Findings from a Scoping Study," *Substance Abuse Treatment, Prevention, and Policy*, 9(34), http://www.substanceabusepolicy.com/content/9/1/34

Royal Commission on Aboriginal Peoples [RCAP] (1994), *The High Arctic Relocation: A Report on the 1953-1955 Relocation*, Ottawa, Canada, https://publications.gc.ca/site/eng/9.829143/publication.html

Royal Commission on Aboriginal Peoples [RCAP] (1996), *Choosing Life: Special Report on Suicide Among Aboriginal People*, Ottawa, Canada, https://publications.gc.ca/site/eng/9.645730/publication.html

Ruhm, C.J. (2021), "Living and Dying in America: An Essay on Deaths of Despair and the Future of Capitalism," NBER Working Paper 28358, http://www.nber.org/papers/w28358

Sahlins, M. (1972), *Stone Age Economics*, Aldine-Atherton, Chicago.

Salzman, M.B. (2001), "Cultural Trauma and Recovery: Perspectives from Terror Management Theory," *Trauma, Violence, & Abuse*, 2(2), pp. 172–191, https://doi.org/10.1177/1524838001002002005

Schmidt, J.J. (2018), "Bureaucratic Territory: First Nations, Private Property, and 'Turn-Key' Colonialism in Canada," *Annals of the American Association of Geographers*, 108(4), pp. 901–916, https://doi.org/10.1080/24694452.2017.1403878

Schultz, J. et al. (2019), "The Church, Intensive Kinship, and Global Psychological Variation," *Science*, 366, 8 November, https://doi.org/10.1126/science.aau5141

Shaw, P.A. (2001), "Language and Identity, Language and the Land," *BC Studies*, pp. 39–55, https://ojs.library.ubc.ca/index.php/bcstudies/article/view/1595/1636

Shneidman, E.S. (1993), "Suicide as Psychache," *Journal of Nervous and Mental Disease*, 181(3), pp. 145–147, https://doi.org/10.1097/00005053-199303000-00001

Silverman, A.R. (1993), "Outcomes of Transracial Adoption," *The Future of Children, Adoption*, 3(1), pp. 104–118, https://doi.org/10.2307/1602405

Silviken, A., T. Haldorsen, and S. Kvernmo (2006), "Suicide among Indigenous Sami in Arctic Norway, 1970-1998," *European Journal of Epidemiology*, 21(9), pp. 707–713, https://doi.org/10.1007/s10654-006-9052-7

Sinclair, C.M. (1998), "Suicide in First Nations People," in *Suicide in Canada*, A.A. Leenaars et al. (eds), University of Toronto Press, Toronto.

Sinclair, C.M. (2015), Honouring the Truth, Reconciling for the Future: Summary of the Final Report of the Truth and Reconciliation Commission of Canada, https://publications.gc.ca/site/eng/9.800288/publication.html

Sinclair, R. (2007), "Identity Lost and Found: Lessons from the Sixties Scoop," *First Peoples Child & Family Review*, 3(1), pp. 65–82, https://doi.org/10.7202/1069527ar

Sinclair, R. (2016), "The Indigenous Child Removal System in Canada: An Examination of Legal Decision-making and Racial Bias," *First Peoples Child & Family Review*, 11(2), pp. 8–18, https://doi.org/10.7202/1082333ar

Singer, J. W. (2000), *Entitlement: The Paradoxes of Property*, Yale University Press, Connecticut, https://doi.org/10.12987/9780300128543

Sinha, V. et al. (2021), "A Review of Literature on the Involvement of Children from Indigenous Communities in Anglo Child Welfare Systems: 1973-2018," *The International Indigenous Policy Journal*, 12(1), https://doi.org/10.18584/iipj.2021.12.1.10818

Slattery, B. (2000), "The Nature of Aboriginal Title," in *Beyond the Nass Valley: National Implications of the Supreme Court's Delgamuukw Decision*, Lippert, O. (ed.), Fraser Institute, Vancouver, Canada, pp. 11–33.

Smith, A. (1759/2000), *The Theory of Moral Sentiments*, Prometheus Books, Amherst, New York.

Smith, H. (2005), *A Seat at the Table: Huston Smith in Conversation with Native Americans on Religious Freedom*, University of California Press, Berkeley, California, https://doi.org/10.1525/9780520940918

Smith, W.A., W.R. Allen, and L.L. Danley (2007), "'Assume the Position . . . You Fit the Description': Psychosocial Experiences and Racial Battle Fatigue Among African American Male College Students," *American Behavioral Scientist*, 51(4), pp. 551–578, https://doi.org/10.1177/0002764207307742

Smits, D.D. (1994), "The Frontier Army and the Destruction of the Buffalo: 1865-1883," *The Western Historical Quarterly*, 25(3), pp. 312–338, https://doi.org/10.2307/971110

Sotero, M.M. (2006), "A Conceptual Model of Historical Trauma: Implications for Public Health Practice and Research," *Journal of Health Disparities Research and Practice*, 1(1), pp. 93–108, https://ssrn.com/abstract=1350062

Southwick, S.M. et al. (2005), "The Psychobiology of Depression and Resilience to Stress: Implications for Prevention and Treatment," *Annual Review of Clinical Psychology*, 1, pp. 255–291, https://doi.org/10.1146/annurev.clinpsy.1.102803.143948

Spillane, S. et al. (2020), "Trends in Alcohol-Induced Deaths in the United States, 2000-2016," *JAMA Network Open*, 3(2), e1921451, February, https://doi.org/10.1001/jamanetworkopen.2019.21451.

Spillane, N.S. et al. (2022), "Trauma and Substance Use among Indigenous Peoples of the United States and Canada: A Scoping Review," *Trauma, Violence, & Abuse*, pp. 1–16. https://doi.org/10.1177/15248380221126184

Stannard, D.E. (1992), *American Holocaust*, Oxford University Press, New York.

Stremlau, R. (2005), "'To Domesticate and Civilize Wild Indians': Allotment and the Campaign to Reform Indian Families, 1875-1887," *Journal of Family History*, 10(3), pp. 265–286, https://doi.org/10.1177/0363199005275793

Stoor, J.P.A. et al. (2015), "'We are like Lemmings': Making Sense of the Cultural Meaning(s) of Suicide among the Indigenous Sami in Sweden," *International Journal of Circumpolar Health*, 74, 27669, http://dx.doi.org/10.3402/ijch.v74.27669

Taiaiake Alfred, G. (2023), *It's All about the Land: Collected Talks and Interviews on Indigenous Resurgence*, University of Toronto Press, Toronto.

Tait, C.L., R. Henry, and R.L. Walker (2013), "Child Welfare: A Social Determinant of Health for Canadian First Nations and Métis Children," *Pimatisiwin: A Journal of Aboriginal and Indigenous Community Health*, 11(1), pp. 39–53, https://gladue.usask.ca/sites/gladue1.usask.ca/files/gladue//resource461-2de50430.pdf

Tajfel, H. (1982), "Social Psychology of Intergroup Relations," *Annual Review of Psychology*, 33, pp. 1–39, https://doi.org/10.1146/annurev.ps.33.020182.000245

Tajfel, H. and J. Turner (1979), "The Social Identity Theory of Intergroup Behavior," in *Psychology of Intergroup Relations*, S. Worchel and L. Austin (eds), Nelson-Hall, Chicago.

Tanner, A. (2004), "The Cosmology of Nature, Cultural Divergence, and the Metaphysics of Community Healing," in *Figured Worlds: Ontological Obstacles in Intercultural Relations*, J. Clammer, S. Poirier, and E. Schwimmer (eds), University of Toronto Press, Toronto, pp. 189–222, https://doi.org/10.3138/9781442674899

Taylor, M.S. (2011), "Buffalo Hunt: International Trade and the Virtual Extinction of the North American Bison," *American Economic Review*, 101, pp. 3162–3195, https://doi.org/10.1257/aer.101.7.3162

Thibodeau, S. and F.N. Peigan (2007), "Loss of Trust Among First Nation People: Implications when Implementing Child Protection Treatment Initiatives," *First Peoples Child & Family Review*, 3(4), pp. 50–58, https://doi.org/10.7202/1069374ar

Throsby, D. (2001), *Economics and Culture*, Cambridge University Press, Cambridge, https://doi.org/10.1017/CBO9781107590106

Thornton, R. (1984), "Cherokee Population Losses During the Trail of Tears: A New Perspective and a New Estimate," *Ethnohistory*, 31(4), pp. 289–300, https://www.jstor.org/stable/482714

Thornton, R. (1987), *American Indian Holocaust and Survival: A Population History Since 1492*, University of Oklahoma Press, Normand.

Tinker, G.E. (1993), *Missionary Conquest: The Gospel and Native American Cultural Genocide*, Fortress Press, Minneapolis.

Thumath, M. et al. (2021), "Overdose among Mothers: The Association between Child Removal and Unintentional Drug Overdose in a Longitudinal Cohort of Marginalised Women in Canada," *International Journal of Drug Policy*, 91, 102977, https://doi.org/10.1016/j.drugpo.2020.102977

Tjepkema, M., T. Bushnik, and E. Bougie (2019), "Life Expectancy of First Nations, Métis and Inuit Household Populations in Canada," *Statistics Canada Health Reports*, 30(12), pp. 3–10, https://www.doi.org/10.25318/82-003-x201901200001-eng

Tobias, J.L. (1983), "Protection, Civilization, Assimilation: An Outline History of Canada's Indian Policy," in *As Long as the Sun Shines and Water Flows: A Reader in Canadian Native Studies,* (eds.) I. A. L. Getty and A. S. Lussier, University of British Columbia Press, Vancouver, Canada.

Tomm, M. (2013), "Public Reason and the Disempowerment of Aboriginal People in Canada," *Canadian Journal of Law and Society*, 28(3), pp. 293–314, https://doi.org/10.1017/cls.2013.2

Trocmé, N. et al. (2004), "Pathways to the Overrepresentation of Aboriginal Children in Canada's Child Welfare System," *Social Service Review*, 78(4), pp. 577–600, https://doi.org/10.1086/424545

Trosper, R.L. (2009), *Resilience, Reciprocity and Ecological Economics: Sustainability on the Northwest Coast*, Routledge, New York, https://doi.org/10.4324/9780203881996

Trosper, R.L. (2022), *Indigenous Economics: Sustaining Peoples and Their Lands*, University of Arizona Press, Tucson, https://doi.org/10.1017/CBO9781107590106

Trovato, F. (1998), "Immigrant Suicide in Canada," in *Suicide in Canada*, A.A. Leenaars et al. (eds), University of Toronto Press, Toronto, pp. 85–107.

Truth and Reconciliation Commission: Calls to Action (2015), Volume 7, Winnipeg, Manitoba, https://publications.gc.ca/site/eng/9.801236/publication.html

Turner, D.A. (2004), "Perceiving the World Differently," in *Intercultural Dispute Resolution in Aboriginal Contexts*, C. Bell and D. Kahane (eds), University of British Columbia Press, Vancouver, https://doi.org/10.59962/9780774850957

Uhlaner, C.J. (1989), "'Relational Goods' and Participation: Incorporating Sociability into a Theory of Rational Action," *Public Choice*, 62(3), pp. 253–285, https://doi.org/10.1007/BF02337745

Van Orden, K.A. et al. (2010), "The Interpersonal Theory of Suicide," *Psychological Review*, 117(2), pp. 575–600, https://doi.org/10.1037/a0018697

van Uchelen, C.P. et al. (1997), "What Makes Us Strong: Urban Aboriginal Perspectives on Wellness and Strength," *Canadian Journal of Community Mental Health*, 16(2), pp. 37–50, https://doi.org/10.7870/cjcmh-1997-0005

Verrocchio, M.C. et al. (2016), "Mental Pain and Suicide: A Systematic Review of the Literature," *Frontiers in Psychiatry*, 7(108), https://doi.org/10.3389/fpsyt.2016.00108

Vizenor, G. (2008), *Survivance: Narratives of Native Presence*, University of Nebraska, Lincoln.

Vowel, C. (2016), *Indigenous Writes: A Guide to First Nations, Métis, & Inuit Issues in Canada*, HighWater Press, Winnipeg.

Waldram, J.B. (2014), "Healing History? Aboriginal Healing, Historical Trauma, and Personal Responsibility," *Transcultural Psychiatry*, 51(3), pp. 370–386, https://doi.org/10.1177/1363461513487671

Wall-Wieler, E. et al. (2018), "Suicide Attempts and Completions among Mothers Whose Children Were Taken into Care by Child Protection Services: A Cohort Study Using Linkable Administrative Data," *The Canadian Journal of Psychiatry*, 63(3), pp. 170–177, https://doi.org/10.1177/0706743717741058

Walls, M.L. and L.B. Whitbeck (2011), "Distress among Indigenous North Americans: Generalized and Culturally Relevant Stressors," *Society and Mental Health*, 1(2), pp. 124–136, https://doi.org/10.1177/2156869311414919

Walls, M.L. and L.B. Whitbeck (2012), "Advantages of Stress Process Approaches for Measuring Historical Trauma," *The American Journal of Drug and Alcohol Abuse*, 38, pp. 416–420, https://doi.org/10.3109/00952990.2012.694524

Walters, K.L., J.M. Simoni, and T. Evans-Campbell (2002), "Substance Use Among American Indians and Alaska Natives: Incorporating Culture in an 'Indigenist' Stress-Coping Paradigm," *Public Health Reports*, 117, Supplement 1, S104–S117, https://www.jstor.org/stable/25747644

Walters, K.L. et al. (2011), "Bodies Don't Just Tell Stories, They Tell Histories: Embodiment of Historical Trauma among American Indians and Alaska Natives," *Du Bois Review: Social Science Research on Race*, 8(1), pp. 179–189, https://doi.org/10.1017/S1742058X1100018X

Weaver, H.N. (2019), *Trauma and Resilience in the Lives of Contemporary Native Americans: Reclaiming our Balance, Restoring our Wellbeing*, Routledge, New York.

Wesley-Esquimaux, C.C. and M. Smolewski (2004), *Historical Trauma and Aboriginal Healing*, The Aboriginal Healing Foundation, Ottawa.

Wexler, L. (2009), "The Importance of Identity, History, and Culture in the Wellbeing of Indigenous Youth," *The Journal of the History of Childhood and Youth*, 2(2), pp. 267–276, https://doi.org/10.1353/hcy.0.0055

Wexler, L.M. and J.P. Gone (2012), "Culturally Responsive Suicide Prevention in Indigenous Communities: Unexamined Assumptions and New Possibilities," *American Journal of Public Health*, 102(5), pp. 800–806, https://doi.org/10.2105/AJPH.2011.300432

Whitbeck, L.B. et al. (2004), "Conceptualizing and Measuring Historical Trauma Among American Indian People," *American Journal of Community Psychology*, 33(3/4), pp. 119–130, https://doi.org/10.1023/b:ajcp.0000027000.77357.31

White, J. and C. Mushquash (2016), "We Belong: Life Promotion to Address Indigenous Suicide," Discussion Paper, Thunderbird Partnership Foundation, Bothwell, Ontario, Canada, https://wisepractices.ca/wp-content/uploads/2017/12/White-Mushquash-2016-FINAL.pdf

White Paper (1969), Statement of the Government of Canada Indian Policy, 1969, https://epe.lac-bac.gc.ca/100/200/301/inac-ainc/indian_policy-e/cp1969_e.pdf

Wiechelt, S.A., J. Gryczynski, and K.H. Lessard (2019), "Cultural and Historical Trauma among Native Americans," in *Trauma: Contemporary Directions in Trauma Theory, Research, and Practice*, J. Brandell and S. Ringel (eds), Columbia University Press, New York, pp. 167–205.

Wieser, M.J. and P. Pauli (2016), "Neuroscience of Pain and Emotion," in *The Neuroscience of Pain, Stress, and Emotion: Psychological and Clinical Implications*, M. al'Absi and M.A. Flaten (eds), Elsevier/Academic Press, Amsterdam, pp. 3–27, https://doi.org/10.1016/C2013-0-16065-5

Wilbur, R.E. and J.P. Gone (2023), "Beyond Resilience: A Scoping Review of Indigenous of *Survivance* in the Health Literature," *Development and Psychopathology*, Special Issue Article, pp. 1–15, https://doi.org/10.1017/S0954579423000706

Wilk, P. et al. (2017), "Residential Schools and the Effects on Indigenous Health and Well-being in Canada—a Scoping Review," *Public Health Reviews*, 38(8), https://doi.org/10.1186/s40985-017-0055-6

Wilm, J. (2020), "'The Indians Must Yield': Antebellum Free Land, the Homestead Act, and the Displacement of Native Peoples," *Bulletin of the German Historical Institute*, 67, pp. 17–39, https://www.ghi-dc.org/fileadmin/publications/Bulletin/bu67/17.pdf

Wilson, D.S. and E.O. Wilson (2007), "Rethinking the Theoretical Foundation of Sociobiology," *The Quarterly Review of Biology*, 82(4), pp. 327–348, https://doi.org/10.1086/522809

Wolfe, P. (2006), "Settler Colonialism and the Elimination of the Native," *Journal of Genocide Research*, 8(4), pp. 387–409, https://doi.org/10.1080/14623520601056240

Wood, E.M. (2002), *The Origin of Capitalism: A Longer View*, Verso, New York.

Yangsom, K., H. Masoud, and T. Hahmann (2023), "Primary Health Care Access among First Nations People Living Off reserve, Métis and Inuit, 2017 to 2020," Statistics Canada, Catalogue no. 41-20-0002, https://www150.statcan.gc.ca/n1/pub/41-20-0002/412000022023005-eng.htm

Ziker, J.P (2007), "Subsistence and Food Sharing in Northern Siberia: Social and Nutritional Ecology of the Dolgan and the Nganasan," *Ecology of Food and Nutrition*, 46(5–6), pp. 445–467, https://doi.org/10.1080/03670240701486743

Use of Copyrighted Material

Part I of this book draws heavily from a published paper of mine:

Eswaran, M. (2023), "The Wrongs of Property Rights: The Erosion of Indigenous Communal Land Rights and Its Welfare Consequences," *Canadian Public Policy*, 49(3), pp. 267–292.

The University of Toronto Press has granted permission for the reuse of this paper.

In Chapter 9, Figure 9.2 is a reproduction with citation of Fig. 29.3 of the book chapter:

Lalonde, C.E. (2013), "Identity Formation and Cultural Resilience in Aboriginal Communities," in *Routledge International Handbook of Clinical Suicide Research*, (eds.) J.R. Cutcliffe et al., Routledge, London, U.K.

Since my use of this figure here is scholarly, limited, strictly for non-commercial purposes only, transformative in the accompanying commentary, and does not impinge on the market value of the original work, I claim fair use (17 U.S.C. § 107).

Index

About the Team

Alessandra Tosi was the managing editor for this book.

Annie Hine proof-read this manuscript.

Jeremy Bowman typeset the book in InDesign and produced the paperback and hardback editions. The main text font is Tex Gyre Pagella and the heading font is Californian FB.

Jeremy produced the EPUB and PDF editions.

The conversion to the HTML edition was performed with epublius, an open-source software which is freely available on our GitHub page at https://github.com/OpenBookPublishers

Jeevanjot Kaur Nagpal designed the cover. The cover was produced in InDesign using the Fontin font.

Hannah Shakespeare was in charge of marketing.

This book was peer-reviewed by an anonymous referee. Experts in their field, these readers give their time freely to help ensure the academic rigour of our books. We are grateful for their generous and invaluable contributions.

This book need not end here...

Share

All our books — including the one you have just read — are free to access online so that students, researchers and members of the public who can't afford a printed edition will have access to the same ideas. This title will be accessed online by hundreds of readers each month across the globe: why not share the link so that someone you know is one of them?

This book and additional content is available at
https://doi.org/10.11647/OBP.0477

Donate

Open Book Publishers is an award-winning, scholar-led, not-for-profit press making knowledge freely available one book at a time. We don't charge authors to publish with us: instead, our work is supported by our library members and by donations from people who believe that research shouldn't be locked behind paywalls.

Join the effort to free knowledge by supporting us at
https://www.openbookpublishers.com/support-us

You may also be interested in:

Stories from Quechan Oral Literature

A.M. Halpern and Amy Miller

https://doi.org/10.11647/OBP.0049

Xiipúktan (First of All)

Three Views of the Origins of the Quechan People

George Bryant and Amy Miller

https://doi.org/10.11647/OBP.0037

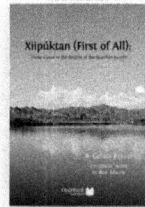

Wellbeing, Freedom and Social Justice

The Capability Approach Re-Examined

Ingrid Robeyns

https://doi.org/10.11647/OBP.0130

Having Too Much

Philosophical Essays on Limitarianism

Ingrid Robeyns

https://doi.org/10.11647/OBP.0338

www.ingramcontent.com/pod-product-compliance
Lightning Source LLC
Chambersburg PA
CBHW071741270326
41928CB00013B/2759